# WILLIAM LAMBARDE
*Elizabethan Antiquary*

WILLIAM LAMBARDE

# WILLIAM LAMBARDE
*Elizabethan Antiquary*
*1536-1601*

RETHA M. WARNICKE

PHILLIMORE

1973
Published by
PHILLIMORE AND CO. LTD.
London and Chichester
*Head Office:* Shopwyke Hall,
Chichester, Sussex, England.

© Retha M. Warnicke, 1973

ISBN 0 85033 077 7

Text set in Linotype Granjon
Designed and printed by
Compton Press, Compton Chamberlayne,
Salisbury

# Contents

# Illustrations

# Foreword

Tudor England was a much, if not well, regulated State. There was scarcely any sort of activity which was not controlled by Parliamentary statute or Council order, and the spacious days of Queen Elizabeth I witnessed a form of government which was totalitarian in intention if not in achievement. Nothing was too trivial to attract the attention of Parliament or Council. What stuff upholsterers should put into bolsters, feather-beds and pillows; the games that labourers may play at Christmas; the apparel permissible to different orders in society; the illegality of retail price maintenance; wages, and 'what time the labourer shall have for his meals and sleep'; the protection of the fry of fish; husbandry; apprenticeship; the making and sale of pins; the licensing of beggars; the improvement of horse-breeding; ale- and tippling-houses; the leather industry; the well garbling of spices; who may bake horse-bread; the making of kilderkins; the prohibition of alms-giving to individuals; the measurement of faggots and billets – these are some of the matters which Tudor Parliaments thought fit to control. As befitted its economic importance, the cloth-industry was the most strictly regulated, and at least 50 statutes were made in the 16th century governing some aspect of the industry.

It was all very well for Parliament to pass statutes and for Council to make orders, but in a country which lacked both a bureaucracy and speedy means of communication, how were they to be enforced? The answer, for the most part, was to entrust their enforcement to that general administrative as well as judicial factotum, the Justice of the Peace. As early as 1485 Huse (or Hussey) the Chief Justice of the King's Bench referred to the numerous statutes with whose execution the Justices of the Peace were loaded, but as Lambarde wrote a hundred years later, 'how many Justices (think you) may now suffice (without breaking their backs) to bear so many, not Loads, but Stacks of Statutes, that have since that time been laid upon them?'. The administration of public business was thus largely dependent on the Justices of the Peace, unpaid officers against whom the Crown had no effective sanction. It is true that a statute of 4 Henry VII provided that a Justice failing to execute his Commission should be put out of the Commission and 'further . . . punished according to his demerits', but if this sanction were employed at all frequently the ranks of the Justices would soon have been depleted and the Crown's business would have remained undone. From time to time a few were summoned into the Star Chamber to be admonished for their remissness, but a more serious threat was uttered by the Lord Keeper in Parliament in 1575: 'The course which Her Majesty hath taken hath been to have her laws executed by men of credit and estimation, for the love of justice, uprightly and indifferently, but, if they shall refuse to do so, forgetting their duty to God, Sovereign and country, then, I say, Her Majesty may be driven, clean contrary to her most Gracious Nature and Inclination, to appoint and assign private men, for profit and gain sake, to see her penal laws executed.' So the alternative to the unpaid Justice was to be a regiment of bureaucrats and trading justices.

It was probably an unnecessary threat. The Justices' backs may have ached under their heavy burdens, but few of them would have had it otherwise. The office conferred prestige and was a sort of official affirmation of the power which the gentry enjoyed as the natural governors of their counties. In practice they could enforce the law as strictly or as loosely as they pleased, and they were in a position to be able to show courtesy to those neighbours who were also friends. Nor do I see any reason why we should assume that the Elizabethan Justice of the Peace was more weakly motivated by patriotism and concern for the public good than his successors of today, or the men and women who serve us in Parliament and on local councils.

Willingness to serve, however, was one thing, ability another. The Elizabethan Justice was faced with a multitude of infinitely varied duties, a plethora of often ill-drafted statutes with which he ought to be familiar, and a never-ending stream of conciliar orders. There was no learned Clerk to be consulted in cases of difficulty, and often he had to work in isolation. A *vade mecum* was what he desperately needed, and it was just that that Lam-

barde provided in his *Eirenarcha,* thereby winning the gratitude
of generations of magistrates. Himself a lawyer as well as a Justice
of the Peace, he wrote his treatise for the benefit of 'such gentlemen as be not trained up in the continual study of the Laws'.

Because he had been trained up in the study of the Common
Law he was conscious of the importance of precedent and because he was concerned about precedent he was concerned also
about history. It is only necessary to look at the works of that
great master (or manipulator) of precedent, Sir Edward Coke, to
see how the Common Lawyer of the end of the 16th and the
beginning of the 17th century inevitably found himself dabbling
in history, however much he may in the process have muddied
the stream. It was as a legal historian that Lambarde wrote his
*Archeion, or a Discourse upon the High Court of Justice in Eng-
land,* and it was as an historian, inspired by an enthusiasm for his
adopted county, that he published in 1576 *A Perambulation of
Kent: containing the description, history, and customs of that Shire.*

Not only was it the first history of Kent, it was also the first
county history to be published. To Lambarde therefore must go
the credit that is due to a pioneer. But the *Perambulation* has
other merits besides that of novelty; it is a well-constructed, sound
and scholarly work that remains of interest and utility four
hundred years after it was written. As the publisher of the 1576
edition said, 'we should unto the author William Lambard Esquire, yielde our verye hartie and perpetuall thanks'.

Just as now we must yield our hearty thanks to Retha Warnicke
for this biography of William Lambarde, antiquary, lawyer, Justice of the Peace, landowner, family man and philanthropist. I
venture to think that it is a work of which the scholarly Lambarde would himself have approved. He was not a native of
Kent, but it is common to find that the comparative newcomer
is more interested in his neighbourhood than those who have
known no other home and who take it all for granted. Perhaps
it needed an American scholar to remind us that Men of Kent
and Kentish Men have been taking Lambarde for granted for
rather a long time. We are in her debt for reminding us of our
debt to an important Elizabethan jurist and our first county historian. 'Good and honest Lambarde' the Queen called him, and
so may we.

*Oxford   April 1973*                                   FRANK JESSUP

# *Acknowledgments*

As this biography is based on my doctoral dissertation, accepted by the Harvard University History Department in 1969, I must first thank my adviser, Professor W. K. Jordan, for his patient and encouraging assistance from those first dark days when my research was just developing into a dissertation to the present time when it is to appear in print. Whenever problems seemed insoluble, he was always ready to provide needed advice and assistance. I am grateful for his experienced and discerning historical approach to the Tudor period. I must also thank Professor S. E. Thorne of the Harvard Law School for important insights into the constitutional development of England. In addition, the staffs of the various Harvard libraries and of the Folger Shakespeare Library, Washington, D.C., introduced me to manuscripts written in 16th-century script (many of them in William Lambarde's hand) and patiently assisted me in learning how to read the style and written variations of that period.

Most of my research, which was financed in part by a Radcliffe College summer grant in 1966, was accomplished in England where I found an abundance of material on Lambarde and his family. His last living lineal descendant, Mrs. S. F. Campbell, kindly permitted me to see her historical possessions which include the Lambarde family diary, various rent and receipt books from the 16th century, and a fine oil painting of the antiquary himself. Of course, I must also thank for their assistance the staffs of the London repositories : the British Museum, the Public Records Office, the Somerset House, and the Drapers' Company. Indeed, the Clerk of the Drapers' Company kindly forwarded the copy of the oil painting of Lambarde that appears in this biography.

Besides providing marvellous research facilities the staff of the Institute of Historical Research, London University, invited me to attend Sir John Neale's and Mr. Joel Hurstfield's seminar. There I was able to discuss some disputed facts about the anti-quary's life and to learn about local collections in England that might be of value to my research, in particular the Sutherland manuscripts at the Stafford Archives Office and some microfilms at the local library, St. John's Park, Blackheath Common. The Stafford archivists were delightful, permitting me to study their numerous manuscripts of Lambarde and other Kentish justices of the peace which at that time had been largely unresearched and unpublished, and the then local librarian at St. John's Park, Mrs. June Burkitts, made it possible for me to view, at my leisure, microfilm copies of Lambarde's rent and receipt books. I must also thank the staffs of Oxford and Cambridge Universities for providing me with various books and materials.

Finally, and in many ways, the most important and most help-ful of the repositories I visited in England was the Kent Arch-ives Office, headed by Dr. Felix Hull at Maidstone. Not only did he make available for my perusal the manuscripts at Maidstone which have been superbly catalogued by him but also those of the Rochester Bridge Corporation at Rochester. In addition, as I was revising the dissertation for publication, both he and his assistant, Miss Elizabeth Melling, carefully read it to help me edit out some unnecessary material and even some foolish inaccuracies about local Kentish customs. Ultimately, Dr. Hull communicated important information about publishing in England and kindly forwarded the prints of various pages of the original manuscript of the *Perambulation of Kent* with their captions that appear in this work. There is no way that I can adequately thank him and his staff for their assistance.

I am most grateful for the Foreword to this work that Mr. F. W. Jessup has so graciously written. His own biography of a Kentish gentleman, Sir Roger Twysden, is a delight to read. Indeed, biographies of members of the Kentish aristocracy, in particular, make for enjoyable research. Mr. Jessup would agree with me, I am sure, that local historical research in Kent, where there is an admirable archives office, is a pleasure.

Of course, the responsibility for organisation and direction of the finished work and for the major decisions in it are mine. I have communicated with two eminent constitutional historians, Sir John Neale and Mr. Paul Ward, who believe that William

Lambarde was the member of parliament who initiated the crisis of 1566, and I am grateful for their wisdom and historical perspectives. It was my decision based on the evidence I found while attempting to put together a comprehensive biography of this important antiquary to argue that he was not that member of parliament. Without more decisive evidence to the contrary, I could come to no other conclusion. Mr. Ward, who has seen many of the Lambarde family records, also read my dissertation and made several helpful suggestions which I have incorporated into this book.

The faculty and administration of Arizona State University at Tempe, where I have been appointed assistant professor, have been a constant source of encouragement and joy to me. At a time when women are seeking to achieve professional status, I thank them both for their financial assistance and their friendship.

From the inception of this research in 1966 to its finished product some changes have occurred in my private life – the most obvious was the birth of a son, Robert, in January of 1968. It is to him and his father, my husband Ronald, that I dedicate this book.

*Phoenix, Arizona*                          RETHA M. WARNICKE

# Important Dates

1536 William Lambarde, the antiquary, was born.

1538 Giles, his brother, was born.

1540 His mother, Juliana, died after the birth of his baby sister, Anna.

1547 His father was elected alderman of London and master of the Drapers' for the first time.

1551 His father was elected sheriff of London and obtained a coat of arms.

1553 The purchase of Westcombe Manor was finalised.

1554 His father, John, died.

1556 He was admitted to Lincoln's Inn.

1566 The parliamentary speech was given by the burgess of Aldborough and William sued his brother in the Court of Chancery.

1567 He was called to the bar at Lincoln's Inn and continued his work on the 'Description of England'.

1568 He had the *Archaionomia* printed and was appointed to a commission of sewers for Kent.

1570 He married Jane Multon of Ightham co. Kent and finished his manuscript on Kent.

1573 He witnessed the Maundy service at East Greenwich and his wife, Jane, died.

1576 He had the *Perambulation of Kent* printed for the first time and opened the almshouse at East Greenwich.

1577 He began his 'Collections on Chancery'.

1579 He was elected as an associate of the bench at Lincoln's Inn and was appointed a justice of the peace for Kent.

1581 His brother, Giles, died.

1582 He had the *Eirenarcha* printed for the first time.

1583 He married Sylvestre Dean Dalison, moved to her home

at Halling, and had the *Duties of Constables . . . and other Low and Lay Ministers of Peace* printed for the first time.

1584 Multon, his heir, was born.

1585 He was first elected to an office in the Rochester Bridge Corporation.

1586 His daughter, Margaret, was born.

1587 His twin sons, Fane and Gore, were born; his wife, Sylvestre, died and he obtained the lease to Halling Palace. The treatise on the House of Commons was written by a W. L.

1589 He was appointed a deputy to the Alienations' Office.

1591 He presented a copy of the 'Archeion' to Sir Robert Cecil.

1592 He was appointed a Master in Chancery and married Margaret Reader.

1597 He was elected a bencher of Lincoln's Inn and was appointed Deputy Keeper of the Rolls.

1598 His lease to Halling Palace ended.

1599 He served as President of Cobham College.

1601 He was appointed Keeper of the Records in the Tower of London and presented the 'Pandecta Rotulorum' to the Queen. In August he died.

*During the splendid reign of Queen Elizabeth, besides those distinguished persons who filled the higher and greater stations of public life . . . there were many others of inferior note and station, whose eminent talents and useful labours justly entitle them to be held forth as an example, and to be honourably remembered by posterity.*
DR. JOHN RANDOLPH, Memoirs of William Lambarde, Esquire: ed. John Nichols, *Bibliotheca Topographica Britannica* (London, 1790), I, 493.

# I

---

# *The Father*

T HE FATHER of William Lambarde, the Elizabethan antiquary and jurist, was John Lambarde, a wealthy London
draper who had been born in Ledbury co. Hereford c.
1500 to a country gentleman named William and his wife, Alice
Baker. John had an older brother who was called Thomas after
their paternal grandfather and two sisters named Elizabeth and
Anne. Because the family estate and fortune were to descend to
Thomas, the elder son, it was decided in 1515 that John should
seek a career in trade, but how that decision was made is not
known. Younger sons traditionally joined the church, obtained
military positions, or went into trade in attempts to earn income
sufficient to support themselves in the style of life they had known
as children.[1]

But once trade was decided upon as a career that John went to
London is not at all surprising. London merchants dominated
the export of broadcloth to the continent in John's day and later
expanded trade in all directions, into the Baltic and Mediter-
ranean Seas and into new lands around the world. This commercial activity was supported by a tremendous increase in the
population of London which doubled and expanded over the City
walls during the 16th century, reaching about 200,000 by the end
of the Tudor era, but that population increase was not effected
by a dramatic rise in the civic birth rate. Indeed, the birth rate
was always lower than the death rate, a statistic which gave the
City a reputation for devouring her own. The growth was sus-
tained by an annual influx into London of provincials like John
Lambarde.

John was undoubtedly given a small legacy in 1515 to aid his entry into the apprenticeship ranks of the Drapers', a livery company first incorporated in 1438 and governed by five annually-elected officials, four wardens and one master, and the members of the Court of Assistants. There were two classes of drapers, the ordinary freemen and the liverymen, drapers who had earned the right to wear the ancient livery of the company. Since the Drapers' Company, like the other big city companies, was not only an economic and social institution but also a political fraternity with great civic influence, membership in it was an important first step for anyone who wished to find fame and fortune in the City.[2]

After his 13-year apprenticeship ended in 1528, John began slowly to advance in draper ranks. In 1534 he purchased his livery and in 1544 he was elected a junior warden at the company's new headquarters, the house built by Thomas Cromwell on the site of the Augustine's dissolved monastery in Throgmorton Street. Often drapers who were elected junior wardens moved up to the positions of upper wardens, but John did not follow that usual pattern. From 1545, when his term as junior warden ended, until 1547, when he was elected master of the company, he held no office except that of member of the Court of Assistants.[3]

In the midst of his successes at the company, he was married, but unfortunately the records failed to reveal the year in which the wedding occurred and gave no personal information about the bride, Juliana, except that she inherited the estate of her father, William Horne of London. Undoubtedly one of her attractions had been her wealth which may have been of considerable assistance in the purchase of the company livery for John. Two years after he became a liveryman, on 18 October 1536, their first child, a son who was called William after his Ledbury grandfather, was born in the parish of St. Nicholas Acon. Later they had two more children, Giles born in May of 1538 and Anna born in the spring of 1540.[4]

A few months after the April baptism of her daughter, Juliana died, apparently from lingering childbirth complications, and was buried on 20 September 1540 in the parish church of St. Nicholas Acon where her sons later erected a monument to her memory and where her daughter, who died at the age of three, was also buried. Thus before his seventh birthday, William experienced the tragic loss of both his mother and his young sister, but fortunately there were also some pleasant childhood experiences. By the time of these personal tragedies it was apparent that his father, John Lambarde, had become a successful businessman.[5]

Seven days before the burial of his wife, John recorded in his book of purchases that he had begun to invest in real estate. Between 1540 and 1548 he obtained lands and houses in London and Shoreditch for almost £800, and like other citizens of Tudor England, as well as those of his own livery company, he did not hesitate to purchase the former monastery land from the crown, thus tying the kingdom more securely than ever to the Henrician Reformation and its accompanying dissolution of the monasteries. In July of 1544, for instance, he obtained the manor of Heddington in Wiltshire, formerly held by Lacock Abbey, for about £400, and further outlays for church property between 1544 and 1546 amounted to over £600.[6]

In August of 1546 he invested in former monastery property in Herefordshire, but he failed to record the purchase price in his book of purchases. Below that entry was found his only reference to the Ledbury property that had descended to him at the death of his elder brother while a student at Oxford University and that was leased out for 23s. a year. With both his brother and his father dead it would seem that the economic reasons which had compelled his move to London no longer existed, but it is unlikely that he ever seriously considered deserting the great expanding and sprawling City where he had gained wealth and stature.

Since the entire Ledbury inheritance, assuming that part of the lands had not been sold and there was no indication to that effect, was leased out for only 23s. a year, it might seem unrealistic for anyone to claim that the Lambardes of Herefordshire were gentlemen. But as status depended on birth rather than wealth, it may have been more than wishful thinking on the part of the antiquiry, in an age when pedigrees were highly prized, to claim that status for his ancestors when he drew up his family tree.[7]

From September 1540 to July 1548 John obtained property at a cost of about £1,900, thus demonstrating that he had become a wealthy man, perhaps because of his wife's inheritance but perhaps also because as a merchant adventurer he had made some shrewd investments in the shipping of broadcloth to the conti-

nent. For whatever reasons by 1544 when the chamberlain of
London asked the Drapers for a wheat money loan, the company
officials recognised the rising value of John's estate by requiring
only one draper to pay more than the £5 demanded of him.[8]

While increasing the value of his estate he was also gaining influence in London where he was elected alderman in 1547 and
where he had first gained political viability when he was admitted
into its freedom as a member of one of the City guilds. The freemen of London, combined in the Common Hall, had various
functions, among them the election of the sheriff and the nomina-
tion of two aldermen, who had previously served as sheriff, for
the office of lord mayor of London. The aldermen, who held
their positions for life, then chose one of the two nominees to be
the new lord mayor and, among other functions, also served as
magistrates for London. As an alderman John represented the
ward of Farringdon Without from 1547 to 1549 and the ward of
Old Aldersgate from 1549 until his death in 1554.[9]

After his election to civic office John was elected master of his
guild for the term of 1547 to 1548 and subsequently served in that
capacity from 1550 to 1551 and again from 1552 to 1553. The
Drapers' records also revealed that from August of 1549 his name
was regularly listed first, even before that of the master, when
the names of those present at the meetings of the Court of Assistants were recorded by the clerk. While he was completing his
second term as company master, the Common Hall elected him
sheriff for London and Middlesex.[10]

His growing political importance was accompanied by a continuing increase in the value of his estate. In 1550 he was assessed
more for a corn money loan than any other draper in his company and he began to make use of that great wealth for the social
advantage of his family.[11] He probably hoped to establish a family
line of country gentlemen in Kent when he began the negotiations that year which led to his acquisition of Westcombe Manor
at East Greenwich. Indeed, his antiquary son later reported in his
history of Kent that the western part of that county was largely
inhabited by people who had moved there after first making their
fortunes in London.[12]

In the winter of 1550 John gave £100 (in addition to a previous
£300) to Nicholas Ballard to require him to transfer the title of
Westcombe to the Lambarde family before 1 November 1552, but

the completion of this transfer was probably delayed in June 1551 when Ballard was convicted by a jury at Old Bailey of raping an 11-year-old girl. By pleading benefit of clergy Ballard saved his life but lost his chattels. It is evident, however, that Lambarde had title to the manor by the fall of 1553 when he began making repairs which had cost him about £200 by August of 1554 when he died.[13]

Because Westcombe was held in socage by the custom of gavilkind, a tenure which did not permit the owner to alienate his property without reserving at least one-third of it for his heirs, John gave 200 silver marks to Robert and Thomas Ballard to void their claims to the manor as the heirs of Nicholas. Later he must have deemed even that amount insufficient, for he recorded in his book of purchases that to clear his title he gave a £10 annuity to Thomas Ballard and his heirs for their share of the manor.

In June of 1551, just before he was elected sheriff of London, John obtained a coat of arms from Thomas Hawley, the Principal Herald and King of Arms of the South, East, and West parts of England. The official description of the coat of arms was:

Geules a Cheueron vair betwene Thre Lambes passant siluer Vngled sable: upon his helme on a Torse siluer and geules a Trogodises hed Rasy and horned Asur, the mayne porfled golde the eares and Tynes of the hornes siluer, the tongue apparente genles manteled asur dobled siluer. . . .

He already had the right to bear the Horne coat of arms, with three musical horns, which had been the property of his wife, Juliana.[14]

The great wealth and influence of John had been won at a time of great religious turmoil in England. He, like most of the members of his guild, escaped persecution during these crises by accepting both the new Anglo-Catholicism and the new Queen of King Henry VIII and, of course, enriched himself from the Reformation's economic settlements. The more radical religious changes of the reign of King Henry's son which took England from Anglo-Catholicism to Protestantism, were also loyally supported by the guild while John again purchased dissolved church property, and just before the death of King Edward VI, he signed the royal will leaving the throne to Lady Jane Grey. In all its actions, then, regardless of the religious issues involved, the Drapers' Company was inflexibly loyal to the reigning monarch and so was John Lambarde.[15]

When Catholic Mary Tudor finally succeeded to the throne, the company transferred its loyalty to her, giving 91 marks toward a suitable gift from the City for her coronation. The following March when she demanded £100 from the Guild toward the expense of keeping a London garrison, she was actually granted 200 silver marks, of which Lambarde paid 30s., but he was no longer assessed the highest amount since Sir William Chester, master, paid 40s.[16]

On 4 August 1554, about a year after Queen Mary's succession, John Lambarde died at the age of 54, probably from an illness like the plague or the sweating sickness since his second wife, Alice, died only eight days later. His funeral was described by Henry Machyn, merchant taylor, who wrote that there were many mourners carrying torches, frises, and the arms of both the Drapers' and the Merchant Adventurers'. John was buried at St. Michael, Wood Street, where a monument was erected to his memory.[17]

The Drapers', in charge of Alice's funeral, had a requiem mass said for her at the Church of St. Michael, Wood Street, where she was buried with John. It was noted by the clerk of the company on 26 August 1554 that John had left the drapers £6 13s. 4d. for a memorial dinner but that Alice had neglected that formality. This problem was solved by John Calthrop, the draper authorised to collect the Lambarde rents during the minority of John's heirs, when he appropriated £3 6s. 8d. from John's estate for a more sumptuous feast in memory of both the deceased Lambardes.[18]

The records revealed very little about Alice Lambarde except that when she married John she was a widow and already had at least one daughter, married to Richard Flower, who was named executor to her will. Two important items in that will were gifts of £10 each to her Lambarde stepsons and several small bequests to the children of her sister-in-law, Elizabeth Lambarde Bond. Greatly concerned with religion and the afterlife, Alice left a cope and other vestments to the church where she was buried and bequeathed her soul to 'God by the mercy of whose previous death and passing I fadfully trust to have clere remission of sinnes'.[19]

John, in contrast to his wife, was loath to discuss religion at all, for in his testament he simply stated : 'In the name of God, amen'. The Lambarde sons could not have learned great religious piety from their father who refused even to express his religious sentiments in a document which would not be made public until after his death. In 1552 when he had drawn up his will, of course, there had been a Protestant king on the throne, while when he died, there was a Catholic queen in England. The shrewd merchant left alone those matters which seemed to touch the royal prerogative.

After his simple statement affirming his belief in God, he made his bequests. To his wife for her lifetime he left Heddington Manor and a house in Cosin Lane, which had probably been the Lambarde home, and to his younger son he left some London property and £150 in cash. William, the heir-at-law, was left £150 and the property not devised to others. John provided a small bequest for the children of his sister, Anne Goodrich, and stipulated that should his own sons die, the £300 in cash left to them was to go to the children of his sister Bond. It was probably because he had made no certain bequests to the Bond children that they were remembered in the will of his widow, Alice.

Finally, John authorised his friends, John Lee, scrivenor, and John Calthrop, draper, to collect the rents from the property and to use whatever was necessary for the upkeep of the estate. He also asked Augustine Hynde, alderman of London, to act as overseer, but since he died eight days after John, the Lambarde brothers were left to the mercy and honesty of the rent collectors.[20]

# The Inheritance

WILLIAM, the heir-at-law of John Lambarde, inherited the Lambarde and Horne coats of arms and property in four counties of the kingdom, but since, at 18 years of age, he had not reached his majority, the crown took possession of one-third of his inheritance, granting to Edmund Hensley, esquire, his body and marriage and an annuity of £20 to begin in August of 1554. Even though a London inquisition recognised that he was of age in November of 1557, a month after his 21st birthday, it was not until 28 June 1558 that he finally obtained a royal licence to enter into all the lands of his inheritance, which brought him annually £160 in rents.[1]

As a landlord in Tudor London William frequently benefited from the rising value of real estate. From two houses he inherited in Cosin Lane, for example, he collected an annual rent of £16 until the middle of the 1560s when he gave them to his brother. Later, in 1581, he re-acquired those two houses and collected an annual rent of £23, £7 more than in the 1560s. The rents of other property which he had on Cosin Lane also rose similarly.

The 1559 sale of the Ledbury inheritance and other sales of property as well as his 1570 move to Ightham, in Kent where he married Jane Multon indicated that he did not intend to re-establish the family home in Herefordshire and that he expected to accomplish what had undoubtedly been his father's goal of establishing a family line in Kent. The other holdings that he sold included the 1570 sale of his property in Wiltshire for £1,400, the sale in 1572 of his London dyehouse for £150 and in 1574 the sale of the Bell Inn and its three tenements in Shoreditch for

£318. The total proceeds of the sale of these holdings came to £1,868, a net gain of £800 over the purchase price his father had paid.[2]

All records that have survived have indicated that John Lambarde, who was constantly adding to his estate in a piecemeal fashion, never sold any property he acquired. William, in contrast to him, had particular goals in mind, that of consolidating his holdings in London and Kent, preparatory to the establishment of a Kentish line, for ultimately, he did settle at Westcombe Manor although it did not become his permanent residence until the 1590s. Westcombe, whose history can be traced to the 14th century, was held in socage by the custom of gavilkind of Dartford Manor in Kent for 9s. 2d. quitrent and a lathe silver charge of 4s. Having the right of a court baron, the lord of the manor could demand a year's rent over and above that year's quitrent on each descent and alienation of land held of Westcombe.

Because in 1554 an inquisition erroneously found that Westcombe was held in knight service of Eltham Manor, William was able to take lawful possession of it when he reached his majority. Several years later his younger brother, Giles, questioned the findings of that inquisition, claiming that the manor was actually held by the custom of gavilkind. Property held by that custom had to be divided equally among all the male children, and if none, among all the female children.

In his attempt to prove that one-half of the manor was his, Giles stole his brother's deeds and sued out a writ of *partition farinda* at Common Law. After the justices acepted the findings of the royal inquisition as valid, William, on 20 August 1566, sued his brother in the Court of Chancery in an attempt to recover his deeds.[3]

Since no final decree has been found in the suit, the brothers probably settled the controversy out of court. It undoubtedly took very little serious investigation on the part of William, antiquary and trained lawyer that he was, to discover that Westcombe was held in socage of Dartford Manor. Ultimately he became convinced that his brother's allegations were correct, for he wrote in his rent and receipt book under the date of 1574 that the manor was held in socage by the custom of gavilkind and of 1593 that the inquisition held in Kent had erroneously found that the manor was held in fee.[4]

It cannot be conclusively proved that the brothers settled out of court, but it is likely that in the 1560s when William gave his brother two Cosin Lane houses and part of the rent from various other property that he was compensating him for one-half of the value of the manor. In 1572 a deed was enrolled on the close rolls to confirm a family settlement whereby all of the Westcombe property which had belonged to John Lambarde was granted to William with the stipulation that should he have no male heirs the manor would revert to Giles.[5]

The treatise on gavilkind written by the antiquary, which has been praised as a valuable contribution to an understanding of the custom, could have been prompted by this family dispute. Even though he did quote in that treatise one author who defended the custom on the basis that younger sons were as dear to their ancestors as the elder ones, William refused to accept it as a tradition for his own family. In 1597, when he drew up his will, he carefully listed all of the property that was to descend to his eldest son, explaining: 'neyther would I have entayled my said other manor and landes but only to prevente the daunger of descent by the custom of gavilkind'.[6]

The view from the old manor house must have been beautiful, with the River Thames, the royal palace and gardens, Shooter's Hill ascending to a height of 242 feet, and Blackheath Common all part of the immediate surroundings. In his history of Kent William later explained that the word, Combe, was a Saxon word that meant camp and that areas around Blackheath Common had been called combes by the Saxons in memory of the invading Danes who had camped on the common during the reign of King Ethelred.[7]

The manor of 16th-century Kent was an 'administrative legal, and fiscal machine for which courts were held and rents collected and which normally consisted of demesne land and freehold tenant holdings'.[8] Of the two the income from leasing out the demesne land was the more lucrative. Like other owners of manors William did not farm the demesne himself but lived off the income of leasing it out. Since the rents from the East Greenwich lands, which amounted to £39 annually, remained stable over a 20-year period from the 1570s to the 1590s, that rural area, despite its proximity to London, was evidently not a profitable place for speculative investments.

At the antiquary's death, Westcombe descended to his eldest son, Multon, who lost 10 acres to the Crown when James I had the royal lands in East Greenwich enclosed with a brick wall. Having refused to go to court, Multon petitioned the King for a remedy but received no compensation for his loss.[9] To continue the history of the manor in the Lambarde family, it passed from Multon to his son, Thomas, a great royalist during the civil wars of the 17th century, who was obliged to sell it in 1649. Five years later he moved to Sevenoaks in Kent which has remained the Lambarde home until modern times.

When he reached his majority, Giles Lambarde discovered that it was no easy task for him to obtain his inheritance. First, he had felt compelled to steal his brother's deeds to win compensation for his half of Westcombe Manor and then he had to resort to complicated legal manoeuvres in an attempt to gain all of his inheritance money from John Calthrop, the draper rent collector named in his fathers' will. Indeed, when both of the Lambarde heirs reached their majority, they discovered that they had been victimised by Calthrop. He had refused to hand over the rents which he had gathered from William's lands until ordered to do so by the Court of Requests.

Giles's problem was not so easily resolved for it was complicated by his having been a draper apprentice of Calthrop's until 1563. When he failed to obtain his money from his former master and when he did not receive what he thought was justice from a draper arbitration board, the method for the settlement of controversies between freemen of the company, he appealed first to the London Court of Aldermen and then to the Court of Star Chamber where he accused various members of the draper arbitration board of conspiracy to defraud him of his inheritance money. There was no point in suing John Calthrop who had already declared himself bankrupt.

Among the many witnesses called in the Star Chamber trial was William Lambarde, who wrote down his testimony on 9 May 1568. His statement confirmed that Calthrop had not turned over all of the inheritance money either to Giles or earlier to William himself, but it did not establish the conspiracy charges against the other drapers. Three years later, on 4 May 1571, the case was dismissed since the court could find no evidence of fraud on the part of the defendants and there was probably none, but it was dismissed without prejudice to the plaintiff.

To be fair to Giles, he had not obtained all of his inheritance money from the bankrupt John Calthrop. Both Lambardes were the victims of a rent collector who attempted to use his legal position during their minorities for his own financial gain, a circumstance not unusual in Tudor England. What makes this incident seem extraordinary is that Calthrop had been chosen collector by their father because he was an old and trusted friend.[10]

Even though William had assisted his brother in the Star Chamber dispute and was his heir-at-law, when Giles died in 1581 without children of his own, he devised most of his property to his wife, Marjory Stevenson, the daughter of a London girdler, and to Thomas Wyckyn, the husband of his cousin, Margaret Bond. The only property that actually descended to William, the 'tenisplace' with its adjoining tenements, was encumbered with rent charges by Giles for his Uncle Horne and Jasper Nicholson, the grandson of Aunt Anne Lambarde Goodrich. In 1595, 14 years after the death of Giles, William noted in his book of purchases that the two tenements adjoining the 'tenisplace' had always legally been his since his father, who had originally purchased them, had not specifically devised them to Giles. An examination of the father's will has confirmed that contention. Even though the tenements were not bequeathed to Giles, he collected rents on them during his lifetime and placed a rent charge on them at his death. It is likely that William did not learn of that legal technicality until after the death of his brother and was unwilling to press his own position at that time.[11]

Status and wealth in 16th-century England were largely dependent upon land ownership. Thus, John Lambarde, the merchant father, invested his funds in land to give his children opportunities for social and economic advancement, and he bequeathed to them a determination to keep their possessions and to add to their value. While the litigious Giles did not always successfully rise to this challenge, it is clear that the elder son's tenacity of purpose and stewardship abilities permitted him to accomplish his father's goals. John gave William the means to establish himself as a county gentleman but it was his own scholarly and personal attributes that transformed him from an aspiring merchant's son into the patriarch of a landed Kentish family that has survived to modern times.

# 3

# *The Student and the Politician*

SINCE William Lambarde failed to record even the most important facts about his early years in London, very little information has survived about his childhood. It is known that he grew up in a wealthy, albeit motherless home, under the guidance of a father who was widely respected and admired in the City, but what religious training that father provided for his family can be only conjectured. If John Lambarde treated his personal matters in the same manner as his business affairs, his son, who was born the same year that Anne Boleyn was beheaded, must have been christened in King Henry VIII's Anglo-Catholic Church and confirmed in King Edward VI's Protestant Church. When Queen Mary completed England's return to Rome, William and his brother must have attended mass with their father, who believed in God but who left doctrinal disputes to others. Surely, the two boys heard the requiem mass at their stepmother's funeral in 1554.

During the years that William was learning to understand and respect the influence of the City of London and to obey and respect the authority of the King in Parliament, he was also learning languages, in particular, Latin, French, and Anglo-Saxon, reading history, and gaining a knowledge of many other disciplines. Where this learning was acquired is unknown. He may have been tutored at home or, since his father could have paid the tuition, he may have attended any one of several primary and grammar schools that were available.

It cannot even be conclusively proved that he attended a university, but in his *Description of England*, a volume written while he was a student at Lincoln's Inn, he made several statements which suggested an intimate knowledge of Oxford University. At one point in his discussion of the two universities he claimed that Cambridge was older than Oxford but carefully noted that his personal feelings had not influenced that decision : 'I confess I owe more to Oxford than Cambridge; but I knowe withal that I owe more to truethe, then to eyther of theim both'. Ruins were of particular interest to him as the author of the *Description*. He supported a rumour that there once had been many more than the then nine small houses at Oxford with the assertion : 'it seameth true by the Ruynes that yet appeare in Sight'. In contrast to that admission, he wrote the following about some Cambridge ruins : 'They that have sene theim gess theim not to be very old'.[1]

Because of his great learning it is tempting to identify him as an Oxford alumnus, particularly since his paternal uncle attended that university, but the evidence in his records is not conclusive and there is no undisputed reference to him in the university registers.[2] Of course, if he had studied at a university for a few years before entering Lincoln's Inn, no record would have been kept unless he had a scholarship, which, as the son of a wealthy London merchant, he did not need, or unless he had received a degree, which, since there were no formal school or age requirements for admission to the Inn, he also did not need.

On 15 August 1556 at the age of 19 he entered Lincoln's Inn, one of the four London Inns of Court for the training of men in the common law. There were three ranks in the society : the benchers, who formed the Council to govern the society, the barristers, and the students, who had to study in residence for several years (after 1596, seven) under the supervision of the benchers before they could be called to the bar. Periodically, the reader, one of the experienced benchers, explained statutes to the brotherhood, although by the 16th century these lectures, called readings, were of more interest for the entertainment that accompanied them than for their educational value. At the moots, the other form of guidance for the students, benchers and barristers argued points of law before the reader.[3]

The students spent most of their waking hours in the hall where they studied, ate, were entertained, and were informed of the society's rules. For private study, of course, they had their own bedchambers, which according to Privy Council directives to all

London Inns, could be shared with only one other member. Since a fire was permitted only in the hall, undoubtedly they did not often study in their rooms. Food for the society was simple; the members had beer and bread at all meals in addition to beef and mutton at dinner except during Lent when fish was served. The hall was where the Council promulgated rules about appearance and other aspects of society life. In June of 1557, for example, it was decreed that no one except knights and benchers could wear light colours, except for scarlet, and that an offender who violated this rule more than once would be expelled. Perhaps this rule was one reason why all extant pictures of Lambarde show him dressed in black, as he did not become a full member of the bench until 1597 when he was 60 years old.[4]

The first reference to him in the records of the Inn, after that of his admission, occurred on All Saints' Day in 1558 when he was one of those named as Master of the Revels, the office charged with Christmas entertainment, but there is no evidence that he ever undertook its duties or the duties of the Steward for Christmas, an office to which he was named with two others in 1559.

On 15 June 1567 it was proclaimed that William Lambarde and 11 other students were to be called to the bar at the next moot, an elevation in status which did not relieve them of the duty to hold society offices. In November of 1573, when Lambarde had been a resident of Ightham, Kent for three years, he was appointed Steward of the Reader's Dinner, but he understandably paid £8 to be excused from serving in that capacity, since that officer's primary function was to finance the dinner with his own funds. If the feast did not meet extravagant expectations, he could expect to pay a fine for niggardliness. As other members later had to pay much larger amounts to be relieved from serving in that position, the Council may have accepted this remuneration in sympathy for Lambarde's recent widower status. His first wife, Jane, died at the end of September of that year. Shortly after excusing him from financing the reader's dinner, the Council appointed either John Master or William Lambarde to serve as Pensioner, an office charged with paying for the repairs to the hall and purchasing necessary eating utensils. The records clearly indicate that Master acted in that capacity.[5]

In February of 1579, when at the age of 42 he was made an

associate of the bench, he was highly praised by the Council:

> He hath deserved universalie well of his comenwelth and
> contrie, and lykewise of the Felloweshippe and Societie of the
> Howse and is like hereaft to wyn greater credytt to himself and
> the Socyete of this Howse . . .[6]

Along with the honour of being elected associate, he was granted
a room 'to sytt amongest the Socyety of the Fellowship of the
Bench, as other associate use to do' and was not required to pay
for it. The Council carefully recorded that this favour was not to
set a precedent for the treatment of future associates. It was not
until 14 June 1597, when he was 60, that the Council unanimously
elected him a full member of the bench, noting that he was a
'man of great reading, learning, and experience'.[7]

After his elevation to bencher, Lambarde was appointed to
various society committees. In June 1599 he was asked to investigate the resignation of the Divinity Reader and in November of
1600 he was asked to draft plans for the construction of a new
building, to be a reader, and to keep a 'vigilant eye' upon the
financial status of the Inn and the manners and learning of the
membership. Once again there was no evidence to indicate that
he performed these tasks but the Council surely would not have
chosen him had he not been willing to participate in a meaningful way.[8]

To be called to the Bar in one of the Inns was a great honour
which brought with it the expectations of monetary and governmental advancement, and two friends of Lambarde at Lincoln's
Inn, John Puckering and Thomas Egerton, were appointed Lord
Keeper of the Great Seal.[9] But membership in an Inn had its
drawbacks as well. The Privy Council regularly assessed the
societies and their membership for loans toward the expenses of
various military operations, particularly in the last two decades of
the reign of Queen Elizabeth I. In 1590 Lambarde was asked to
contribute toward the relief of Geneva and in 1599 and 1600 he
was asked to loan money toward the pacification of Ireland. One
witness at court reported that even though much courtesy was
used in requesting the Irish loans, those assessed 'must give'.[10]

In 1562 when Lambarde had been a student at the Inn for six
years, Queen Elizabeth's second Parliament was summoned. One
man named William Lambert, who has been identified as the

antiquary, was asked to represent the Yorkshire town of Aldborough in the House of Commons. From the first session, which lasted from 12 January to 2 October 1563, no record of any activity of that burgess has survived.

In the second session, which was convened on 20 September 1566 and which was ended on 2 January 1567, he helped to foment a constitutional crisis when, after Queen Elizabeth had denied the plea of the House to name a successor to the throne, he rose to give a 'learned oration' for the 'reiteration of the suit to the Queen to limit the succession'. The next day, 9 November 1566, when the House was requested by royal messenger to refrain from that line of discussion, Paul Wentworth challenged the royal right to deny their freedom of speech. Finally, as she found herself confronted with the possibility of losing her supplies in a hostile house, the Queen revoked her commandments to be silent and remitted one-third of the badly-needed supplies.[11]

When Parliament was dissolved she had not given way on the issue of limiting the sucession and throughout her long reign she steadfastly refused all petitions which requested her to name a successor. This refusal was based partly on her own vanity and on her reluctance to give one of her ambitious rivals the advantages of being singled out as her official heir. But the most formidable obstacles to settling the question were the religious and dynastic problems that would arise were Catholic Mary, Queen of Scots excluded, as the House of Commons evidently desired. Presumably the Queen of Scots had the military support of Catholic Europe to challenge any such exclusion, particularly since if the will of King Henry VIII were set aside, she seemed to have, as a descendant of the king's elder sister, the best hereditary claim to the throne after Queen Elizabeth, herself.

William Lambarde, the antiquary, has been identified as this learned parliamentary orator, but the evidence must be closely examined.[12] The main argument supporting this conclusion focuses on a treatise entitled 'Some Certaine Notes of ye Order, Proceedings, Punishments, and Privileges of the Lower House of Parliament', gathered by W. Lambert. Since the author of this treatise confessed that he had been the Aldborough burgess, if it can be proved that it was written by the antiquary, he automatically becomes the Member of Parliament.

The treatise has not been found in the antiquary's handwriting; the 16th-century copy[13] that has survived has no marginal corrections by Lambarde and does not seem to be in the hand of a professional scribe. The bibliography, listed on folio one of the treatise, indicated several manuscripts and books as the author's source material, but none of them, as far as it can be determined, was ever in the antiquary's possession. One item listed in the bibliography is of special interest as the author referred to the 'fragment of my writing'. By 1587, the year the treatise was written, the antiquary had written nothing specifically about the House of Commons. To be sure, he had begun the *Archeion* almost a decade before the treatise was penned, but in that volume he did not discuss the procedures or customs of the House of Commons.[14]

Most authorities have agreed that the treatise was a well-written, scholarly work. It would be too coincidental, it has been argued by them, that two 16th-century men named William Lambert could have written scholarly works, but at least two William Lamberts, neither of whom was the antiquary, attended Cambridge and Oxford Universities, thus presumably qualifying as scholars. It is, of course, senseless to argue the question of coincidence.[15]

That the manuscript was not published until 1641 and then anonymously has raised another obstacle to accepting his authorship. In 1641 Lambarde's grandson, Thomas, was carefully guarding his ancestor's manuscripts, and only six years earlier, with no little effort, had the publication of an unauthorised edition of his grandfather's *Archeion* cancelled. Thomas Lambarde would not have permitted an anonymous publication of any of his ancestor's manuscripts unless, and this is unlikely, that he was unaware that it was his grandfather's work, or unless, after all, that it had not been written by the antiquary.[16]

Modern Tudor historians have generally agreed that the author of the treatise was familiar with the sessions of Parliament that were held from 29 October to 2 December 1586 and again from 15 February to 23 March 1587. The author was not a Member of that Parliament but judging from the precedents cited in the treatise, he knew much about the proceedings of the first session and possibly those of the second. Lambarde, the antiquary, was as usual in London during term time, but as Conyers Read noted, he was in Kent serving on the Commission of the Peace during parts of both sessions.[17]

In addition to the treatise, the text of the *Description of England* has been used to prove that Lambarde was the burgess from Aldborough. In the section on that town he revealed that he had received some brass coins from there and continued : 'It is at this Day notable for no other Thinge, than it sendeth Burgesses to Parliament'. In the same work he also noted that Scarborough had the right of parliamentary representation but no one, on the basis of that assertion, has argued that he served Scarborough in Parliament.[18]

Lambarde even referred to the session of 1566 in his *Description* when he explained that the Lord Viscount Montague, the owner of the dissolved Battel Monastery had displayed in that Parliament a royal charter that had been granted to the monks by Henry I. Since he gave a detailed account of the seal and the Latin inscription on it, he had undoubtedly examined the charter closely. Had he been the Aldborough burgess he would surely have been given the opportunity to inspect it, even though there was no indication that it was displayed in the Commons as well as the Lords.

Still it would be tempting to place too much emphasis on his knowledge of the charter since there were several individuals who could have brought it to his attention. Well acquainted with Lambarde were Dr. Matthew Parker, Archbishop of Canterbury, who had loaned him his own manuscripts, and Sir William Cordell, Master of the Rolls and Member of that Parliament, who later collaborated with him on the *Archaionomia*, the work on Anglo-Saxon laws.[19] It was remarkable, moreover, that this, the only statement about the 1566 session unquestionably made by the antiquary did not refer once to the constitutional crisis or even to the Catholic sympathies of the Viscount. To him the most important event of that session was the discussion of the old charter.

Finally, it has been noted that the representative for Aldborough was chosen by Sir Ambrose Cave, Chancellor of the Duchy of Lancaster, and suggested that since the antiquary was acquainted with various members of the governing hierarchy of England that he must have also known Cave. It is true that his friendships with the Archbishop of Canterbury and with the Master of the Rolls have been well documented, but it is also true that there is no evidence that directly links him to Cave.

While the arguments placing Lambarde in Parliament depend heavily upon reading more into the evidence than is actually there, the arguments denying he was the burgess depend greatly upon the silence in his records. At the same time that the treatise on procedure was being written the antiquary was keeping a family diary in which he recorded all the important events of his life. It would seem appropriate, since the author of the treatise referred to his role in Parliament, for him if he were the antiquary, to enter the event in his diary, kept regularly since 1554, but none of the entries for the decade of the 1560s referred to Parliament even once. In the diary, the year of the constitutional crisis was most memorable because of his suit against his brother, Giles Lambarde, in the Court of Chancery. Another note in the diary causes the silence about Parliament to seem even more remarkable. Under the date of 9 October 1563, one week after the first session of the Second Parliament was prorogued, Lambarde recorded that because of the plague the courts had not met at Westminster. Had he been a member of that Parliament, surely he would have noted the date of the prorogation.[20]

Presumably the Lambert who spoke out about limiting the succession desired the naming of a Protestant heir. The antiquary, of course, was a Protestant but to argue that he was a potential martyr or Puritan leader exaggerates too much his commitment to Protestantism. It is true that he frequently rebuked medieval Catholics, but it is also true that he judiciously refrained from criticising 16th-century Catholic royalty and nobility. In his diary, without a word of comment, he noted the marriage and death dates for Queen Mary Tudor. As the Queen of England she had represented justice in the kingdom and had deserved public obedience. Indeed, in the many marginal notes he made as he read John Proctor's *The Hystorie of Wyatt's Rebellion*, there was no indication of regret that the uprising had failed.[21]

It is reasonable to expect that the burgess who wished to limit the succession disliked the Catholic claimants, particulary Mary, Queen of Scots, but in the antiquary's only reference to that Queen, he made no personal comment about her. In 1568 he wrote in the *Description* that Queen Mary was at Tutbury, but he did not comment on her religion or her claim to the English throne, a remarkable omission.[22]

The opinion has been expressed that if any student of history cared to prove that the antiquary had not given the parliamentary speech in 1566 she would have to identify for the scholarly world the Lambert who was that burgess. In addition to the two William Lamberts who attended the universities, there were many other William Lamberts. Of course, the name Lambert, or Lambarde, or Lambart or however else the unpredictable Elizabethans spelled it, was not as common as John Brown or John Smith, but there were still enough 16th-century William Lamberts to cause some modern-day confusion. First, since Aldborough was in Yorkshire, it is possible that a local man was chosen. It is interesting to note that a William Lambert, who lived in Burneston, in Yorkshire, was granted a pardon by the Queen on 25 April 1570, for treasons committed since 1 November 1569.[23] Among other possibilities were William Lambert of Hampshire, gentleman, who died in 1588, the year after the treatise was written, and a William Lambert who was appointed to a royal commission for Surrey on 15 June 1566, about five months before the speech in the House of Commons.[24]

One final manuscript, a letter which was written by a William Lambert and which is important to this discussion, has survived. The letter, written on 16 July 1585, probably to Lord Burghley, warned that if the government did not champion the cause of the Low Countries, conspiracies similar to those against Queen Mary Tudor would abound, but predicted that if the Queen came to their defence, all of the other Protestant countries would join her in what he thought would be a short, cheap war. He continued, 'I have told her Majesty of late sundry things of good consequence, proving true, but I have had Cassandra's luck'. Finally, the writer closed his letter with the explanation that he was weak and sick.

The writer was a man who was acquainted with the foreign service, who wrote frequently to Queen Elizabeth, who was probably old enough to remember the reign of Queen Mary, who was educated, since he used many Latin and French phrases, and who was ill in 1585. The antiquary has often been identified as the author of the letter which has survived only in printed form, but there is no corrobative evidence that Lambarde of Kent ever communicated with foreign ambassadors or that he was ever concerned with foreign policy except as it affected local law and

order. He had no great love for the Dutch whom he charged
with corrupting the morals of Englishmen that were returning
in 1588 from the Dutch Wars.[25]

In 1585 when the letter was written the antiquary was probably in good health. It was at that time that he studied Camden's
manuscript of the *Britannia* and returned it with a cover letter on
29 July 1585, 13 days after the letter to Burghley was written, in
which he apologised to Camden for keeping the manuscript so
long, but he did not give the convenient excuse of illness for the
delay. Because the copy of the letter to Burghley has not survived
in the hand of Lambarde and also because of his own knowledge
of the antiquary's character, Conyers Read has argued that it was
'almost certainly from someone else more closely associated with
the Queen'.[26]

Could not the William Lambert who gave the speech in Parliament and who wrote the treatise on parliamentary procedure be
the same man who communicated about foreign policy with Lord
Burghley in the 1580s and who as a student earned his B.A. in
1561 and his M.A. in 1565 at Oxford University? This conjecture
is as good as any that has been made about the identification of
the burgess.

None of the arguments advanced to prove that the antiquary
was the Member of Parliament withstands close examination, for
they really do little more than work with the idea that he was an
educated man with the same name as the antiquary. Since there
were other William Lamberts with the proper education and
social background, it is only speculative to conclude from the evidence that Lambarde of Lincoln's Inn was the Member of Parliament. Furthermore, because there is no evidence in his personal
life and records that clearly establishes him as the Aldborough
representative, it is a fair conclusion to state that it is highly unlikely that the antiquary was ever a Member of Parliament.

# 4

## *The Antiquary*

THE ANGLO-SAXON scholar who researched ancient manuscripts with William Lambarde while he was a student at
Lincoln's Inn was Laurence Nowell of London, a cousin of
Laurence Nowell, the Dean of Lichfield, with whom he has often
been confused. From about 1564 to 1567 they transcribed old
chronicles which belonged to noted churchmen like Dr. Matthew
Parker, Archbishop of Canterbury, and Dr. Nicholas Wotton,
Dean of Canterbury and York, but an end to their studies came
when Nowell sailed for France to acquire a better knowledge of
learning abroad.[1]

On 4 October 1568, about one and a half years after Nowell's
departure, Lambarde had the *Archaionomia*, which was a pioneer
effort in the translation of Anglo-Saxon laws to Latin, printed by
John Day. In addition to the 124-page text, which presented the
laws in Anglo-Saxon on one page facing the Latin translations on
the next, it contained a letter of introduction and sections on the
Anglo-Saxon customs, their invasions, their kingdoms, and the
laws of King William I and King Edward I.[2]

In the letter of introduction, dated September 1568, Lambarde
explained how the volume was conceived and why he was having
it printed, an explanation at variance with the modern version of
the translations. It has frequently been asserted that when Nowell
went abroad he left a collection of Anglo-Saxon laws, some already translated, in Lambarde's possession and that those transcripts formed the bulk of the final work. Many historians have
all but claimed that Nowell was the author of the *Archaionomia*.[3]

Before Nowell left for France in March of 1567, the letter revealed, he had earnestly pleaded with Lambarde to translate the laws into common Latin. At first the antiquary had been reluctant to embark upon such an enormous project, but when he received encouragement from many of his friends, including Sir William Cordell, he decided to fulfil Nowell's wishes. In an attempt to prove that the laws were genuinely Anglo-Saxon, he also disclosed that most of them had been taken from manuscripts then preserved in the library of the Archbishop of Canterbury.

This letter, which was published in the *Archaionomia*, credited Nowell, who was called Lambarde's friend not his mentor, with suggesting the project but not with translating the laws into Latin. Long after the work was published the antiquary continued to borrow manuscripts from Parker and for another year at least to correspond with Nowell in Europe. Anything less than the truth in this letter would have cost him their friendship and would have brought discredit to his scholarly efforts.[4]

Once the project was underway he decided to dedicate it to Sir William Cordell, a bencher at Lincoln's Inn, who had been appointed Master of the Rolls and Privy Councillor by Queen Mary, and who, at the accession of Queen Elizabeth, was permitted to continue as Master of the Rolls but was dropped as a Councillor. He was elected to the second Parliament in 1562 and later became the first president of the Lambarde almshouse at East Greenwich in Kent. The work was dedicated to him because he was greatly distinguished in the interpretation of the law, because he had been diligent in preserving old manuscripts, and because the translator wished to thank him for his assistance with the translations. So pleased was Lambarde with his patron's help that he expressed the desire to work with him again on a similar project.[5]

After thus showing his appreciation to Nowell for suggesting the project, to the Archbishop of Canterbury for lending the manuscripts, and to the Master of the Rolls for his assistance, Lambarde revealed why he had decided to accept the challenge of this endeavour. First, he explained that he thought that laws were of tremendous importance to society and compared their value to that of a town's walls. The laws protected the people from enemies on the inside while the walls protected the people from the enemies on the outside. To maintain inner peace, he warned, a constant vigilance by the magistrates had to be kept in effect and severe penalties against lawbreakers had to be meted out. He also believed that since there was no sharp break in the history of England at the Norman Conquest and since the laws and customs of the Anglo-Saxons had continued as the basis of England laws to his own time, it was important for him and his contemporaries to study their Anglo-Saxon past in order to understand their own society.

He further confessed that he had proceeded with the project despite his own inabilities, because as these laws had never before been translated into Latin, he feared that any further delay would mean their total loss to the world, for the paper on which they had been preserved was already old and decayed. Finally, he feared, he said that his book would not be read with the respect the laws deserved because of the inept workmanship, but his aim had been to present the volume as a challenge to the learned, as an aid to the unlearned, and as a delight for all.[6]

The study of Anglo-Saxon culture by many 16th-century scholars like Lambarde was popular for at least two basic reasons. First, a feeling of nationalism was rising in Europe in conjunction with the emergence of nation states. When national identification began to supersede and replace old provincial ties, those who desired to glorify their nation and their race were motivated to search their past for examples of greatness and splendour. Lambarde, who was of that English movement, not only lauded the kingdom's Anglo-Saxon heritage but he also frequently expressed vivid contempt for other national groups.[7]

Another cause for the scholarly interest in England's antiquity was the severing of Papal ties during the Reformation. By an exhaustive study of history Lambarde and others hoped to prove that the Church in England, once pure and uncorrupted, had been lead astray by Papal direction. If they could find a historical basis for their theory, they could justify the Reformation that had ended the link to Rome and could glorify the Tudors who had expelled idolatry.

After a thorough study of the *Archaionomia*, Dr. Felix Liebermann, a noted authority on Anglo-Saxon law, concluded that since Lambarde was a 'pioneer in an unknown land', his work was good. Naturally modern Anglo-Saxon scholars have recognised his book as that of a beginner who not only made errors in the translations but who also chose inaccurate texts. Nevertheless, for the 16th century it was a marvellous accomplishment and was widely read by the scholars of the day.[8]

England's Anglo-Saxon heritage was praised not only in the *Archaionomia* but also in the *Alphabetical Description of the Chief Places of England and Wales*, a work which was in progress in 1567, the year that Lambarde began the translations and the year that he was called to the bar at Lincoln's Inn. It is likely that he had begun to transcribe old manuscripts for this volume at least as early as 1564, when he and Laurence Nowell began to collaborate on scholarly endeavours although there is no definite evidence of that early date in the work itself. He must have been neglecting his legal training during the years of research with Nowell, moreover, for he was in residence 11 years at the Inn before he became a barrister.[9]

Probably by 1570 most of this manuscript was completed, at least in rough form, for in a letter in January 1571 to Thomas Wotton of Kent he revealed that he had used his notes on many histories of England to form a historical dictionary or 'store house', out of which he intended to draw suitable information for histories of all the shires in England. He continued to add to the manuscript at least as late as 1577 but finally forsook the project after Camden sent him a manuscript copy of the *Britannia* to review and criticise. In July of 1585 he returned the manuscript to Camden with a covering letter in which he lamented that he 'may not nowe . . . dwell in the meditation of the same things that you are occupied withal'. He must have been convinced that his own manuscript was of little worth when compared to Camden's great achievement.[10]

Lambarde arranged his manuscript like a dictionary, describing in alphabetical order all the most important historical places in the kingdom. While his own personal observations did form a part of the work, the bulk of the dictionary was taken from old chronicles and ancient histories. A reading of it reveals that the author was particularly interested in Anglo-Saxon history and name derivatives of the places he described.

He did not hesitate to criticise the various historians and chroniclers who were quoted in the manuscript. For instance, because he was particularly proud of his own ability to read Anglo-Saxon, he often ridiculed other writers who were unable to do so. He charged that Polydore Vergil had mis-named the abbess of the Monastery at Shaftesbury because of his 'Ignorance in the Saxon', and that Fowler was a 'man belike unlearned in the Saxon Tongue'. Even the Venerable Bede was rebuked for relying too heavily upon hearsay, as was Gyraldus Cambrensis who told of a hill which miraculously grew in size under a speaker's feet. The antiquary quickly dealt with his style: 'I wish his Booke was not so longe that he needed any mery Tale to refreshe the Reader'.[11]

For his own part he attempted to evaluate in a critical manner the information made available to him. In his discussion of London he wrote that John Ross had identified Caesar as the founder of that City but that he was sceptical: 'But I (reading no suche thinge in Caesar's own *Commentaries*) dare not afferme so muche, least I be noted (as Leland hath noted Ross) a man of more Diligence than judgement'.[12]

In addition to revealing his approach to evidence and his attitude to the chroniclers he quoted, the *Description* disclosed some of his own prejudices and opinions. As a scholar who knew Anglo-Saxon, French, and Latin, he was interested in the development of English from those tongues. One particular criticism he had of English was that the language 'consisteth of woordes of one syllable', and to demonstrate how words had become shorter and shorter throughout history, he cited the change of the name of a town called Genlademouthe by Bede to Glademouthe in his own day. He agreed with Erasmus that spoken Engish sounded like a dog's barking, 'baw, waw, waw'.[13]

Other opinions of his can be found in this volume. He bitterly lamented the loss of Calais as did many of his contemporaries, including Queen Elizabeth who tried to reclaim it, and he had an unfavourable opinion of Stonehenge which he believed had been built in honour of the deaths of British noblemen. He wrote that he had not seen anything impressive about the stones for 'they hange with no more Wonder then one Post of a House hangeth upon another . . .' Perhaps he would have been more impressed with the monument had it been built in honour of Saxon noblemen.[14]

In addition to using his own research in this work, Lambarde revealed in his letter to Thomas Wotton in 1571 that he had used the research of many of his friends who had taken notes out of ancient books for him. Had he, himself, had the work printed, he might have named those who assisted him and the extent of their contributions, but the manuscript was published posthumously. There are historians who have claimed that the *Description* was written almost entirely from transcripts Nowell left when he sailed to France in 1567.[15]

Too much credit has been given to his contributions to this volume, which, when published in 1730, had over 5,000 references to more than 150 different chronicles, histories, and charters. After his discovery of 20 volumes that had passed from Nowell's ownership to that of Lambarde, the late Robin Flower concluded that those transcripts formed the primary source material for the *Description*. In addition to the volumes discovered by Flower at the British Museum, another 20 have been identified as having been in the possession of both scholars, but only 31 of the total 40 were probably used as sources for the *Description*. Another 40 books and manuscripts which were cited in the work and which were never in Nowell's possession have likewise been traced.[16]

Flower included in the list of Nowell transcripts which he thought had formed the bulk of the research materials for the *Description*, four questionable titles. He believed that Nowell's 1562 copy of the Itinerary of Wales by Giraldus Cambrensis was used but that hardly seems likely when Lambarde had owned a copy of it since 1560. There is no evidence to support the claim that he used his friend's copies of the Peterborough Chronicle or the Alfredian translation of Bede's *Ecclesiastical History*. Indeed, Lambarde had probably seen several copies of both of those works. Finally, according to Flower, the shorter history of Matthew Paris was transcribed by both Lambarde and Nowell from a manuscript then owned by Lord Arundel and in the possession of Archbishop Parker, but Dr. John Randolph reported that it was in the hand of Lambarde alone.[17]

This present study has revealed that even though Nowell's transcripts were undoubtedly of great significance in the writing of the *Description*, they were not as important as those of Lambarde. Even if the antiquary had used all the Nowell materials on Flower's list, except for the Cambrensis and Paris transcripts but conceding the copies of Bede and the Peterborough Chronicle, since he referred to them only about 1,500 times in a work with over 5,000 references, they provided at most about one-third of the research for the *Description*.

After the slow process of accumulating this vast amount of research, a difficult task in Reformation England with its destruction of the monastery libraries, it was a major undertaking to
organise the material into a history that was coherent. There were
few in England, until Camden, who were willing to contemplate
such a painstaking project, but Lambarde was one of them.

Not only did Robin Flower state that Lambarde had done little
if any of the research for the *Description*, but he also suggested
that the Nowell transcripts had been secured by devious means.
In 1571 Lambarde testified in the Court of Requests that his
friend had freely left the transcripts with him when he departed
for the Continent in 1567. This case had arisen when three
Nowell relatives requested that the Court order the release of
some bequests that Laurence had left in the custody of William
Lambarde. It was thought at the time that Laurence, who had
been missing in Europe for two years, was dead, and, indeed, he
probably never returned to England.[18]

Since Lambarde confessed that his *Perambulation of Kent*,
printed in 1576, was drawn from information in the *Description*,
Nowell's research must have been of some importance to that
work. Although about 60, slightly more than a quarter of the
275 references, may have been made to nine of the Nowell transcripts, there is some question about the use of two of them, the
copies of Bede and Huntingdon's 'Leges Conquestoris'. Unfortunately, when he referred to Huntingdon, the antiquary, who
had read three treatises and a history by him, did not specify
which one of his works he meant to cite. Thus the 10 references
to that author surely did not all depend on the Nowell transcript
of the 'Leges Conquestoris'. As there were 20 references to Bede
and as Lambarde probably had seen more than Nowell's transcript of it, suspicion is attached to 30 of the 60 citations.[19]

It is true that some information from the *Description* was included in the *Perambulation*, but the Kentish history was greatly
enlarged. In addition to 30 new scholarly sources, 29 more
Kentish towns were discussed, and of those towns that were re-
peated, much more information was given. For example, in the
*Description* he noted that he believed Stouremouth was in Kent
but that he had not had time to inquire about its exact location.
Later, in the county history, he identified it as Kentish and devoted three and one-half pages to its history. There were also de-

letions. Four towns previously claimed for Kent were found to be in other counties.[20]

There were other distinguishing characteristics. First, since the *Perambulation* was prepared for publication by its author, it has survived in a more polished form than the earlier work which was not published until 1730. Secondly, since it was impossible for Lambarde to have the same familiarity with the topographical history of all England to the same extent as that of only one county he was forced to rely more heavily upon written sources for the survey of England than for the history of Kent.

It is apparent that he visited Kent often and knew the county well, since he discussed with some authority its climate, the people and their customs, the land and its vegetation, the rivers and the ships that sailed them, and the tenures of land and their history. Although the chroniclers and their narratives formed a major portion of the work, the *Perambulation* has a significant historical importance because it contains many of Lambarde's own personal observations about 16th-century Kent.

Usually he began his description of the Kentish towns with a discussion of their histories, but occasionally, as with the village of Teynham, he permitted his own feelings to take precedence :

> I woulde begin with the Antiquities of the Place as commonly I doe in others, were it not that the latter and present estate thereof far passeth any that hath been tofore it. For heere have wee, not onely the most dainty piece of all our Shyre, but such a singularitie as the whole British Island is not able to patterne.

This passage is particularly delightful to read because it was he, and not some distant chronicler, who described the village as both 'delightsome', and 'beautiful'. In contrast, the paragraph on Teynham in the survey of England was confined to a story about King John and his troubles.[21] Modern historians, of course, lament that he did not more often dispense with the antiquities and dwell on the Kent that he knew, but even though his personal comments were limited, it is obvious that he loved the county that he chose for his home.

He permitted some of his own prejudices and beliefs to show when he explained that, even though he was saddened by the great decay of Canterbury and other religious places, which had been caused by the dissolution of the monasteries, he still had to praise God that the temples of wickedness that had housed the sinful nuns and monks had been destroyed.[22] He also ridiculed those who kissed the shoe of Becket, a saint he particularly abhorred because he had 'opposed himself against his Prince (Gods lawfull and Supreme minister on earth) . . .'.[23]

The framework or vehicle by which he presented the history of Kent was totally different from the one used in the *Description*. He chose to perambulate the two dioceses of the county, first Canterbury and then Rochester. Before the perambulations, he inserted 70 pages of information, including a letter of introduction, a section on Anglo-Saxon Kent, a chapter on the estate of Kent, lists of administrative details, a short essay on early Britain, and a map of the beacons in the county.[24]

The original map of the beacons has probably been lost but copies of the Philip Symonson map, which Lambarde had printed in the 1596 edition of the *Perambulation* and which he praised as the best map of Kent that he had ever seen, have survived.[25] The map, he explained, was printed as a public service to the inhabitants of Kent who seemed to be ignorant of the significance of the beacons and unaware of their positions. At times of a threatened invasion from the sea, the beacons were lighted to warn the countryside to arm for the defence of their homes. Anticipating that there might be criticism of the printing of the map, he carefully noted that the enemy would gain no advantage from learning the beacon positions and that it would surely aid in the defence of the country.[26]

By January of 1571 he believed that the manuscript was ready to be printed, but since he first wished to have the opinion of someone who was familiar with the county, he sought the aid of Thomas Wotton of Boughton Malherbe, Kent whose deceased uncle was Dr. Nicholas Wotton, Dean of Canterbury and York. In choosing Thomas Wotton, a former sheriff of Kent, as his first critic, Lambarde singled out a local gentleman whose support would be important to the ultimate success of the history among Kentish gentlemen.[27]

Wotton may have assisted Lambarde in obtaining the loan of his uncle's manuscripts since the Dean's transcript of the 'Memorandum de Ponte Roffensi, etc.', was cited in the *Perambulation* and his copy of the 'Taxation of the Temporalities of dyvers religious Houses', was used in the *Description*. Because the Dean

of Canterbury and York died in 1567, when work on the topographical manuscripts was just beginning, it is not unlikely that
Thomas Wotton loaned his uncle's transcripts to the antiquary.[28]

The copy of the *Perambulation* was sent to Wotton in January
1571, but for over two years nothing further was written about its
possible publication. Finally, in May 1573 Archbishop Parker
sent to Lord Burghley a treatise of Gervasius Tilberiensis and a
description of Kent, whose author he described as an 'honest and
well learned observer of tymes and historyes'. Cautioning Burghley to remain silent about the volume on Kent, Parker explained that the author had not wanted the manuscript discussed
in public until he had received the opinions of his friends, and
also indicated that the author had helped him in the recent revision of his own works.

Two months later the Archbishop again wrote to Burghley
about the county history, this time because he had learned that
the Queen was planning to visit Thomas Wotton during her progress in Kent. He had failed, he pointed out, to inform Burghley
that the manuscript was to be dedicated to Wotton and was for-
warding a copy of the dedication to him so that he could read it.
Once again he cautioned him not to reveal that the work was in
his possession.[29]

No further reference was made to the manuscript for a period
of two and a half years. During that time Lambarde lost his first
wife and began preparations for the founding of his almshouse,
but he did not neglect his antiquarian studies. Searching for old
manuscripts and adding new information to the county history
consumed much of his time. One manuscript which he discovered
was the 'Textus de Ecclesia Roffensi', an old volume collected by
Ernulfus, Archbishop of Canterbury in the 12th century. Since
marginal notes in the volume indicate that Lambarde examined it
first in 1573, it had not been available as a source material for the
*Archaionomia* but citations to it were added to the Kentish history before it was printed in 1576. He shared the discovery of the
'Textus' with Archbishop Parker who asked him to write a passage in it about Lanfranc, Archbishop of Canterbury during the
reign of William the Conqueror.[30]

His close friendship with Parker can be traced at least to 1565
when he borrowed an ancient copy of Matthew Paris from him.
In 1568, of course, he claimed that most of the Anglo-Saxon

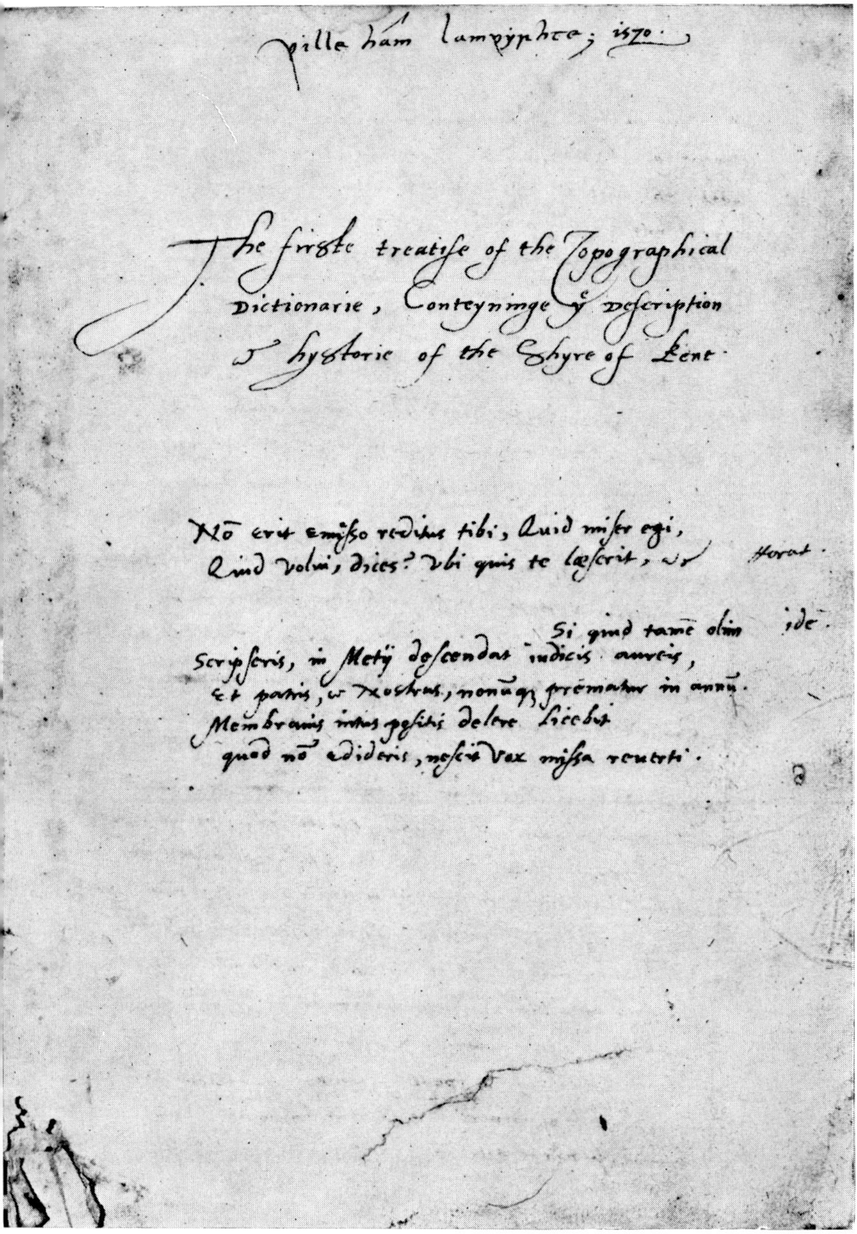

_gilla ham lampzphca; 1570._

_The firste treatise of the Topographical_
_Dictionarie, Conteyninge y<sup>e</sup> description_
_& hystorie of the Shyre of Kent_

Nō erit emisso reditus tibi, Quid miser egi,
Quid volui, dices? vbi quis te læserit, &         Horat.

                                    Si quid tamē olim   ide.
Scripseris, in Metij descendat iudicis aureis,
Et patris, & nostras, nonūq̃ prēmatur in annū.
Membranis intus positis delere licebit
quod nō edideris, nescit Vox missa reuerti.

PLATE I. PERAMBULATION OF KENT, 1570

The title page in Lambarde's hand to the MS. of the 1576 edition, the
property of the Kent Archaeological Society [K.A.O.: U47/48 Z1].

PLATE II. PERAMBULATION OF KENT, 1570

Two pages from the MS. of the 1576 edition. Both the map and the text
are in Lambarde's own hand. The MS. volume belongs to the Kent
Archaeological Society [K.A.O.: U47/48 Z1].

The exposition of this mappe, of the Inglishe
Heptarchie, or seven kingdomes.

To thende that it may be vnderstoade, what is ment by the tearmes
of Eastsaxons, westsaxons, mercia, Northumberland, & suche other,
of wch theare is comō mentiō in this treatise followinge, I haue
thoughte good to prefixe a chorde, of the seuen sundrie kingdoms, into
the wch this realme was sometyme deuyded. & for the better & more
playne explicatiō therof, it shalbe good to knowe, that al theise
nations followinge haue had to doe within this countrye: the bryttons,
the Romanes, the Scottes & pictes, the Saxons, and the Normanes. The Nation
(after the Semothess, Plineus &c) were the greate same in our hystorie) the most auncient inhabitantes of this land and
The bryttons

Jul: cæsar (the Romane) invaded them; for so muche may a man gather of
Horace his wordes, wheare he sayeth, Intactus aut Brytanus,
                              Sacra vt descenderes cute natus via: or

                    therfore weare by Jul.
Theise Cæsar sobdued to the Romane empyre, & made their countrye a prouince;
in wch case they continued many yeres together, vntyl at the lengthe beinge
greiuouslie vexed wth the pictes & Scottes, their neighbours in the northe,
& beinge vtterlie voyde of al hope of aide, the Romanes their patrons,
(who at the same tyme weare sore afflicted, wth the invasiō of the like Barba=
rous nations) they weare enforced to seke for further helpe. And therfore sent
into Germanie, to whence they receaued hyred souldiours, vnder the conducte
of Hengist & horsa, who brethe, &c, were valiant capitaines.

Theise Scottes (as them selues write) weare a people that came first into Spayne,
then into Ireland, & from thence to the north part of Brytaine, wheare they
yet inhabite; & weare called Scottes, or Scyttes, of Scyttan, wch is to
shoote. The pictes came after them, & occupied the partes, whence west &
morland & Galoway now be. And they weare so called pictes, either for that they vsed
to paincte their bodies, to seame the more terrible, or of the worde vextes,
wch signifieth, a champion, by reason of their great hardines.
The Saxons, Jutes, & Angles, weare the germans that came ouer, & ar ade of
the bryttons. of wch the first sorte inhabited Saxonie, the second weare of Gotland,
& therfore called gates, or gottes; The thyrd weare of Angia, a countrye
adioyninge to Saxonie, of wch the duke of Saxonie is lord tyl this day, &
the name in his stile, or title of honour, & of theise weare al be called Englishe me

Theise germanes, for a season serued against the Scotter & pictes; but afterward,
(enticed by the pleasure of this countrie, & the fraude of the Enemies) they ioyned
hondes wth theym, & al at once set vpō the Bryttons that broughte them in, And so
dryvinge them into fraunce, wales, & Cornwall, possessed their dwellinge &
deuyded the countrye amongest them selues. howbeit, they also wanted not their
                                                                    plague;

manuscripts which were translated into Latin for the *Archaio-nomia* belonged to Parker. Later the Archbishop praised Lambarde's ability in his work, *De Rebus Gestu Aelfredi Regu* and loaned him a roll about gavilkind for his treatise on that subject in the *Perambulation.*[31]

Less than one year before the *Perambulation* was printed, on 17 May 1575, Archbishop Parker died, leaving behind many mourning friends, among them Lambarde who recorded in his diary the death of his 'amans' in 1575. When the *Perambulation* was finally printed, in part because of the efforts of Parker, it contained a letter of introduction, dated 16 April 1576 and written by Thomas Wotton who stated that the manuscript of the work had been 'lately' sent to him. He dedicated it to the gentlemen of Kent because 'there is nothing either for our instruction more profitable or to our minds more delectable . . . than the studie of histories . . .'. Hoping, he further added, that the Kentish gentlemen would receive pleasure from reading the book, he called upon them to give thanks to Lambarde for his learned labours.[32]

Since the book was a great success, Lambarde issued a new edition in 1596. During the 20-year period between printings, he had continued to learn many new facts about Kent which were incorporated into the new edition. For example, during his visit to Quinborough Castle in 1579 he discovered a man trying to manufacture brimstone and copper. He also introduced a new discovery to the world since he was the first to suggest that the hill above Hillborough was a Roman burial mound. It was the discovery of an earthen pot on the hill by a neighbour that led the antiquary to search that area and to find the burial mound.[33]

The 1596 edition is also notable because of its references to Camden who was called the 'most lightsome antiquarie of this age'. In the 1576 version Lambarde had stated that the name of the county was derived from the British word Cainc which meant woods, but in the second edition he included Camden's explanation in the *Britannia* that the name Kent was derived from Cant or Canton which meant an angle or corner of land. The ninth and final reference to Camden occurred at the end of the perambulation of the diocese of Rochester. There Lambarde had previously called upon learned men in all shires to write their local histories, which could then be joined together in one giant topographical work of England. In the 1596 edition, however, he claimed that even though Camden had partially fulfilled his wish, he still believed that the 'Inwardes of each place' were known best by men who lived there and that they should write their own histories.[34]

The printing of the *Britannia* by Camden terminated Lambarde's topographical dream of writing a history of England which was to be created from shire histories, but it did not end his wish that the local works should be written. Indeed, his thorough sense of organisation and timing may have been somewhat undone by the appearance of Camden's work before the completion of the shire histories. What is certain is that, after Camden's achievement, except for an occasional new Kentish discovery for the 1596 edition, Lambarde's antiquarian research, already inclined towards legal topics, became immersed in them.

According to one modern scholar, Thomas Kendrick, Camden owed all of his knowledge of Anglo-Saxon history to other Elizabethan antiquaries, among them Laurence Nowell, William Lambarde, and Francis Tate. That Camden asked Lambarde to criticise his manuscript implied that the scholarly world must have thought highly not only of his Anglo-Saxon scholarship but also of his knowledge of the history and topography of Kent. Indeed, at the beginning of the Kentish section in the *Britannia*, Camden wrote that Lambarde was the source for his history of that county. From Camden this was welcomed praise.[35]

Although the history of Kent was highly praised by Camden there was at least one contemporary who was somewhat more critical of the work. Because he was a deputy-lieutenant who supervised the beacons of Kent, Sir Roger Twysden was particularly interested in Lambarde's discussion of them. He recorded in his Book of Musters that he disagreed with the antiquary's assertion that the beacons were first used by the Saxons and cited Bede as his source. He also doubted Lambarde's claim that they were made of stacks of wood prior to the 11th year of the reign of King Edward III, for as the deputy-lieutenant complained, 'I confesse I have neyther met with that Record of 11 Ed. 3 nor yet is ther proffe to seeke it by hym mentioned'.[36]

Naturally as a pioneer in the writing of county histories, Lambarde was bound to err occasionally. One modern scholar has discovered that the antiquary confused the historical identities of

Old and New Romney.[37] Another modern criticism of Lambarde is that he was unconcerned about the why and how of an event and was interested usually in discovering only what had occurred and when. On the few occasions when he searched for the cause of an event, he often found the answer in the mysterious and unfathomable movements of God. This kind of answer sufficed for his explanation of the death of King Hardacanute: 'At the length, God, taking pitie upon the people, took suddenly away King Hardacanute'. As a lawyer and as a historian, he was 'precedent-minded' not 'historical-minded'.[38]

The greatest modern criticism of the county history is that the author dwelt too long on the antiquities of Kent, particularly its Saxon past, and not long enough on the county of his own day. Primarily a Saxon scholar, Lambarde was not interested in the ancient Britons and had very little to add to that period of English history. Indeed while discussing the revival of Saxon learning in England, Thomas Kendrick said, 'The return of the Saxons was a calamity for the ancient Britons.' Kendrick also revealed that Lambarde evidently accepted without question not only the story of the Trojan Brutus but also the proposal that Samotheans had first inhabited the island. Because these matters did not seem to concern him, he did not thoroughly investigate their validity. As he saw it, his aim was to evaluate and criticise those chroniclers who wrote about Anglo-Saxon England.[39]

On the favourable side, Dr. Felix Hull of the Kent Archives Office has called Lambarde one of the giants among the historians of Kent and has revealed that his history of Kent is still significant for at least four reasons: first, that it represents a pioneer effort in the field of county histories; second, that it represents Kent of the late Tudor period; third, that it is good reading; and fourth, that it is still of great value for a knowledge of Kentish customs.[40] That Lambarde was able to place his great knowledge of topography and local history into a thoroughly readable and enjoyable narrative that still has great value for the modern world, is an achievement of no little consequence for a man whose avocation pioneered the writing of local history.

# The Son-in-Law

S INCE William Lambarde was not called to the bar until
1567, 11 years after he had entered Lincoln's Inn, his efforts
at transcribing chronicles and translating Anglo-Saxon
laws, while he was studying to be a barrister, undoubtedly
delayed his promotion. In the succeeding three years he similarly
demonstrated a greater interest in his antiquarian research than
in his legal practice, a career which may have been limited to the
drafting of a will in 1568 for a Kentish gentleman, whose needs
probably came to his attention during one of his trips to Kent to
gather material for the *Perambulation* or to survey the marsh-
lands of that shire as a commissioner of the sewers.[1]

In July 1568, along with William, Earl of Pembroke, and William, Lord Cobham, he was appointed to a Commission of Sewers
for the area of Lombards Wall to Gravesend Bridge in Kent. If
he had not previously made the acquaintance of Lord Cobham,
this appointment, which authorised them to oversee repairs to the
sea walls, the cleansing of rivers, public streams, and ditches, and
especially the drainage of marshes and low-lying ground near the
watercourses, began a long association that was to end only with
his lordship's death in 1597. It was undoubtedly in 1568, after his
appointment to this service and after publication of the *Archaionomia*, that he began writing the *Perambulation*.[2]

Apparently he served on several commissions since there is
scattered evidence of his activity in overseeing the drainage of
lands for the next 31 years. He probably kept a record of those experiences but only one reference has been found to his book of
sewers and that was in 1599 when he sent it to his friend, Sir John

Leveson of Kent, because he had to remain at the Court of Chancery in London. It was probably as a commissioner of the sewers that he held the post of Collector for the Greenwich Marsh from October 1579 to October 1580. As this officer it was his duty to see that the landowners and tenants of the Marsh, who were responsible for embanking and draining the land, paid for their share of the upkeep. Since he was the chief landowner of the Marsh, which was liable to extensive flooding if the banks were not properly looked after, the co-operation of the other owners was of significance to him.[3]

Because the roads were extremely poor in the 16th century, riding on horseback and transport by water were the only practicable ways to travel, but unfortunately many of the rivers in Kent were made impassable by weirs or small dams which diverted water for the driving of the mill wheels. They not only caused obstruction to water traffic but were also responsible for flooding the countryside. As a sewer commissioner and as the lessee of Halling Palace on the Medway River from 1583 to 1589, Lambarde had ample opportunity to become acquainted with the prolonged disputes over the weirs and the flooding they caused.

In 1600 Sir John Leveson, who was trying to resolve one of those disputes, asked his friend, Lambarde, to assist him with a review of the Medway, but the antiquary, who was then living at Westcombe in East Greenwich, replied that he saw no need to participate in another investigation since he, himself, who had been made aware of the Medway's weir problems through service on various commissions, and the legislators, who had outlawed the erection of weirs by statute, were already confident of their damage to the countryside. He further expressed the opinion that his honest and kind friend had been lured into the fray by neighbours who were weir owners with no concern for the property of others. Despite continued protests, it was not until the middle of the 18th century that they were finally removed from the Upper Medway River.[4]

Besides increasing his Kenish contacts through his scholarly and governmental business, Lambarde further cemented his ties there by a marriage alliance with Jane Multon of Ightham in Kent. In 1570 while he was polishing his draft of the *Perambulation* he was also courting his future bride, the 16-year-old daughter of George Multon, owner of St. Clere's Manor. When they first met and how long their courtship lasted are not known, but they were wed on 11 September 1570, a month before his 35th birthday and on the eve of her 17th birthday. Instead of taking his new wife to his home in East Greenwich, William chose to live with her family at St. Clere's, which had been a part of Aldham Manor in the reign of King Edward III and which had not been granted by the Crown to his father-in-law, then of Hadlow, until 1547.[5]

This was an advantageous marriage alliance for both partners. Lambarde, a barrister and landowner as well as an acknowledged expert on Anglo-Saxon law, was a good match for Jane whose ancestry was far from illustrious, since her mother, Agnes Polhill, came from a family of yeomen. Her father's ancestors, the Multons, were gentlemen who had settled in Kent as least as early as the reign of King Edward III. A record of their marriage settlement has not been found but there is evidence of the value of Jane's dowry in the Lambarde rent and receipt books. Until 1583, the year of his second marriage, Lambarde received £10 7s. annually in rents from lands in Ightham and Pickham, but the major part of the dowry was the lease of St. Clere's which was given to him for 39 years from October 1571 and which he leased back to George Multon for an unspecified rent. After the death of his father-in-law in May 1588 Lambarde traded this lease to the Multon heir, George, for £300 in money and the lease of the demesne of Otford Manor, then valued at £100.[6]

When he agreed to accept the Otford lease he was well acquainted with the property, since he had served on a commission to review its manor house, which, after its conveyance by Thomas Cranmer, Archbishop of Canterbury, to King Henry VIII, had fallen into a ruinous state. In 1573, a commission, composed of Thomas Wotton, the gentleman who then had a manuscript copy of the *Perambulation*, George Multon, the father-in-law, and the antiquary himself, reported that repairs of £1,729 9s. 10d. were needed to renovate the manor house. Despite this report, and others, the crown permitted the house to lie in ruins until it was sold in 1601.[7]

In addition to her dowry, there were other practical and unromantic reasons for the antiquary to choose Jane Multon for his wife. Since she was young, presumably she would be able to bear him many children, and since her father was a respected justice of the peace, he would be able to introduce his new son-in-law to the community and to the administration of law on the local level. Surely, Lambarde, the son of a London merchant, needed this entry into Kentish society if he hoped to become a local dignitary, such as a justice of the peace. Undoubtedly he followed the traditional middle-class pattern of wedding his wife, however alluring, for reasons other than mere romantic love.[8]

Their marriage was only three years old when Jane died on 21 September 1573, at the age of 20. Recording her death in his family diary, William noted that his pious and beloved wife had died after six days of illness, probably from smallpox. In the corner of the parish church of Ightham behind the font, a monument was erected to her memory.[9]

Since he continued to live at St. Clere's for a decade after the death of Jane, a close relationship with her father must have developed during the years of their marriage. Indeed, not only did the two gentlemen co-operate on commissions like the one to survey Otford Manor, but they also invested in horses and exchanged books. In 1577 Lambarde purchased horses from Multon that they had previously owned together and in the *Perambulation* he quoted from a transcript of the customs of Kent which had been given to him by Multon. After his second wife gave birth to a son in October of 1584, Lambarde confirmed the continuance of the great love and affection he had for his father-in-law at Ightham, who seems to have been his father substitute, by naming the child Multon Lambarde.[10]

With his move to Ightham, Lambarde established himself as a gentleman of Kent, but, of course, he still possessed his chamber at Lincoln's Inn and continued to visit the City during term time. He transferred his residence from that urban area of about 100,000 people in 1570 to a county with approximately the same number of inhabitants since by 1600 there were about 145,000 people in Kent. The largest towns of the county, Greenwich, Rochester, and Sandwich, had a population of between 1,000 and 2,000 inhabitants. Excluding the county of Middlesex, the shire of Kent, which was ninth in total area in the kingdom, had a high urban population for Tudor England since about 15 per cent of its people lived in towns. It was no small and insignificant county that Lambarde chose as his home.[11]

Since Lambarde's manor was located in East Greenwich, a town only four miles southeast of London, it is possible that he

established his residence at Westcombe after he was called to the
bar in 1567 and before his marriage to Jane Multon in 1570, but
there is no evidence to suggest that he did so or even that he lived
there for any length of time, although he undoubtedly visited the
area frequently to survey his holdings and to gather material for
the *Perambulation*. Even though he resided at St. Clere's from
1570 to 1583, the central government, well aware that he possessed Westcombe Manor, listed him among 100 others assessed
for a Greenwich subsidy in 1571.[12]

Historically, Tudor Greenwich was important because a royal
residence had existed there since the 13th century. Queen Elizabeth I, who had been born at Greenwich, was particularly fond of
the palace and usually moved there each year in May for the
summer, but she was present early enough in the spring of 1573
to celebrate Maundy Thursday at Greenwich. William Lambarde witnessed this celebration, whose origins go back to 600
A.D. in England, but why he was permitted this privilege can
only be conjectured since in the detailed record he kept of the
service he did not explain the reasons for his presence. It has been
suggested that Archbishop Parker interceded for him and it is
true that two months later Parker brought a manuscript of the
*Perambulation* to the attention of Lord Burghley, but there is no
evidence to support the claim that he also won this favour for his
antiquarian friend.[13]

The hall at Greenwich Palace was prepared for the service by
the placing of a long table on each side of the room and another
at the upper end. After the necessary equipment was assembled,
39 poor women, numbering the age of the Queen, entered the
room and stood by the side of the tables. The yeoman of the
laundry, followed by the sub-almoner and the almoner, performed
the ceremony of washing all the women's feet in a silver basin
with warm water and flowers, of wiping them with a towel, of
making the sign of the cross above them, and of kissing them.
Then the Queen entered, knelt on cushions before the end table
to hear a service and then performed the same ceremony. After
the traditional gifts were disbursed to the women, the Queen
heard the choir for a few more minutes and then left as the sun
was setting. The description was written with great beauty and
reverence by the antiquary who was not offended by the Catholic
ritual of the service.[14]

That Lambarde was interested in subjects other than the topography of England and the development of the Common Law was evident by the assortment of books he obtained in the 1560s and the 1570s. In 1564 he owned Philip Melancthon's *Chronicon Carionis* and in 1574 he added to his collection, Theodore Zwinger's *Morum Philosopha Poetica*. He also obtained in 1571 Conrad Heresbach's *Rei Rusterae Libri*, a volume which contained information on hunting, bowling, and fishing. Some time between 1571 and 1577 he drew up a cycle of years for the period 1571 to 1600 in which he computed the date on which Easter would fall every year in that period, as well as the date of the first Sunday in Lent, of Whitsunday, and of many other religious days. Even though the cycle was drawn with great care for detail, he did err in his figures and recorded on the parchment that 'The Numbres of the Indication by mystaken and Therefore drawe it backe by one, throughe out the whole circle'.[15]

Although he continued to study law and to learn the practical side of administering justice in the 1570s, it cannot be proved that he was an active counsellor-at-law. The only records which indicate that he represented clients were those which concerned the missing Laurence Nowell and those completing the sale of some property to Robert Bing, justice of the peace, from Lord Cobham's brother, Sir Henry Cobham. Since Lambarde was in London during every term from Hilary Term of 1558 to Hilary Term 1588, presumably he had business to conduct at the courts although no other record of it has survived. It was, of course, in 1579 that the Inn elected him an associate of the bench and praised him for his great abilities.[16]

Although he may not have had extensive legal business between 1567 and 1579, he increased the value of his estate by buying and selling property. In addition to adding a few acres called Thistlecroft to the Manor at East Greenwich, he also obtained in 1567 for £200 a 20-year lease of the parsonage of Rowde in Wiltshire. This investment may have come to his attention on one of his trips to that shire to survey his holdings there which were not sold until 1570, the year of his marriage, when he began to consolidate his holdings in Kent and London.

Both the rise in London land values and Lambarde's shrewd business sense were demonstrated in the transactions concerning four Maiden Street houses which he purchased in April of 1571 for £300 and which he leased for an annual rent of £19. Two and a half years later he sold them to the Haberdashers' for £440, earning a £140 profit in addition to the rents that he had collected during those years. These houses were sold on 1 November 1573 to acquire enough ready money to endow his almshouse at East Greenwich.[17]

From 1575 he kept a record in his rent and receipt books of his annual worth in cash and goods, which came to £178 in 1575, not including the value of his St. Clere's lease and 13s. 10d. in quitrents. It was not until 1577 that he again reckoned his worth which came to £375, more than double his first estimate, but he failed to explain the reason for the increase. During every October thereafter he reckoned his worth in cash and goods. In 1578 it was £375, including jewels and plate worth £39, ready money of £8, leases worth £120, and debts of £160. This estimate did not include the St. Clere's lease, his rents, his books, or his horses. In October 1579 he estimated his worth at £365 with the same exclusions.

The debts which were a part of his annual worth usually referred to loans that he had made to tenants, relatives, and friends. He often lent money to his relatives, especially to two of his first cousins, Thomas Wyckyn, draper, the husband of Margaret Bond, who was a child of Elizabeth Lambarde Bond; and Charles Bond, draper, brother of Margaret. Margaret and her husband, Thomas, were evidently close friends of the Lambardes, for Giles devised most of his London property to her and her children, two of whom were named William and Giles. In addition to the Bond cousins, William also had at least one other first cousin in the City, Christian Goodrich, one of the daughters of Anne Lambarde Goodrich. Christian married John Nicholson of London, currier, and had six children. Lambarde recorded that he gave her £10 for her marriage in June 1575 and that he made loans to her new husband, usually in the amount of £5.

Two other relatives were indebted to him in the 1570s; in 1573 his brother, Giles, owed him £36 and in 1575 his sister Lambarde, owed him 15s. 2d. No matter how close the relative and no matter how small the amount involved, William kept a meticulous and detailed record of the loan and its repayment, a habit that undoubtedly he had learned from his merchant father and one that evidenced a close stewardship of his possessions. It is obvious that although he chose to become a gentleman of Kent he maintained a close relationship with his London relatives.

He also lent money to friends and associates. One such friend was Humphrey Windham, called to the bar at Lincoln's Inn in 1569 and Lambarde's roommate from the early 1570s when he occasionally borrowed £5. Another of Lambarde's debtors was Robert Bing, justice of the peace of Kent, who borrowed £30 in 1578 and again in 1579. Actually after 1578 the antiquary had other business transactions with Bing, who owned lands which were held of a manor that had been granted to the Lambarde almshouse.[18]

The rent and receipt books left not just a record of wealth but also gave proof of his love for horses. In his reckonings he unfortunately did not include the value of his horses, except for those which he owned with his father-in-law, but he did keep records of the animals he purchased. The horses for which he admitted a great weakness and which brought him so much joy were more than just a hobby in Tudor Kent where they were a necessity for travel. He found this true when he became a member of the Commission of Peace for Kent in 1579.[19]

# 6

## *The Proctor for the Poor*

UNDOUBTEDLY because at 37 years of age he was a widower with no children of his own and because he had a strong conviction that it was the responsibility of private citizens to provide for the poor, Lambarde endowed an almshouse in East Greenwich with over one-third of his inheritance. In February 1575 he completed the transaction to exchange his plot called Thistlecroft (purchased in 1563 for £73 6s. 8d.), the release of its 23d. yearly quitrent to Westcombe Manor, and £20 in cash to Edmund Chapman, principal joiner to the Queen, for a close of seven acres in the west end of East Greenwich to be the site of the almshouse, and for eight acres of woodland called Ballingsborough Grove to provide fuel for the inmates.[1]

The almshouse, erected on the close in time to admit the first inmates in October 1576, was a brick building with a tile roof and a courtyard with a pump. Besides a common room and a prayer room, it had 20 chambers for the poor, each measuring 20 feet by 20 feet, with two glass windows, a chimney, and an oven. On the north side of the building lay an enclosed fenland and behind the building were 20 gardens for the almsmen and a hemp plot.

In November of 1576 to provide more fuel for the inmates, he purchased for £16 a five-acre woodland, Hicson's Grove, which, along with the site of the college and Ballingsborough Grove, was leased to Richard Bromhead, the lessee of the demesne of Westcombe Manor, for 20 loads of faggots for fuel and the ploughing, dunging, sowing, and enclosing of the hemp plot. For income to provide the pensions of the almsmen and the upkeep of the almshouse, Lambarde granted the college lands worth £2,035 with yearly rents of £83 6s. 8d. and two capons.[2]

In his book of purchases he reckoned the cost of founding the almshouse at £2,739, broken down into two parts : £2,139 for lands and £600 for the building.[3] That he was able to make such a generous grant gave proof of his own shrewd stewardship and of the rise in the value of real estate in 16th-century England. He had, of course, obtained these resources primarily from the sale of his inheritance in Wiltshire and London, which, along with the unsold portion, had been appraised at only £1,900 in 1544, less than the total value of the charitable endowment some 20 years later.

The Letters Patent incorporating the almshouse as the College of Queen Elizabeth in November 1574 identified the founder as William Lambarde of Lincoln's Inn in the county of Middlesex, gentleman. They stipulated that 20 people were to reside in the college and that the Master of the Rolls was to act as president while the upper wardens of the Drapers' Company were to serve as governors. During his lifetime the antiquary was to retain full control over the college and the number of inmates was to be limited to 10. Many Elizabethans, like Lambarde, named institutions they endowed in honour of the Queen, although he may have been personally inspired to do so by his memories of her celebration of the Maundy at East Greenwich in the spring of 1573.[4]

Of the 20 poor to be housed in the almshouse two were to be chosen from anywhere in the kingdom, one by the Master of the Rolls and another by the two upper wardens. The others were to be selected from places within Blackheath Hundred, with eight coming from the parish of East Greenwich because it had more poor people than any other and because the College was located there.[5] The electors of the inmates who included the parson or whoever was resident in the parish for the administration of the sacraments, the churchwardens, the sidesmen, the collector for the poor, the surveyors for the poor, and the constables or borsholders or both were to hold the election at the church or in the common vestry on either the first or second Sunday after the announcement of a college vacancy.

After his selection the new candidate was to be sent with two sureties and a letter of introduction to the two upper wardens who were authorised to give him a key to a chamber at the almshouse when they had ascertained that he was qualified for admission. (During his lifetime, of course, Lambarde had the right of final acceptance or rejection.) If the parish could not find two persons who were willing to put up £20 for the good conduct of the new almsman, it forfeited its election turn.

In order to be chosen, an individual must have been supported for three years by the selecting parish and must have shown himself to be an honest and godly person who could recite the Lord's Prayer, the Articles of the Christian Faith, and the Ten Commandments of God. If he were married, his mate had to meet the same moral and religious requirements or the candidacy was denied. When a married couple qualified, they entered the college as one person, were given one room, and granted one pension of 6s. a month. A person residing at the college because of the election of his spouse was required to leave at his partner's death unless he was then selected in his own right.

The antiquary set up other guidelines for the choice of inmates. In order of preference he suggested that the aged should be chosen first, then the sick, lame, or maimed, after that the blind, then the victim of a sudden casualty, after that the ones who were continually sick, and finally those overcharged with children. If the electors had to choose between two people of equal decree, they were to prefer a man to a woman, the married to the unmarried, the long-time Protestant to the newly-converted Papist, the 'unnotorious' to the notorious, and the one who had lived in the parish the longer.

The almsmen were to select from their midst a warden who kept the keys to the front gate and the house of prayer and an underwarden who held the keys to the back gate and the common room. These two, elected for life, were to lock the gates from 8.00 p.m. to 6.00 a.m. from All Saints' Day to the Pacification of the Blessed Virgin Mary and from 9.00 p.m. to 5.00 a.m. during the rest of the year. Each morning before the opening of the gates and each evening before their closing, the almsmen were required to assemble at the front gate on the second ringing of a handbell to pray a prayer written by Lambarde with the advice of John Yonge, Bishop of Rochester, who gave his seal to it on 11 June 1578, for a fee of 10s.[6]

The prayer service, which included a recitation of the Ten Commandments, of the Articles of Faith, and of the Lord's Prayer, ended with the following plea :

God save his Church Universal, our gracious Prince (by name) the Nobility and the Councellors, the Master of the Rolls, the Company of the Drapers', and the whole Clergy and Commonalty of the Realm. The Grace of God the Father, the Peace of our Lord Jesus Christ and the Fellowship of the Holy Ghost be with us all now and ever. Amen.

After this service it was the duty of the warden to name those absent from prayer, an offence that carried a 4d. fine. The names of those absent overnight without a licence were read after the morning service and they were fined 12d. Because the founder wanted the behaviour of those whom his endowment supported to be carefully supervised, an impossible goal if they did not live at the almshouse, special permission had to be obtained for overnight absences.

The almsmen took turns ringing the handbell which signalled morning and evening prayers, and the one whose turn it was to be the bellringer also had to keep watch in the courtyard until 1.00 a.m. At the end of his duty he delivered the bell to the one whose watch came after his. Among other requirements, they had to wear badges, which Lambarde purchased for 4s. in May of 1587, for easy identification when they were away from the college. Finally, they were forbidden to sell their portions of the hemp crop, grown in the plot behind the almshouse, but were required to work it into cloth or to have one of the other inmates weave it for them at the cost of one half their portion.

All of their activities were closely supervised and the infractions of the rules were met with rather severe penalties on second and third offences. Among the penalties were a 2d. fine for refusing to hear divine service and for swearing in the college after two months' residence, a 6d. fine for fighting, a 13d. fine for refusing to work in Blackheath Hundred for 1d. a day, for being caught in the tippling house, and for breaking hedges. Most of these infractions carried a 6s. fine for a second offence, which was a whole month's pension for an almsman, and expulsion from the college for a third. Finally, the founder thought it wise to expel immediately anyone caught damaging the building.

Approximately one year after the Letters Patent were enrolled, the founder met with the two upper wardens of the Drapers' Company, Sir William Chester and Nicholas Wheeler, at the home of Sir William Cordell, Master of the Rolls. Since Lambarde had referred to Cordell as his patron in the *Archaionomia*, it was undoubtedly because he still held the office of Master of the Rolls that its holder was selected to serve as president of the college. At this meeting the seal of the almshouse was displayed, the upper side engraven with the arms of the Master of the Rolls and of the Drapers' Company. This portion of the seal was to remain in the custody of the president while the lower part, depicting a hand 'yssuing owt of a cloude poynting to a certen scrowle', was left in the possession of the upper wardens who were to serve as the college governors. It had earlier been agreed by the president and the governors that the college was to lease its lands to William Lambarde and his assigns for 50 years.[7]

Only one of many charitable institutions founded in Elizabethan England, the almshouse was not the first private Protestant endowment in Kent after the Reformation as it has been credited, but like other Kentish institutions it was based upon London wealth. Professor W. K. Jordan, the investigator of these endowments, has estimated that 40 per cent of all funds for charity in that county actually came from London and that 80 per cent of that amount was given for relief of the poor. The vast amount of funds contributed to charity by lay people in the 16th century was, of course, a great secular achievement.[8]

Lambarde's own secular orientation is nowhere more evidenced than by his decision to choose a non-religious corporation to administer his almshouse. He could have authorised some officer of the church, such as the Bishop of Rochester, to oversee it, but instead he entrusted it to the Drapers' Company despite the earlier dispute between its members and his brother. Another example of his secular bent of mind can be found in the name of the college, itself. It was not named after a saint of the universal church but rather after Queen Elizabeth, the living symbol of a national church in which the state had the final authority.

That he was willing to identify himself and his endowment with the Drapers' indicated that he, like many other professionals of the 16th century, saw no need to reject his mercantile background. Professor Louis B. Wright has asserted that the 'eschewing' of these origins did not occur on a wide scale until after the Restoration and that many of the professionals of the Elizabethan age actually shared the ideals of the commercial groups from which they sprang and with which they were associated.[9]

Because he was pleased that the drapers agreed to administer the college after his death, he gave them, when they returned from divine service on 4 August 1578, a cup of silver and gilt, which had a cover bearing the arms of England, of the Master of the Rolls, and of the Drapers' Company. The cup for which he paid £10 is presently the most valuable silver possession of the Company which lost all of its other pre-Commonwealth plate during the turmoil of the 17th century. Measuring 12½ inches tall and weighing 25¼ ounces, it was made with beautiful workmanship and lovely proportions, probably by John Bird of London in 1578. Around the rim is engraved, 'A Proctour for the poore am I remember theim before thou dye, 1578'. In addition to the cup, he gave them a small 'rundelet' of three gallons of ipocras with the request that the last drink at their annual election dinner be ipocras from the Lambarde cup.[10]

As definite arrangements for the endowment before the date of November 1573 have not been found, the death of Lambarde's first wife, Jane Multon, the previous September was undoubtedly the pressing reason for his charitable design. He was then a widower with no children to carry on the family name, but in 1583, a decade after Jane's death, he married Sylvestre Dalison, who by 1587 had borne him three sons and a daughter. It was with concern for the future of these children, born to him somewhat late in life, that he obtained an agreement from the Drapers' Company in 1591 to lease the college lands only to his descendants for the same rents that he was paying. Later, in his will, written in 1597, he encouraged the keeping of that agreement by extinguishing a £5 rent charge on the college lands and by adding the lease of the Lilly lands to the endowment.[11]

In August 1601 when he lay on his death bed, his thoughts naturally dwelt upon the future of his children, and unwilling to rely on the previous arrangements, he sought the opinion of his friend, Sir Thomas Egerton, Lord Chancellor of England, Master of the Rolls, and President of the College, who, in response, approved the plan to lease the lands only to Lambarde's descendants for the rents then paid. To encourage further the Company's compliance, the founder informed them of Egerton's consent and increased the college revenues by another £5. On 21 August 1601, two days after his death, the members of the

Court of Assistants of the Drapers' Company ruled that they
would keep their promises to him.[12]

After the birth of his four children Lambarde must have feared
that he had beggared them by granting away much of his property to the college without safeguards to reserve the use of the
lands for them and their descendants. Since the rents of his other
property in Kent had remained relatively constant, he probably
anticipated the rents would remain stable on the college lands.
Consequently, by the bargain with the Company, it can be argued
that he intended to guarantee both a stable income for the almshouse and the use of the lands to his family for reasonable rents.
Whatever the reason of the founder, it cannot be denied that
ultimately the bargain was prejudicial to the best interests of the
college, itself. In the early part of the 19th century the 200-year-
old agreement was struck down by the Court of Chancery which
decreed that since the founder had granted the lands to the
college by deed, he could not alter the basis of that legally-binding
agreement by petition of will or by any other petition. Thereafter the Company was required to lease out the lands for the
best possible rent.[13]

Even before the antiquary's death testators began to leave gifts
to the poor of the college. In June of 1587 Joan Tallis left a rent
charge of 10s. on two houses in Greenwich for them, in 1596
Ralph Rokeby left £100, and in 1610 William Stanton left a £2
rent charge on a Greenwich house. In the 18th century over
£1,200 worth of South Sea annuities, however worthless, were
bequeathed the almshouse along with various sums of money.
Not only did people bequeath gifts but they also copied the
college's organisational scheme. William, Lord Cobham, who
founded a college in 1597, and Sir John Jolles, who founded
several in 1618, both adopted the statutes of Queen Elizabeth's
College at Greenwich.[14]

One of the bequests was left by Ralph Rokeby, a good friend
of the founder and a fellow member of Lincoln's Inn. From
Rokeby's admission to the Inn in 1567 their friendship must have
flourished, for he gave Lambarde a horse for a Christmas present
in 1577, a generous gift which evoked the following thanks:

I can not but . . . receave him, if not as myne of youre guifte,
yet as youre owne in my custodie, lease eyther you should think

me disdainfull in refusing youre great kindness or daungerous and squaymishe to become hereby so much the more indebted to youe.[15]

10 years later Audrey Multon, the wife of George Multon, the younger, of Ightham, gave further evidence of the continuing close relationship between Rokeby and Lambarde when she asked her former brother-in-law to plead with Rokeby on behalf of her uncle whose case was to be settled by him.

The next year, 1588, Lambarde wrote to his good friend as a Master of the Court of Requests for a favour. Since he admitted that he had 'hitherto forborne to sollicite' Rokeby's assistance in cases pending before him, it is unlikely that he intervened on behalf of Audrey's uncle. He was boldly asking for his friend's aid in this instance, he continued, because the problem concerned not just one private person but many poor people of the county of Kent whose charitable endowments were being successfully withheld by greedy men because many of the deeds and papers authorising the charities were missing. Heretofore, he explained, 'as a professed proctor of the poore', he had tried, but unsuccessfully, to obtain justice for them in the spiritual courts and in the Court of Chancery, and he was then sending the suit to the Court of Requests with the hope that justice would triumph there. Not only did the antiquary found a college for the poor but he also acted as their advocate to gain their legal rights.[16]

Rokeby, himself a champion of the poor, bequeathed Lambarde's college £100 which he placed in the custody of the Drapers' Company in exchange for their agreement to pay £5 or its equivalent in cloth annually to the inmates. In September 1597, giving further evidence that until his death he kept complete control of the college finances, Lambarde asked the Drapers' to discharge the £5 rent on a house he was leasing from them in St. Peter the Poor, in return for his discharging the £5 they owed to the college from the Rokeby estate. The request was granted. Whether Lambarde, himself, paid the extra £5 to the almshouse is unknown, but since he had complained to Rokeby in 1588 about greedy men withholding legacies from the poor, it does not seem likely that he would be guilty of retaining the income for his own personal use.[17]

As executors for the Rokeby estate, Sir Thomas Egerton and

William Lambarde had to dispose of £1,970 6s. 2d. in bequests, many of them for charitable purposes. It was a heavy responsibility which was not completed until June 1600 when Lambarde certified that all the bequests had been paid, although much of the disbursal of funds was accomplished shortly after Rokeby's death in 1596. When Lambarde became ill in August of 1596 he accounted to Egerton for the legacies, promising that God willing he would continue to 'discharge the trust layed upon [them both] but undertaken by [him] aloane'.[18]

One of the many Lambarde letters dealing with the various bequests and revealing some of the problems he encountered was sent to Sir Julius Caesar on 24 December 1596. He noted that he had enclosed an order for the immediate payment to Caesar of £53 and that £300 had already been spent to free 200 debtors. Those transactions were under investigation since it was suspected that the creditors and the debtors had conspired to claim inflated debts so that they could split the difference between the alleged and real amounts. Disclosing that £1,600 of the legacy money had been disbursed, he promised that another £100 would be placed at Caesar's disposal and asked him to pay the letter-bearer's fee from the legacy money. He was not prepared to spend his own funds to carry out his duties as executor, even for a friend.[19]

From 1591 Sir Julius Caesar worked with Rokeby on the Court of Requests and at his friend's death succeeded him as Master of St. Catherine's. As early as 1584 he became a Master in the Court of Chancery and laboured with Lambarde on that court after his appointment to it in 1592. They must have been good friends since Caesar not only assisted with the disbursal of the Rokeby funds but also sent Lambarde for critical review a book he had written entitled *The Ancient State, Authoritie and Proceedings of the Court of Requests*. In the book Caesar contended that Masters of the Court of Request had the right to be members of the Privy Council, but Lambarde disagreed, writing in the margin, when he perused it in October 1598, that since the oath a Master of Requests took simply required him to affirm that he was a faithful servant to the Queen's Majesty, he did not deserve such an exalted position.[20]

In 1614 Sir Julius Caesar became Master of the Rolls and President of the Queen Elizabeth's College. During his presidency the poor sent at least four petitions to him to complain that they were being deprived of their rightful income. In one petition they charged that the clothes, wood, and other items the Drapers' Company gave them did not equal the full value of their legacies. In still another petition they claimed that since the accession of King James I one of the owners of the Tallis houses had refused to pay his share of the 10s. rent charge. Since they had heard that the founder's son, Sir Multon Lambarde, had obtained the house, they hoped that Caesar would talk to him about the payment of that rent charge.[21]

The finances of the college prospered even though its lands were leased for antiquated rents and despite allegations that the true value of its legacies was withheld. By the early 19th century the inmates were living in a new almshouse, rebuilt at the cost of £4,729 3s. 11d., a sum obtained from the sale of timber off the college lands and were receiving a monthly stipend of 35s. By 1868 the gross annual income was £1,608 8s. 10d. Today it is still standing on Greenwich Road as a haven for the poor and still governed by the statutes enacted by the founder almost 400 years ago.[22]

If ever the antiquary had been considered an outsider by the gentle families of Kent, the publication of his *Perambulation*, with the support of a leading Kentish gentleman, Thomas Wotton, and the incorporation of his almshouse must have laid that prejudice to rest. In the space of one year, 1576, he publicly lauded the beauty and history of the county and opened an almshouse for the shelter of its poor. As a newcomer to the county he was more enthusiastic about its attributes and more concerned about its social problems than many of its ancient families. When, after almost a decade of residing at Ightham with his father-in-law, George Multon, Lambarde was appointed to the Commission of the Peace for Kent, he must have already won the acceptance and respect of his neighbours whom he could surely call his friends.

# Justice of the Peace: The First Decade

O N 6 August 1579 Sir Thomas Bromley, Lord Chancellor
of England, issued Letters Patent naming a new Kentish
Commission of the Peace, which included for the first
time the name of William Lambarde, and indicated those who
were on the *Quorum*. Since the *Quorum*, a prestigious position
for senior and responsible justices, was expanded from one-
third to three-quarters of the commission in the reign of
Queen Elizabeth I, Lambarde quickly attained that status.[1]

The duties of those on the commission were many and
varied. In maintaining law and order, a justice of the peace,
acting alone, could investigate crime, could bind the accused
to appear at court or imprison them to await trial, and could
treat with breaches of the peace. With slightly more authority,
two or more justices working together could also bail prisoners
out of jail, regulate alehouses, deal with recusancy, and order
the punishment of parents of illegitimate children. When they
assembled at their county quarter sessions, they had the
authority to hear and determine all criminal cases which were
not serious enough to require trial in the royal courts. They
were also heavily encumbered with administrative tasks: the
overseeing of road repairs, the binding of apprentices, the fix-
ing of the wage level, the regulation of grain prices, the assisting of the lord-lieutenant in military affairs, the overseeing of
the honest poor, the raising of taxes, and the performing of
any other service the central government required. Besides
accomplishing these formidable tasks, they also acted as an in-
valuable means of communication, receiving new orders and

decrees from above and passing on information about local matters.

In April, before his official swearing in on 3 June 1580, Lambarde assisted several justices of the peace with the musters, first at Shorne and Frindsbury and later at Malling, Tonbridge, and Borough Green. He did not thereby exceed his authority because, as he explained, 'The commission of the muster was a general commission by itself, etc.'.[2] He apparently did not function as a justice of the peace until June after his swearing in, when he noted in his 'Ephemeris', the record book of eight of his years on the commission of the peace, that he and his father-in-law, George Multon, with whom he performed judicial inquiries until 1583, questioned several individuals about a robbery.[3]

The purpose of the musters which were held three times a year, during Easter week, at Whitsuntide and at Michaelmas, was to train all able-bodied men between the ages of 16 and 60 for home defence. The men were armed by the constables under the supervision of at least two justices of the peace and under the overall direction of the lord-lieutenant and his deputies. The lord-lieutenant, who in the 1580s in Kent was Sir William Brooke, Lord Cobham, had the supreme local authority to raise levies of men, to collect loans and subsidies, to enforce ecclesiastical laws, and to regulate grain prices. His assistants were more than 80 justices of the peace and several deputy-lieutenants, among them John Leveson, a close friend and associate of William Lambarde.[4]

The lord-lieutenant was not only required to call routine musters but he was also ordered to send men abroad for military service. Lambarde's term as justice of the peace fell in part during the last 15 years of the reign of Queen Elizabeth when the counties were drained of able-bodied men for fighting abroad to defend Protestantism from attacks generated by the Counter-Reformation and by King Philip II of Spain. Between April 1584 and July 1601, the county of Kent, with a population of about 145,000, furnished more than 15,000 men for duty to places such as Ireland, the Low Countries, and France, plus another 2,000 for Calais who were discharged before they sailed, and 18,000 for home defence during the Armada crisis.[5]

The first evidence of Lambarde's assisting with the levying

of men for service overseas survives in a Privy Council directive requiring 5,000 men for the suppression of the Munster Rebellion in Ireland. On 11 May 1584 the commissioners of the muster, Sir Thomas Fane, Sir Thomas Scott, and William Lambarde met with the muster master to discuss the progress of that levy and the expense involved.[6] A year later, in July of 1585, when Kent was ordered to train 150 men for overseas duty, Lord Cobham raised the subsidy for supplying those troops by parish, William Lambarde paying 6s., John Leveson 6s., and Margaret Dene, the mother of William's second wife, 15d.[7]

It was in July 1586 when Kent was required to supply 1,500 men and 18,000 pounds of powder and lead for the war in the Low Countries that Lambarde began assisting John Leveson, the deputy-lieutenant who was also a justice of the peace, with his military duties. On 20 July they sent out all constables in the area where they lived, the northern division of the lathe of Aylesford, letters berating them for falling behind in their raising of subsidies and purchases of military furniture.[8] That same year Lambarde purchased some armour in Rochester for £4. Perhaps he, too, was preparing for military duty, but it is more likely that he wished to appear at the musters in a dress suitable to his status as master of Halling Palace, his home from 1583 to 1598. Not only as a local official but also as a private citizen was he thus affected by the mustering of Kentish men for war.

Because of the danger of the Spanish invasion the government continued to call up men from the shires for military duty. In June 1587 when the lathe of Aylesford was required to furnish 50 of the 300 men to be raised in Kent, Leveson and Lambarde apportioned the cost among the various parishes of their lathe. That same month, on 23 June 1587, Lambarde recorded in his memorandum book that 13 of the 50 allotted to his lathe had been sent to the Low Countries, that each man had been given 2s., and that the captain had been given 10d. per soldier for military clothing and furniture. Later that year, in November and again in December Lambarde and Leveson wrote to Lord Cobham to complain that the cost of sending men abroad and training local bands for defence against invasion was impoverishing the shire.[9]

The next year, of course, military preparations continued at a feverish pace because of the threat of the Armada. Kent furnished 18,000 men for the home armies and was assessed £5,000 toward the costs of that defence. In April of 1588 Sir Thomas Fane wrote to Leveson and Lambarde about some military matters, but, unfortunately, their reply, if they sent one, has not been found. There is no other direct evidence linking Lambarde's activities to the Armada crisis although he probably assisted Leveson with a muster held at Rochester in late July and continued to work with him on military affairs after the English victory.[10]

Of course, the destruction of the Armada did not end the threat of the invasion and the English continued to train men to fight the Catholic menace abroad. Early in 1589 the Privy Council ordered Kent to send 200 soldiers and 75 pioneers to Gravesend for service under the command of Sir John Norreys and Sir Francis Drake, who planned to attack Lisbon (then under Spanish rule), and also ordered Sir Henry Cobham, John Leveson, William Lambarde, and William Sedley to feed the troops while they remained at Gravesend. Later that year the Council asked the same justices to report on the contents of the storehouse of munitions and powder at Chatham and on the soldiers who appeared at the regular muster.[11]

During his first decade as a justice of the peace Lambarde often assisted Lord Cobham with the supervision of the beacons, which were used to warn the countryside of an invasion. The lord-lieutenant, as the officer in charge of the county's defence, was required to oversee their use and maintenance; his deputies were ordered to see to their repair and the several captains in the county militia were charged with providing the proper quantities of pitch for their firing. The Privy Council sent out letters to remind the lord-lieutenants of the maritime counties every spring that it was time to begin the watch and every fall that it could be discontinued.[12]

The Privy Councillors kept up-to-date information about local changes in the beacon watch. In 1586 they congratulated Lord Cobham on reviving the ancient sea watches at the Isle of Sheppey, Romney Marsh, and other places, a revival based on information that Sir Thomas Scott and William Lambarde had found in the ancient records to prove their existence in ancient times, and they also requested Lord Cobham to send all who disputed the revival to London to answer to them.[13]

Occasionally, because of the expense involved, altercations did arise between communities about who had the traditional responsibility of maintaining a beacon watch. In 1587 Lambarde was asked to arbitrate a dispute which had originated in 1585 when Lord Cobham ordered the Seven Hundreds to send 12 men to Denge Marsh for the watch. Because of the danger of an invasion and because of their desire to obey Lord Cobham, the inhabitants had followed his orders, but under protest, for they claimed that the residents of Lydd had performed that service in the past. After spending £9 to keep the men at Denge Marsh in 1585, the Seven Hundreds thereafter refused to comply with Cobham's orders.

By the time the lord-lieutenant referred their case to Lambarde in 1587 they had already had one hearing at Ashford where his lordship's agents had decided against them. Armed with new evidence from some ancient records, they pleaded their case a second time before Lambarde who admitted to Lord Cobham that he was impressed with their evidence and believed that there was some truth to their assertions. As Lord Cobham was then going to Flanders, he asked the Seven Hundreds to resume the watch and wait until his return to England for his final decision, but they refused to co-operate and even during the Armada crisis no watch was kept at Denge Marsh.

The next year, 1589, when Lambarde, along with his good friend, Humphrey Windham of Lincoln's Inn, was once again asked to hear the dispute, he decided that the case should be settled at Common Law, but Lydd refused to go to trial. In the meantime, the Privy Council intervened to order the Attorney-General and the Solicitor-General to settle the matter, but there were delays and as late as October 1600 no solution had been found.[14]

Lord Cobham had probably asked Lambarde to arbitrate this dispute because it was well known that he read and understood ancient records and that he had written a section on the beacons in the *Perambulation*. This section was read carefully by Roger Twysden, whose duty as captain was to keep sufficient quantities of pitch available for their firing. In the late spring of 1588, just before the Armada arrived, Twysden, noting that there was a shortage of pitch and remembering that Lambarde had reported in the county history that great stacks of wood were used in ancient times, ordered wood to be made available as a precaution against running out of fuel.[15]

The antiquary not only gave advice about the beacon watch, but he, himself, was involved in overseeing it. In June 1589 Sir Henry Cobham, deputy-lieutenant, advised Leveson, Sedley, Lambarde and others to keep the watch and to meet with him later to certify their progress. Throughout the 1590s orders were sent to the maritime counties about the beacons and even though no further record of Lambarde's activities in that regard has survived, it can be assumed that he assisted the lord-lieutenant and his deputies whenever he could.[16]

As a justice of the peace he was also concerned with the orderly return to civil life of soldiers he had helped muster to war. Their return from abroad created many problems, especially in the maritime counties, even though the Privy Council supplied them with passports and conduct money at the ports of debarkation and allowed only a specified number of days for travel to their homes. Notwithstanding the passports wandering ex-soldiers became such a nuisance in London that on 10 November 1588 the Lord Mayor was required by the Privy Council to confer with the justices of the peace of the counties of Middlesex, Surrey, and Kent, but especially with Francis Alford and William Lambarde, 'men of good experience and discretion', about this problem.[17]

This recognition of Lambarde's 'good experience' may have been a reference to his successful plan for the erection of a house of correction for the incarceration of the Kentish idle. He recorded in his 'Ephemeris' on 4 March 1583 that at the Rochester assizes the members of the Commission of Peace 'agreed upon a draft for the house of correction which [he] had penned' and on 20 July 1583 that he had written to all the constables of his division about the need of taxation to support the gaol and the house of correction.[18]

These entries probably referred to a manuscript entitled 'Ordinances for the house of correction at Maydstone, agreed upon by the Justices of the Peace at the Easter Sessions of the Peace in the 25th yeare of the reigne of Queene Elizabeth, to be put into execution within the Lathes of Aylesford and Sutton-at-Hone, in the said countie'. The information in this manuscript provides ample evidence of the actual working of the Statute of 1576 which was enacted to solve the problems of vagabonds by requiring the erection of two houses of correction in every county. Healthy beggars who were residents of the county and who refused to work were to be sent to the house where they were first to receive 20 lashes of the whip and then to be put to work. Foreign rogues, over 14 years of age, were to be taken to the gaol at Maidstone to await trial, and, under 14 years of age, were to be whipped and sent out of the county. Resident rogues under 14 were apprenticed. Only those beggars who were disabled or ill received gentle treatment. They were conveyed to the parish of their birth, whether in Kent or another county, where the inhabitants, however unwilling, were expected to support them.[19]

While rogues remained in the house of correction, they were required to say morning and evening prayers and were to receive 2d. a day for food, but if it was believed that extra punishment was necessary, part of that allowance could be withheld. To keep them working, which was the reason they were forced to remain there, four wheels to grind malt and three or four troughs for the beating of hemp were supplied. The house was also furnished with eight bedsteads and bolsters of straw in canvas, four for women and four others for men. Their incarceration was not terminated until they were either released at the quarter sessions or delivered by the justice of the peace who had committed them. In the 'Ephemeris' when Lambarde recorded three instances of the deliverance of inmates, he noted that his willingness to release two of the three was based upon certain knowledge that jobs awaited them.[20]

Because the local officials wished to avoid an excessive charge to the county for the maintenance of the rogues who were sent to the Maidstone gaol, three sessions, one on the Thursday after St. Andrew's, one on the Friday after Twelfth Day, and one on Tuesday in Whitsun week, were set aside for the delivery. Lambarde attended two of these sessions in the 1580s, one on 14 June 1582 when seven were punished and the second on 21 May 1583, when 'divers were bound and whipped'. Of course, both native and foreign rogues were delivered at the first session since the house of correction at Maidstone had not then been founded.[21]

At both gaol deliveries, at many quarter sessions, and at special sessions, Lambarde gave the charge to the grand jury, which, when printed in the *Eirenarcha*, his handbook for justices of the peace, filled about 75 pages and took over two hours to read aloud even in abbreviated form. Why he assumed that responsibility is not known but Conyers Read conjectured that Thomas Wotton, who, as *Custos Rotulorum*, was probably responsible for giving the charges, delegated that authority to his friend, Lambarde.[22]

Despite the great length of the charges the antiquary almost always preceded them with an exhortation or prologue. According to Read, these exhortations, given at both special sessions and quarter sessions by Lambarde, are the only ones of their kind that have survived from the Elizabethan era except for the rough draft of one in the Thynne Papers at Longleat. Since the giving of these prologues was apparently not a customary procedure, Lambarde probably introduced them into Kent. Indeed, the antiquary reported in the *Eirenarcha*, which was first published in January 1582, that they were traditionally given at assize courts and that he wished they were also used at the quarter sessions.[23]

The Grand Jury was usually composed of two constables of each hundred as well as others from the lower gentry, and occasionally they must have had very small incomes, for Lambarde pleaded in the exhortations that no one assume the office of constable unless he could read and write and unless he was assessed in the subsidy of books at £6 in lands or £12 in goods. The duties of the grand jury, of course, were first to make inquiries and then to bring that information to the justices of the peace for further action.[24]

In the prologues at the gaol deliveries of 1582 and 1583 Lambarde hoped to impress upon the jurors the need to present all the information they had about idleness in the county. He admitted to them that in times past the severity of the laws, which during the reign of King Edward VI had provided for temporary enslavement and the branding of an ear, had caused some to hesitate to present information against vagabonds, but, he continued, the present just laws, which punished by whipping for the first offence and by the cutting of the ear for the second, should encourage them to do their duty. The jurors must remember, he admonished them, that the laws of England were based on the general law of God: 'In the sweat of thy brows shalt thou eat thy bread'. In short, since God detested idleness, it was the duty of all good Christians to seek to punish by legal means those who refused to work.[25]

Besides believing that he was administering the will of God, Lambarde had a more immediate and worldly reason for ridding the county of idle ex-soldiers and other rogues, as he was convinced that they consumed food that rightfully belonged to the hardworking and disabled poor for whom he had great sympathy and concern. Indeed, during the famine of 1587, which was so severe that the government intervened by special commandment to order the relief of the poor, one of the ways Lambarde and Leveson hoped to increase the quantity of grain available was to give greater attention to the expulsion of ex-soldiers from their division.

Even before the royal commandment reached them in January 1587, Lambarde and Leveson had ordered constables in their division to send 'inholders, alehowsekeepers, and other Typplers and fellowes of Ale, Beere, or Breade' to appear at Stroode Church in Shamele on 11 January 1587 for questioning. With information gained in this manner they suppressed about 30 alehouses and forbade the owners of others to sell cakes of white bread and strong drinks worth more than half-pence a quart.[26]

They were in the midst of these operations to restrain the use of corn when the royal commandment arrived, ordering them to hold a special session and to inquire about grain growers in the county. Obedient to the new orders, they attended a grain session at Frindsbury on 29 January 1587 where Lambarde told the Grand Jury that God had plagued the kingdom with the famine because the people by 'unsatiable avarice and niggishness' dishonoured Him. Since it was the Queen, he reminded them, who wished to prevent the starvation of her people, the jurors should present all the information they learned from questioning large grain growers in the county.[27]

By 2 March 1587 Lambarde and Leveson, whose activities had been limited to the northern division of their lathe, could report that they had obeyed the orders issued by the Crown that January. Using information obtained by the jurors they had bound every corn grower to deliver grain to the poor of his parish and to sell provisions at the open markets. By these measures they obtained for poor relief about 290 quarters of grain in Shamele, 186 in Toltingtroe, 101 in Chetham and Gillingham, but only 60 in Hoo where because the inhabitants were not able to provide enough to feed the poor, an increase in taxation was necessary. Altogether they had raised 618 quarters for distribution to the poor, a charitable enterprise that was to be supervised by the parish officials.

They had also made provision for 896½ quarters of grain to be taken to several markets in their division; Maidstone to receive 243, Rochester 161, Gravesend 326, Dartford 19, Sevenoaks 134, Malling 4½, and Milton 8. The price of the best wheat was set at 4s. 10d. per bushel, the best rye at 3s. 4d., the best barley at 2s. 8d., the best malt at 2s. 4d., the best oats at 12d., and the best pease at 2s. 4d. The justices, themselves, planned to oversee the markets, but because Gravesend and Milton were at least five miles from the homes of any of them, three men were appointed to supervise these two markets to ensure that the orders were obeyed.

Articles for the direction of the markets were drawn up by Lambarde and Leveson. The names of all those who were required to bring grain to the market and the amounts allotted to them were to be listed in a register book. When the grain arrived, it was to be set in the market in open sight of all but was not to be sold before 10.00 a.m. For the first two hours it could be sold in quantities of two bushels or less, and after 12.00 noon, licensed Kentish and foreign bakers, brewers, and badgers could purchase in larger amounts. If some produce remained, the grain seller was required to store it and bring it to the next market in addition to the supply he had been scheduled to bring at that time. The governors, of course, were ordered to report the progress of their markets to the justices at regular intervals.[28]

During this famine, the justices, particularly the antiquary, who in December 1586 had complained to Lord Cobham that the London buyers of grain in Kent were causing much suffering among the poor, hoped to restrain purchases by out-of-county millers. It is possible that the Kentish justices began to limit drastically the amount of grain available to London millers, a move which understandably was not popular in the City and which probably caused the Privy Council in February 1587 to order the sheriffs and justices of several counties, including Kent, to permit licensed London bakers, who were not able to obtain sufficient grain in London to feed the citizens, to purchase provisions in their areas. No doubt because of this order Lambarde and Leveson were careful to arrange for foreigners, who were properly registered, to purchase corn at their markets.[29]

Another foreign consumer of corn in Kent was the Crown, represented by its purveyors, who probably compounded for grain during the famine of 1586–87 and who were highly unpopular because they normally paid a lower price for the provisions than the market price, keeping the difference for themselves. Lambarde recorded in his 'Ephemeris' that on 4 March 1583 the entire Commission of the Peace assembled at the Rochester assizes wrote on behalf of a constable who had been arrested at the complaint of a purveyor and that in July 1585 he had bound Hugh Wilson of Higham, another unpopular purveyor, to appear at the quarter sessions where witnesses planned to give evidence against him. During the decade of the 1590s abuses by the purveyors must have continued at an alarming pace, since in 1596 Lambarde called for a full-scale investigation of their uses of carts and in 1598 the Privy Council ordered inquiries into their actions in Kent where it was admitted that had not 'delt dutyfullie' with the inhabitants.[30]

The purveyance exactions, like the military and grain subsidies, were apparently supervised by the justices who, because of the Crown's compounding for many more kinds of provisions and in greater quantities, were asked to form a more structured organisation. At the Michaelmas quarter sessions of 1592 a deputy for each lathe was selected to take charge of 'collecting all somes of money unpayd for any of ye said purveyance due to be paid before Michaelmas laste'. Chosen for the lathe of Aylesford was Sir Thomas Fludd who wrote to Sir Thomas Scott, deputy for Shepway, on 13 December 1592 to discuss the new demands of provisions for her Majesty's household and to propose a conference with Sir John Leveson and William Lambarde. Almost two weeks later, on Christmas Eve, Fludd noted that Lambarde was planning a purveyance meeting.[31]

According to Conyers Read, editor of the 'Ephemeris', Kent compounded for wheat as early as 1588 and not for other provisions before 1602, but other evidence at the Stafford County Archives Office has proved that many different kinds of provisions were exacted before 1588. Since the earliest evidence of Lambarde's performing his purveyance duties occurred in 1586, even though the kind of goods compounded for was not identified, apparently something, if not wheat, was exacted that year.[32]

Further evidence to support the contention that many different kinds of goods were demanded before 1588 has survived in a letter dated in December 1587. In it the author, possibly Leveson, complained that the purveyors were not only exacting more and more kinds of provisions but in larger quantities as well and exclaimed that everyone who lived within 25 miles of London would happily pay her Majesty to be freed from that charge. Finally, Lambarde, himself, drew up a list which clearly indicated that both oats and oxen were compounded for in 1589. There is no doubt that many kinds of provisions were exacted before 1602 and that as early as 1587 there was at least one royal official in Kent who thought that the purveyors were impoverishing the shire.[33]

As more information is learned about the activities of Elizabethan justices and of Lambarde in particular it becomes even more apparent that upon their shoulders rested the ultimate success or failure of royal policy on defence, beacons, musters, rogues, poor relief, corn prices, purveyance, and any other endeavour performed on the local level. Impressed with the zeal of these officials, the government almost yearly added new duties to their already heavy load. In 1563, for instance, the Statute of Artificers, which required among other things that the rates of wages be certified to the Court of Chancery by the justices of the peace, was passed, but it had been considered a dead letter by some historians until the discovery of Lambarde's manuscript entitled 'Rates of Wages' which proved that the statute was enforced, at least in Kent.[34]

In this manuscript were listed the wages for artificers, servants, and other labourers in Kent, probably for the year 1589, since it was under that date that the antiquary noted that each year since the passing of the act in 1563, the rates had been certified to the Court of Chancery, 'without any change'. The words of his, 'without any change', were significant since at least three times in the late 1580s the Privy Council informed the Lord Chancellor that they had received from him the 'several rates and taxacions' of the servants' and labourers' wages that officials from all over the kingdom had certified to him but that many of the rates, unfortunately, had been changed from those of the previous year.[35]

Besides performing duties specifically required by statute and decree, the justices had the discretion to grant licences or certificates in cases where they thought such action proper. In an eight-year period, 1580 to 1588, Lambarde issued two licences for the keeping of victualling houses, eight for the keeping of alehouses, one for a man to beg, one for a woman to marry a vicar, and one to a man for safe-passage to Westmorland.[36]

Since much of his time was devoted to administration, it is reasonable to expect that he would record that function in his 'Ephemeris', the memorandum book of his first eight years on the Commission of the Peace, but instead most of his entries were about judicial inquiries, although he did not even include all of them, and about the recognizances he took.[37] Of the 237 entries in the book, 178 concerned judicial investigations, which were preliminary inquiries and not trials; 28 noted attendance at various sessions; five concerned the behaviour of constables, and 26 were about miscellaneous non-criminal matters. Of the crimes reported the most popular was larceny with 52 entries about theft; the next most popular was breaking the peace with 42 references to people bound to keep the peace; and the third popular crime, in recorded numbers, was fornication with 22 entries about the births of illegitimate children.

During the eight-year period there were only nine bodily injuries: three murders, one manslaughter, three unexplained cases of injury, one poisoning, and one rape, but other recorded violations may also have involved that kind of injury, for there were six felony charges—the specific kind of felony left unexplained —two riots, and one assault. Among other infractions were six violations of alehouse rules, one case of counterfeiting, one contempt charge, one perjury, one licentious statement, and several arrests for the wearing of disguises.

Many of the accused were bound to appear for trial at the next quarter sessions in the western division of the county which were held at Maidstone. Lambarde attended the Michaelmas sessions of 1580 (the first at which he had official status as a justice of the peace) and 1581[38] and was present at both the Easter and Michaelmas sessions from 1582 to 1585. Having missed the September assemblies in 1586 and 1587, he attended both in 1588 and 1589. The reasons for his absences were not stated in the 'Ephemeris' but at least two of them can be accounted for. In September 1586 he was in Ashford on business for Lord Cobham and in September 1587 his wife died, a loss which probably prevented his attendance at the Michaelmas sessions but which did not prevent his imprisoning a Scot on 14 September for fathering an illegitimate child.

Since the first extant rolls for the quarter sessions in Kent date from the 1590s most of the evidence about Lambarde's activities at them stem from notes in the memorandum book and from the prologues he gave to the juries. Besides certifying and releasing recognizances, he also supplied any pertinent information he had and at least once, on 7 April 1583, renewed the Register Book for the poor at Ightham. Never in any entry in the 'Ephemeris' did he refer to the speeches he made to the juries.

Between Easter 1582, the date of the first prologue at the quarter sessions, and September 1589, Lambarde attended 14 sessions, but only nine prologues have survived. In them the jurors were exhorted to seek information about crimes, which were daily increasing, and to reveal all they knew about misdemeanours as well as felonies :

Let us not be afraid to cut off treason, murders, witchcrafts, rapes, and other felonies that be the highest and top boughs, as it were, of this tree of transgression . . . but let us also hew in sunder the master roots and mores of idleness, unlawful games, wasteful apparel, alehouse haunting, dissolute living, cony stealing, and all other lewd and deceitful practices, which, as they do send the sap of nourishment to the rest, so being once stricken off, the whole tree, both in bough and body will by little and little pine away and die together.[39]

One evil Lambarde considered particularly grievous was the jurors' incorrect presentment of evidence, which he dwelt upon at some length in the exhortation dated 1587. First, he reminded them that they were sworn to present all the knowledge they had had about crime in the county not just that which had been offered in evidence by others, for they were the 'eyes of justice', and second he warned that it was their duty, regardless of fear or sentiment, to make presentment against their betters, their kinsfolks, and their friends since to withhold evidence 'leadeth to perjury'. Another error was the tendency of some to obtain revenge by giving false information against their enemies, but this showed, he declared, that they cared nothing for the hard-won English traditions of justice and that they 'wreak their malice . . .

upon themselves . . . when they achieve their desire by this abuse of their oath, office, and duty'.[40]

In none of these exhortations did he emphasise national affairs. For example, the speech given at Michaelmas, 1588 ignored the defeat of the Spanish Armada, but, of course, no one at the time realised the true historical significance of that event since other armadas were built and the Spanish war lingered on until the 17th century. Still, even if he had known of its importance, he would not have wished to add to the complacency of the jury by congratulating it and the country on a great victory. What he did wish to do was to arouse the jurors to a sense of their duty in maintaining law and order by elaborating upon the problems created by war, such as the increasing number of vagabonds and the bad habits brought back by the returning soldiers who 'will do nothing but booty and rob'.[41]

Indeed, his eye was always cast toward local problems of law and order. The speech given at Michaelmas, 1585, which had actually been written in 1584 before war had broken out in the Low Countries, concentrated upon the dangers of the happy peace enjoyed by the realm :

> But what increase of good manners . . . hath this so long and sweet peace engendered? Nay, rather hath not the cold and re- miss handling of laws in these peaceful days of ours begotten the like dangerous disobedience and contempt that very war and hostility itself would have brought forth amongst us?[42]

Because in peace there was slothful attention to justice and in war there were crimes caused by 'inflamed hearts', he hoped to arouse a zeal for law and order among the jurors in all seasons.

In addition to the quarter sessions held twice a year in the western division of Kent, there were other assemblies that the justices attended. Some like the gaol deliveries for rogues were routine but others like the grain sessions were called at times of great distress in the county. One special session, held on 22 March 1582, was called because of a grave crime at Longsoleshothe where during the night of 13 March 1582 some 20 men on horse- back cut down the four principal posts of a house that had been built by Thomas Culpeper and that was inhabited by a poor labourer and his wife.

In his prologue to the jury at this session, Lambarde marvelled at the act and, as he said, only because such a crime was 'unthought of . . . no special punishment hath been hitherto appointed for it'. As these men, who had frightened the poor labourer and his wife, deserved the 'full revenge of the law', he called upon the jurors to make diligent inquiry to hasten the discovery of their identities. Since this session convened only one week after the crime (an example of great haste considering communication problems of 16th-century England), and was called even though the regular quarter sessions, scheduled for 24 April, were only a month away, the crime apparently caused widespread consternation in the county. It is to be wished that more evidence were available about the progress of the investigation.[43]

Besides participating in quarter sessions and special sessions, Lambarde also attended 12 royal assizes held in Kent where he certified recognizances and examinations to the assize justices who handled both civil and criminal matters. These assemblies, which lasted about two days, seemed to have been held twice a year, in February or March and again in June or July, and were convened usually in Rochester, although three were probably held in Maidstone. The most important function of the assizes was to deliver the gaols. At least two general gaol deliveries, probably unconnected with the assizes, were also attended by Lambarde, one in Maidstone and one in Sevenoaks.[44]

When the justices assembled together at the assizes, they sometimes performed other administrative work. It was at the assize on 4 March 1583, in Rochester, that plans for the house of correction were completed and that the letter in support of a constable was drawn up. The next year at another Rochester assize, on 20 February 1584, Lambarde was put in the commission of *oyer and terminer*, an appointment which gave him the authority to hear and determine all treasons, felonies, and misdemeanours in conjunction with at least one other justice and after an inquiry by a grand jury.[45]

During his first decade as a member of the commission the evidence overwhelmingly proved that Lambarde and the justices in the division where he lived devoted tremendous amounts of time to their official functions. Besides the routine inquiries and the sessions they attended (usually more than four a year), they found that special problems, like war preparations, famine, and vagabonds, required even more of their efforts. All of these duties Lambarde performed diligently and without protest except for occasionally complaining that the wars were draining the county of all able-bodied men. It was local officials like himself, unpaid for their services and not privy to policy-making decisions of the kingdom, who loyally forsook their pleasures, especially during years of crises like 1587 and 1588 when the realm was attacked by famine from within and the Armada from without, and enforced laws to feed the poor and to win the war. That Lambarde and others left evidence of the existence of crime and confusion in the countryside during this decade not only proves that they were performing their duties but also demonstrates their commitment to law and order whatever the cost in labour and time.

In these first years as a justice, he performed a multitude of duties and gained great experience in criminal justice and local administration, but even before he acquired that experience, he had begun to write the *Eirenarcha*, the best handbook for justices of the peace in the 16th century. It was his appointment to the commission of the peace which prompted him to begin the book that first appeared in print on 29 January 1581/82. It was revised in 1588, but even after eight years in office, Lambarde made surprisingly few changes, the most important differences being the shift from two books or sections in the first issue to four books in the second and the addition to the later edition of an appendix of documents and an index.[46]

He presented a copy of the 1581/82 edition to his friend, Sir Thomas Egerton, then Solicitor-General to the Queen, and also gave him a copy of the 1588 edition, probably as a Christmas present, with a note thanking him for his many favours. Besides the second edition, several others were issued during his lifetime, in 1591, 1592, 1594, and 1599. There are copies of all of these editions at the British Museum, which also has a preliminary outline of the book in manuscript with the date of August 1579 on the title page. The *Eirenarcha* continued to be popular in the 17th century and was published with *The Duties of Constables Borsholders, Tythingmen, and such other Low and Lay Ministers of the Peace*, also written by the antiquary.[47]

The handbook on justices was dedicated to Sir Thomas Bromley, Lord Chancellor of England, whom Lambarde praised for his knowledge of the law and whom he then petitioned to correct errors in the commission, which, according to him, was out of date, since it omitted many duties of the justices that he, himself, had discovered while doing research for his book. Despite this plea, the commission was not revised until 1590 and then by order of the Privy Council. Obviously pleased with this development, Lambarde included a list of the revisions in the 1591 edition of his handbook.

According to the dedicatory letter in the first edition, he had not only read the statutes of the realm, but also the books of the Common Law, Sir John A. Fitzherbert's book on justices, Thomas Marowe's *De Pace Terre et Ecclesie et Conservacione euisdem*, and an anonymous work on the justices, all of which were used as the sources for his own work. He gave particular credit to his good friend, John Tyndall of Lincoln's Inn, who had read many of the statutes and had arranged them so that he could refer to them easily.[48] After a careful study of the *Eirenarcha* Dr. Bertha Putnam agreed that Lambarde had used almost all of the legal literature available to prepare his work and displayed a 'keen historical and legal sense' in its writing. Of all the authors he read, she continued, Marowe, a lawyer of the reign of King Henry VII, was apparently the most important:

> It is certainly only just to Marowe to remember that quotations from his reading form a very large part . . . On the other hand, it is due to Lambarde to point out that it was his shrewdness that produced a volume which combined sound scholarship with practical common sense and which therefore met the needs of the country gentlemen on the commission.[49]

The *Eirenarcha*, itself, later became the basis for other works on the justices of the peace.

In his work Lambarde explained that justice, which existed in the kingdom only by royal pleasure, was maintained by the justices of the peace, whose responsibility was not to transform the spirit of the people from a quarrelsome one to that of universal love and brotherhood but rather to suppress the eruption of violence and lawlessness whenever it occurred. The man, he continued, who could best perform that function, had to be a good and lawful gentleman with lands and tenements worth £40. Those who qualified for the office had to take two oaths, one of allegiance to the Queen as the supreme governor of the Church of England and one, which he printed in verse :

> Doe equall right to rich and poor,
>     as wit and law extends;
> Give none advice in any cause,
>     that you before depends :
> Your Sessions hold as statutes bid :
>     the forfeits that befall;
> See entered well, and then estreat
>     them to the Chequer all :
> Receive no fee, but that is given
>     by King, good use, or right :
> No precept send to party self,
>     but to indifferent wight.[50]

He ended the handbook with the hope that he would be pardoned for anything that was done 'amis' for it had not 'proceeded of wilfulnesse'. His attitude, of course, was unnecessarily humble since the quality of this work, which went through 13 editions between 1582 and 1619 despite some competition from John Goldwell of Gray's Inn and Richard Crompton, was superb. Lambarde noted on his copies of the works of his competitors that they were inferior to his own. Even Blackstone could recommend the book to law students and lawyers of his day.[51]

After the antiquary gained personal insight into the role of a justice of the peace he realised that to be effective he had to have the co-operation of the lower Kentish officials, whose negligence sometimes increased the problems of law enforcement. On 8 July 1581, for example, Multon and Lambarde issued a warrant for the arrest of a constable who had captured a felon and had not delivered him to a justice. Concluding that a handbook to instruct them in their duties was badly needed, he wrote and had printed for the first time in 1583 *The Duties of Constables Borsholders, Tythingmen, and other Low and Lay Ministers of the Peace*, a work printed 14 times between 1583 and 1619. That it was popular and useful there is no doubt, but after a study of Lambarde's exhortations to the jurors, who were mainly constables, it is difficult to believe that its message was altogether effective. In his first exhortation after the book was issued, he begged the jurors not to be seduced by the evil examples of their predecessors, but seduced they must have been, as he continued in later years to charge that their neglect of duty had led to increased lawlessness in the county. In all the prologues to the jurors he left no doubt that law and order depended upon their vigilant and earnest co-operation with the justices of the peace.[52]

To suggest from this evidence that there was a breakdown in the administration of justice in 16th-century Kent would be unfair to these local officials. The constables and jurors, berated by the justices of the peace, who were, in turn, pressured to perform by the Privy Council, kept the institutions of local justice operating on an admirably high plane in the face of great economic changes, the stresses from constant warfare, and the ever-increasing population of Tudor England. Often unrewarded and unthanked, they worked against great odds to prevent anarchy and to punish quickly flagrant lawlessness and routine misdemeanours.

# The Master of Halling Palace

WHILE the antiquary was achieving fame as the author of handbooks for local officials, his personal life was undergoing a number of changes. The death of his brother in 1581, leaving a widow, Marjory Stevenson, was of some importance to Humphrey Windham, his roommate at Lincoln's Inn, who, after a short courtship, married her on 17 July 1582, less than one year after she was widowed. William apparently approved of the match, although there is no evidence that he purchased them a wedding gift, and in later years when he drew up his will he entrusted the Windhams with responsibilities for the settlement of his estate and the care of his children.

Another important change in his life was the taking of a second wife, Sylvestre Dean Dalison, in 1583. Sylvestre, the only child of Robert Dean, the son of a Rochester alderman, and his wife, Margaret, the heiress of Edward White, had at the age of 19 married William Dalison of Gray's Inn and had borne him two children, a girl named Sylvestre and a boy named Maximilian. Four years after her marriage, her father died, leaving her husband, since she was the sole Dean heiress, 22 messuages, lands, tenements, rents, profits, and reversions in Halling and Snodland by virtue of a lease made with John, Bishop of Rochester, on 1 November 1551. At his own death in 1581 William Dalison, in turn, left Sylvestre, his wife, a lease to Ponashe, some household articles of her father, and the right to occupy the Halling and Snodland lands which were to descend to their son, Maximilian, at his 24th birthday.[1]

A wealthy 29-year-old widow with a reputation for being a beauty, Sylvestre apparently had the qualities Lambarde sought in a wife and in 1583 he began to court her. Whether they had been acquainted before her widowhood is not known, but undoubtedly the Dalison family knew the Multons who lived only 10 miles from Halling at St. Clere's. On 14 March 1583 Sylvestre agreed to marry him and on 15 May 1583 he moved to Halling, although the wedding did not take place until 28 October 1583, shortly after his 47th birthday.[2]

With their marriage he began to record the purchase of personal items in his rent and receipt books for the first time. On 1 November 1583 he spent over £4 for wine, gloves, and a firepan for Christmas; in February of 1584 he obtained fish and wine for Lent at a cost of £5; and in May 1584, shortly before the birth of his first child, he obtained a bed of walnut for £5 5s., perhaps for his wife's lying-in. As head of a family and alone responsible for the management of his home, he also found it necessary to retain domestic servants and in 1584 employed a gardener and a cook.

Within four years of their wedding she bore him four children : on 15 October 1584 a son and heir named Multon in honour of George Multon the elder of Ightham; on 8 January 1586 a daughter named Margaret after her maternal grandmother; and on 6 August 1587 twin boys named Fane and Gore, probably in honour of Sir Thomas Fane of Badsell co. Kent and Thomas Gore, grocer of London and cousin to Lambarde, who frequently acted as his banker. When the two cleared accounts, as they did frequently, Lambarde noted in his rent and receipt books that they owed each other nothing but love, and until the death of Gore in 1597 that close relationship continued. Sir Thomas Fane, after whom the other twin was named, was a justice of the peace of Kent and an important figure in the county since in 1573 he had been knighted by Robert Dudley, Earl of Leicester, in the presence of Queen Elizabeth I and the following year had married Lady Mary Neville, the only daughter of Henry, Baron Abergavenny.[3]

Sylvestre did not recover from her fifth lying-in and died on 1 September 1587 just a little over two weeks after the birth of the twins. Like other country gentlemen of Tudor England William must have desired a male heir and must have been delighted with his wife when she presented him with not one but three sons and a daughter as well. In tribute to her great achievement, he had erected in Halling Church a monument with the inscription that no woman was full of more reverence for God and with the figures of a woman, presumably Sylvestre, lying in bed, and of her six children placed around her. Altogether the illness, the funeral expenses, and the monument cost £40.[4]

The death of his wife created a special problem for Lambarde because he feared that he would lose his right to remain at Halling. After their marriage in 1583 he had decided to live at the palace, an edifice that had probably been erected in the 14th century by Hamo de Hethe, bishop and counsellor to King Edward II, because the manor at Greenwich needed extensive renovation and because of his many friends and associates in the Rochester area. At Sylvestre's death, the Dalison heir, Maximilian, became a royal ward whose inheritance, including the lease to Halling, lay at the disposal of the crown and of executors.[5]

Apparently even before his wife's death, he had had a request forwarded to Lord Burghley by his 'favourable and fatherlike good Lord Cobham' to ask for the custody of Maximilian and a lease to the palace. When his petition was granted a few days after Sylvestre's death, he thanked his benefactor, the Lord Treasurer, for restoring his 'halcyon days' and apologised for not expressing his appreciation in person but the subsidy and his recent loss kept him occupied in the country. Both the step-children continued to live with him until 1591 when Sylvestre went to join her paternal uncles in Lincolnshire.[6]

He restored and repaired the palace buildings while he resided there, always keeping a careful account of his stewardship in his rent and receipt books. For example, on 1 November 1583, shortly after his second marriage, he paid 50s. to a glasser, a carpenter, and a bricklayer for work there and in 1592, the year of his third marriage, he paid £10 for 53 yards of lead pipe to convey water to the palace. He continued making repairs until 1595 when he noted that at a cost of £4 he floored, glassed, and sealed the schoolhouse and chamber where the children were probably tutored, and when he chose to add some beauty to his home by obtaining for £11 a Turkish carpet and eight pieces of leather-gilt hangings. Altogether during his 15 years there he disbursed well over £90 for restoration, an indication that as long as he possessed the lease, which had been granted him by the executors of William Dalison for £40 a year until 1598, he did not permit the buildings to fall into decay. During those years he expended no money on renovation at Westcombe probably because the funds he had available for repair were allotted to his wife's home.[7]

In addition to his love for the palace and his devotion to his wife who bore his children there, Lambarde apparently enjoyed the Rochester area because of the many friends who lived nearby. Of course, his patron, whom he called 'his favourable and father-like good Lord Cobham', and John Leveson, his associate on the commission of the peace, lived within walking distance of his home. Several letters written by the antiquary to Leveson in which he not only asked him for favours but also thanked him for many presents have survived to attest to that close relationship which endured even after Lambarde moved to Westcombe with his third wife in 1598.[8]

He also had good relationships with other neighbours and must have had the reputation for being a peacemaker, for in 1586 he mediated a dispute between his neighbour, a Mr. Tilghman who may also have been his clerk, and his wild carefree son. After another friendly neighbour had sent him some wine, Lambarde wrote a note of thanks to the giver, Mr. Owen of Ludgate, expressing his embarrassment at receiving the gift since he had never even given him a 'cuppe of water'.[9]

Besides leaving him, alone, responsible for rearing four children, the death of Sylvestre encumbered him with obligations to fulfil wishes expressed by her father and her first husband in their wills. As early as 1 October 1587, one month after her decease, Lambarde was administering the will of Robert Dean, paying £50 of his legacies, a duty he continued to perform until 1598 when he noted that all of them were cleared. The same month that he began paying the Dean legacies he paid some creditors of Dalison and in 1593 noted that he still owed over £4 on one of those annuities.

Partly because of the death of his wife in 1587 Lambarde's estate increased in value, an increase that can be seen by a study of the annual reckonings he made of his worth in cash and goods. In 1580 his estimate was £430 6s. 8., broken down as follows: debts owed him £224, plate and jewels £34, ready money 40s., leases of Rowde and the Lilly Lands £140, and the stock with his father-in-law £50. He did not include in that reckoning the value of his St. Clere's lease, the rents due on his lands, his clothes, or his books. The following year, with those same exceptions, his estimate was £415, but in 1582 the figure dropped to £212 6s. 8d. because of his purchase of some Dowgate Houses and the stock he shared with Multon for over £200 and the Cosin Lane Houses from the Wyckyn cousins for £250.[10]

Shortly after his marriage to Sylvestre in 1583 he estimated, with the usual exceptions, that he was worth in cash and goods about £270, broken down as follows: debts £63 6s. 8d., plate and jewels £40, the usual leases £140, ready money £20, and an annuity of £7. From 1583 the value steadily increased: In October 1584 it was £300; in 1585 £340, and in 1586 £540. The £200 increase from 1585 to 1586 can be accounted for in part by the sale of some houses for 100 marks that had escheated to him in 1580. Then in October 1587, one month after the death of Sylvestre, he reckoned, without including the value of his Dalison leases, that he was worth £790, about £250 more than in 1586. For the 1587 estimate he noted that he had £400 in ready cash, double the amount on hand in 1586 and that the value of his jewels and plate had increased to £120, £80 more than in 1586.[11]

Apparently he had inherited from his wife about £200 in money, the Dean plate (the Dalison plate having been willed to Maximilian by his father), and the lease to Ponashe, about 150 acres held from Lady Mary Abergavenny for £12 rent annually. With the aid of this inheritance he purchased Turkesplace in 1588 for almost £500 and still reckoned his worth in cash and goods at £298 in 1589. Like his merchant father who was a shrewd steward of the family estate, William invested in real property whenever his funds permitted.

During this decade he continued to make loans to friends and relatives. In 1580 John Nicholson, the husband of his cousin Christian Goodrich, owed him £20, Thomas Wyckyn and Charles Bond jointly £40, and Uncle Horne, Robert Bing, and others various sums of money. One new cousin appeared in his personal records when he noted that Thomas Langton, cousin, repaid £10 which he had borrowed some time before. The antiquary immediately returned 53s. 4d. of that sum for Langton's son and his godson. Besides loaning £100 toward the new building at Lincoln's Inn, an amount repaid in 1585, he even loaned £60 to his close friend and associate, John Leveson, when he went to France in September 1589, probably as a captain in the army.[12]

Lambarde's rent and receipt book also gave evidence of his continued interest in horses and of various transactions with Richard Bromhead, the lessee of the demesne of Westcombe Manor. He not only sold and traded horses with Bromhead but also commissioned him to buy for him at a cost of £6 a dark grey gelding that was six years old. Despite all of this horse trading and buying, he apparently still lacked a suitable mount for his wife in 1586 when he wrote to Leveson to beg the loan of his 'bonny nag' for her trip to Malling.[13]

While his material wealth was increasing, Lambarde was not neglecting his intellectual pursuits and probably joined the Elizabethan Society of Antiquaries that was founded in 1586. The Society, whose goal was to further research into England's past, had many lawyers and knights among its members, and since Lambarde was held in great esteem by the outstanding antiquaries of the age, he, too, was probably a member. John Stowe gave his 'loving friend' credit for suggesting the form for the *Survey of London*, and Camden not only depended upon his knowledge for an understanding of Kent but also asked him to review the *Britannia* before it was printed. Clearly two of the most noted antiquaries of Elizabethan England knew and respected his scholarship. That the society had so many lawyers and knights in its membership indicates that by the late 1580s gentlemen commonly studied antiquity, but Lambarde, of course, was a pioneer in awakening his contemporaries to the value of that study since his historical research had begun some 20 years before the founding of the society.[14]

Lord Burghley, who had been sent a manuscript copy of the *Perambulation* in 1573 by Archbishop Parker, also esteemed Lambarde's work and in 1584 asked him for a description of the City of Lincoln. Lambarde searched through his papers, probably those he had collected for the *Description*, and sent him some notes about that City and also about Stamford, the home of Burghley, with a letter in which he apologised for their poor quality and stated that they were 'as rudely tumbled together, as if my promise had not bound me, and your honourable acceptation (of things savouring of learning) not emboldened me, I durst not have directed them towards you'. He was undoubtedly delighted to send the material not only because he, himself, loved studying antiquity, but also because he must have been anxious to please someone so powerful as the Lord Treasurer.[15]

Throughout the decade of the 1580s Lambarde continued collecting a wide variety of books. A copy of Holinshed's *Chronicle of 1586* was given him by the printer, Ralfe Newbyre, in 1587 and copies of Hieronymus Osorio's *De Gloria Ejusdem de Nobilitate Civil Christiana* and Rene Chopin's *Parisiis apud Martinum Juvenum* were in his library. In 1581 a book was published under the title of *A brief Conceipte of Inglishe policy* by W. S., but when Lambarde learned of its publication he wrote in his transcript of the work which he had owned since 1565 that it had been written either by Sir Thomas Smith or John Hales. In 1585 he obtained F. Beurhusius's *Analysis Epistolarum et Evangeliorum dominicalum Scholastica* to which he appended an index; this book provides excellent evidence of the thorough way in which he read and studied his prized possessions.[16]

As important as historical research was to him, he did not neglect a study of Tudor laws, with the intent to update and revise them. There is extant a manuscript entitled 'An Acte for punishment of the injurious taking of goods as wrecked at the Sea', which was dated 1580 and which provided various fines and penalties for theft of shipwrecked merchandise. He may have been asked by the Privy Council to revise this act because of the notorious seizure of goods off a Genoan ship, the *St. John Baptist*, in May 1580 by Derick van Bleke of Holland, a crime which caused the central government to order all justices of the peace to inquire about the whereabouts of van Bleke's ship, but even if that seizure was not the occasion for the examination of that law, as a justice of the peace in a maritime county, he must have been especially concerned about shipwreck.[17]

In 1580 he also revised another law at the behest of the government, this one entitled 'An Act to Restrain the Licentious Printing, selling, and uttering of unprofitable and Hurtfull Englishe books', in which it is evident that he approved of lay rather than religious control of censorship since all control was taken away from the Bishop of London and given to the Inns of Court and that he approved of stringent licensing of books and of heavy penalties for violators of the law. An entry in his diary, dated 2 November 1579, about the severing of the right hand of John Stubbs, proved that he was personally interested in licentious

books. Stubbs, of course, was the author of 'Discovery of a Gap-
ing Gulf wherein England is like to be Swallowed by Another
French Marriage', which has been described as an 'intemperate
puritanical pamphlet, grossly libelling the royal family of France'.
Written in response to the courtship of Queen Elizabeth I by the
Duke of Alençon, brother of the King of France, this pamphlet
enraged the Queen since it suggested that she was too old to be
married, and she insisted that justice, which meant the chopping
off of the hands of the publisher and the author, be done. The
heavy penalties in Lambarde's revised law did not include the
barbaric practice of mutilation but provided for fines, loss of
printing licences, and relegation to the social and economic position of menial servants.[18]

Eight years later the Privy Council once again requested that
Lambarde as well as three others, including John Tyndall, of
Lincoln's Inn, several barristers of the Middle Temple, of Gray's
Inn, and of the Inner Temple study the statutes and recommend
changes to the next parliament. The antiquary probably obeyed
these orders which were signed by both the Lord Treasurer and
Lord Cobham but no copies of revised statutes from that year
have survived.[19]

Various central courts at London called upon his knowledge
of the law and of local affairs during this decade. He joined
Thomas Fludd, William Baynham, and Robert Rudston on a
special commission for the Court of Exchequer in 1583 to investigate the whereabouts of Benedicta Horne, a recusant who
had fled to France, and became a member of the subsidy commission in 1585. In his personal records he noted that he paid
£3 4s. for the first payment of the subsidy after the rate of £24 in
lands.[20]

Besides appointing him to various commissions the government
also ordered him to inquire into disputes over property. In 1582
the Court of Chancery asked him to investigate a complaint sued
in that court by William Cromer, and in 1586, he, along with
Henry Willoughby, was required by Sir Francis Walsingham,
principal secretary to the Queen, to examine some individuals
about a hearing scheduled for the Court of Star Chamber. The
controversy was over the disposition of rents from lands owned
by a Mrs. Sprinte, with her present husband claiming that they
were his, and with her son from a previous marriage insisting

that they had been earmarked for his education. Lord Cobham was personally involved in this dispute because it was he who held the lease to the lands and needed to know the disposition of the rents. Over Mr. Sprinte's objections, Lambarde and Willoughby decided that Mrs. Sprinte would have to be called to testify under oath, but that was all the further they ventured in the case which was settled by the Court of Star Chamber.[21]

In addition to attending to official duties, Lambarde also had private matters to handle. One of these concerned a misunderstanding about a promise made by William Pelsant the elder at the marriage of his son, George, to Margaret, the daughter of Christopher Dunne. In 1586 Lambarde and a barrister of Gray's Inn were requested to draft covenants disposing of the disputed property in a way that would appease all of the interested parties. He was also appointed overseer in at least two wills that have survived from the 1580s. One was for John Somers, whose widow called upon Thomas Randolph, Thomas Fludd, and him in 1589 for advice about her remarriage and the other was for Robert Rudston of Boughton Monchelsea in Kent whose will was probated in 1590. Rudston, undoubtedly the same gentleman who served on the Court of Exchequer commission to investigate the whereabouts of the Horne family, left Lambarde, 'his loving friend', a cup of silver worth £6 13s. 4d. It is noteworthy that the antiquary had an associate and loving friend in Boughton Monchelsea, the home of his third wife, Margaret Reader, whom he married in 1592.[22]

Having lived as a bachelor for 47 years, except, of course, for his three-year marriage to Jane Multon when he was not held responsible for managing a household since they lived with her family at St. Clere's in Halling, Lambarde seems to have adjusted well in the 1580s to assuming the role not only of a husband but also of the father of a growing family and of a master of his home. He evidently disposed of his personal and domestic problems without too much difficulty during those years of happy births and the sad loss of his wife, even though he was spending increasing amounts of time performing his duties on the various commissions to which he was appointed, was continuing his personal surveillance of the almshouse, was reading about a great variety of subjects, as well as working on at least three major manuscripts, the *Eirenarcha*, the *Duties*, and the *Archeion*, was enlarging his estate and his worth in cash and goods, and was maintaining personal and political friendships both in Kent and in London that would endure for the rest of his life. As he aged he did not slow down the pace of his life. If anything, it seemed that the older he became the more he attempted to accomplish. The wonder is that everything he did he seemed to do so well.

# Prince of Legal Antiquaries

S INCE at least as early as 1579, the year of his appointment to the commission of the peace, Lambarde had begun to write the *Archeion or, a Discourse upon the High Courts of Justice in England*, a pre-eminent work which has prompted one historian to call him a 'prince of legal antiquaries',[1] his activities as a barrister and as a justice did not prevent him from continuing his scholarly pursuits. A copy of the manuscript, which was not completed until 1591, was sent to Sir Robert Cecil, son of Lord Burghley, but it was not published until 1635 and then twice, once in March by Daniel Frere and again in July by both Henry Seile and Daniel Frere with a note added on the title page of the second version that it was 'Newly Corrected and enlarged according to the Authors Copie'. The note, signed with the initials, T.L., was inserted by Thomas Lambarde, the author's grandson, who had not authorised the first printing and who, according to his own words, sought, by having the second edition printed, to correct the many errors of the first. Paul Ward, who joined Charles McIlwain in editing a modern version, has placed the responsibility for those errors on the carelessness of Frere who apparently did not proof-read the copy before it was printed.[2]

Further, Ward has shown that the second version, with its six pages on the Lord Chancellor's authority and its 41 pages on the statutory offences of the Court of Star Chamber also differed textually from the first printing. There were two reasons for this difference. First, the Frere issue in March essentially reproduced the 1591 presentation copy to Sir Robert Cecil while the edition of July was taken from the antiquary's own copy which he continued to amend after 1591. Second, Thomas Lambarde, the grandson, had ordered another manuscript of the antiquary included in the July version of the *Archeion*. It has been suggested that he inserted the manuscript, entitled 'Star Chamber' and written in 1589, because as a royalist during an era when the Court of Star Chamber came under heavy attack, he wanted to 'dignify' his grandfather's defence of that court.[3]

Throughout the antiquary's discussion in the *Archeion* of the relationship of the central courts and the council to each other and to the Common Law, he recognised no irreconcilable conflict or rivalry among them but rather a continuing co-operation that resulted in the dispensation of justice. In particular, he praised the courts of equity which meted out the first kind of justice known to mankind, that of the conscience of the father or elder of a household before there were written laws. For his own age he admonished the English people to be thankful that the Queen had appointed men of great ability and integrity to the equity courts, among them Sir Thomas Egerton, Lord Keeper of the Great Seal, who not only used great moderation in the dispensing of equity, but who, by his own training, was well versed in Common Law. This section praising Sir Thomas was obviously added after 1596 when he became Lord Keeper and was, of course, missing from the 1591 manuscript sent to Sir Robert Cecil.[4]

In the section on the equity courts he also warmly defended the royal use of the Court of Star Chamber where the King and council sat in judgement or, as he said, sat 'at the sterne, and . . . governed the Shippe of the Commonwealth'.[5] It was there that the rare and great matters which needed to be handled by the forces of 'absolute power and irregular authoritie' were heard. Like most lawyers of Tudor England he believed that without this power great offences such as unlawful maintenance, the giving of liveries, the bribery of juries, and riots would go unpunished, and anarchy rather than order would prevail in the kingdom. It was this section, according to Charles McIlwain, that made the *Archeion* important historically. Written, McIlwain said, at a 'critical period in the development of the English constitution', the *Archeion* is a 'record of favourable contemporary opinion about a court system that many, a half-century later, considered to be an intolerable burden'.[6]

Parliament Lambarde described as the highest court in England, the origins of which he traced to the days of the Anglo-Saxons except, as he explained, in those days it was called the Witan. Representing the three estates of the kingdom, this court had the king at its head with the nobility (lords spiritual and temporal) and the commonalty (knights and burgesses) as its body. He went on to claim that the king in parliament could act only with the consent of the body so that even though various old statutes like *Magna Carta* ran 'in the Name of the Prince onely, yet the other two Estates were supplied, in all good understanding'.[7]

In the dedicatory letter dater 22 October 1591, he complimented Sir Robert Cecil on his worthiness to hold high public office and spoke of the time when he, the son of that 'renowned Nestor and onely Atlas of the English Countrie', would inherit his father's political power. It has been suggested that the manuscript was dedicated to Cecil purely for political reasons and that had the antiquary followed his own personal inclinations, he would have instead honoured Sir Thomas Egerton of Lincoln's Inn to whom he had given at least three gifts in the previous nine years—a copy of Fitz-Neal's 'Dialogue of the Exchequer' in 1587 and two presentation copies of the *Eirenarcha*, one in 1582 and one in 1588.[8] Furthermore, despite this apparent evidence of friendship between Cecil and Lambarde in 1591, no other communications between the two exist although he must have had some personal knowledge of Cecil from 1589 when he married Elizabeth, the daughter of Lord Cobham.

To accept the suggestion that Lambarde would have preferred Egerton to Cecil assumes that it was his inclination to dedicate his books to personal friends without reference to political and business matters, but that preference is not evidenced by three of the works that were published in his lifetime. There is no reason to believe that he was an intimate friend of Sir William Cordell, Thomas Wotton, or Sir Thomas Bromley, to whom he presented his works on Anglo-Saxon law, the history of Kent, and the justices of the peace. Instead, they were singled out because of their close association with and knowledge of the topics treated and because their support would lend credence to the worth of the books, presumably aiding in their sale and circulation. It is well to keep in mind that in 1591 Sir Thomas Egerton had not yet advanced to an important position in the Chancery.

There also seems to be an assumption in the suggestion that Egerton was his personal preference that Lambarde could not admire Cecil, but there is no evidence that he abhored his character or believed that he was cunning and treacherous. Indeed, of the two leaders, Sir Robert Cecil and Robert Devereux, Earl of Essex, who were beginning to vie for power at court, it can be assumed that Lambarde, basically stable and hardworking, would prefer Cecil with his studied knowledge of affairs to Essex, a handsome, mercurial courtier who could not concentrate on the routine of government for his excursions to win glory, beginning with Lisbon in 1589 and ending tragically in Ireland in 1599.

In 1591 it was not so obvious that the struggle between Cecil and Essex, who at the time was with the army in France, would be fought so openly and furiously, and, indeed, what Lambarde saw at court was that the persevering Lord Treasurer, who had kindly supported the publication of the *Perambulation*, had granted him the custody of Maximilian Dalison, and had offered him a position in the Alienations' Office, was grooming his younger son for the affairs of state. By dedicating the manuscript to that son, Lambarde indicated his support of the continuance of the Cecil family in royal government. Since clearly in 1591, three years before he began to work with Egerton in the Court of Chancery and three years before the Cecil–Essex struggles began in earnest, Lambarde's patrons were Lord Burghley and Lord Cobham, the father and father-in-law of Sir Robert respectively, he probably never even considered dedicating the manuscript to Egerton.

Two years before the presentation of the manuscript, Lambarde was offered by the Lord Treasurer a position in the Alienations' Office where fees for licences to alienate, for pardons of alienations, and for writs of entry in recoveries were collected for lands held of the Crown in chief as well as for writs of covenants. Until 1576 when the Queen created the Office by leasing the farm of those fees to Robert Dudley, Earl of Leicester, who continued as farmer until 1588, the Court of Chancery had performed that service.

At the end of Hilary Term, 1589, Lord Burghley became the new farmer with a lease that extended until 1595, when it was renewed for seven years with the addition that the fines for writs of entry in recoveries on lands not held in chief were also to be collected. The officials of the Office were three deputies, a receiver, three clerks, and a Justice of the Assize or a Master in Chancery to take oaths from the suiters as to the value of their lands. Of these officials, only the deputies were given an allowance of £20 per term and the others depended upon fees from the suiters.[9]

When, on 4 October 1589, Lambarde responded to Burghley's offer of the position of deputy in the Office, he admitted his pleasure at receiving the appointment for it was an 'infallible messenger' of his lordship's favour, but he also suggested that he should accept it only on probation to discover whether or not he was equal to the task. He gave two reasons for doubting his abilities: the decline in his eyesight and his discontinuance from study. It is true that his sight had been weakened because of the endless hours he had devoted to studying ancient manuscripts, often only by the light of candles, but despite this decay, he continued to punish his eyes in those endeavours after 1589. The other reason he gave for doubting his abilities was even more invalid, for he had not, as he suggested, terminated his studies. In the year 1589, alone, he began his treatise on Star Chamber and was probably adding material to the *Archeion*, and the year before that he had gathered information about the mint and had prepared a second edition of the *Eirenarcha*.[10]

Lambarde's apologetic letter reveals not a reluctance to assume the position as many have supposed but rather a desire to appear appropriately humble and subservient to the powerful Lord Treasurer. In subsequent years there is no evidence that he hesitated to become a Master in Chancery, the Deputy Keeper of the Rolls, or the Keeper of the Records in the Tower of London, any of which posts might well have required far better eyesight and greater historical knowledge than the Alienations' Office position which he did not relinquish until his death in 1601.

Neither his declining eyesight nor his previous discontinuance from study prevented him from writing a treatise about the Office, which he completed in 1590 but to which he added an appendix in 1595. He had little sympathy, he explained in the manuscript, with those who complained about the fines due to the Office, for they were an ancient revenue of the Crown, but he did admit that they were often inequitable as it was impossible to ascertain the exact land value for lack of specific information about its fertility and its location in the kingdom. To pacify its critics, and there were many in Tudor England who objected to these feudal exactions, he revealed that the Office was conducted more efficiently than it had been under the leadership of the Earl of Leicester.

A suitor to the Office first had to swear an oath to a Justice of the Assize or a Master in Chancery about the value of his land and next present his affidavit to the receiver who charged him the appropriate fee. After paying the fine, the suitor then gave his affidavit to a clerk who entered the information on it into a book and issued a writ, licence, or pardon which had to be approved and endorsed by one of the deputies.

The special Master in Chancery Lambarde titled a doctor in 1590 when he wrote the treatise, and since until that time most of the masters had been trained in Civil Law, it has been suggested that Lambarde, who was trained only in the Common Law, was appointed a Master in Chancery in 1592 so that he could perform the duties of the master assigned to the Office. There are two reasons why this suggestion is unlikely: first, he was appointed by a friend, Sir John Puckering, the newly-named Lord Keeper of the Great Seal, and second, the deputies could, when no master or justice was available, compound the value of the land with the suitors. In those cases the suiter took his composition, instead of his affidavit, to the receiver and thereafter followed the procedure of those who had sworn oaths. Surely when Puckering appointed his friend Master in Chancery he had reasons other than his fortuitous position in Alienations![11]

Before his appointment to the Office, the three deputies had been Thomas Dudley, Robert Wrote, and Thomas Wigges, but since Wrotes' name did not appear in the records after Easter Term, 1589, Lambarde evidently replaced him even though he did not begin his duties until Michaelmas Term, 1589. During this first term he reviewed the clerks' accounts of licences and pardons for alienation six times but in the shorter terms he normally certified them only three or four times. He also reviewed their records of the writs of covenant as frequently as those of the licences and pardons but not always on the same day. During his first Hilary Term, for instance, he endorsed both accounts on 23 January and 12 February but reviewed only those of the writs of covenant on 18 and 20 February and those of the licences and pardons on 28 February.[12]

Even though the other deputies certified the accuracy of the clerks' accounts, it was not until 1596 that one of them, Thomas Fortescue who had replaced Thomas Dudley in 1594, certified the licences and pardons more frequently than Lambarde and not until 1598 that he examined the writs of covenant more frequently than the antiquary. Furthermore, from 1595, the earliest date of surviving records of writs of entry in recoveries, Fortescue and Lambarde shared about equally the reviewing of those accounts which had to be endorsed about twice as often as the others.[13]

Since frequently during term time all three deputies had to endorse summaries made in the clerks' books of the income on the various writs, despite the small amount of routine checking that Wigges and Dudley did, they were still required to assume responsibility for the accounts. Besides the figures in the clerks' books, the receiver's records indicated how much revenue was collected, and at the close of each term he certified his totals to the deputies, who signed his report if they found it in order. When they had gathered all the information, they reported their total profits to the crown, as, for example, in June 1596 when Lambarde, Fortescue, and Wigges calculated that their profits for the Trinity Term and the preceding vacation were £524 3s. 3¾d.[14]

In 1595 critics claimed that by preventing many writs from passing under the Great Seal, the Alienations' Office was responsible for her Majesty's loss of revenue. Since that was the year that Burghley's farm was renewed, they probably hoped thereby to gain his disgrace and to influence the Queen not to renew his lease. Perhaps at the behest of the Lord Treasurer, Lambarde, Fortescue, and Wigges wrote a treatise entitled, 'An Appolligie to the obsertions of the diminutions of the profitts of the Greate Seale of England', in which they claimed that if, indeed, some revenue were lost to the Queen, it was not their fault as the Office was administered under rules formulated in the days of the Earl of Leicester, but, in which they also asserted that to their knowledge none of the writs issued by them had ever passed under the Great Seal.[15]

Because the Lord Treasurer, himself, was concerned that some of the revenue of his Office sent to the Exchequer was siphoned off before it could be spent by her Majesty's government, he requested his deputies to investigate one source of income, the post fines paid on writs of covenant. Reporting on this fine from Easter Term, 1594 through Hilary Term, 1597, Lambarde, Fortescue, and Wigges calculated the total income collected by them but could 'make no conjecture' from their records about what percentage of the fines was actually retained by the government and suggested that the information could be obtained at the Exchequer. The problem, as they saw it, was that holders of franchises with the benefit of recovering post fines collected by the crown sometimes expanded the territory covered by their grants. For example, they claimed that whenever any part of a town extended into a lord's franchise, he often illegally collected the post fines from the Exchequer on writs of covenant issued to everyone in the town. At fault also were local bailiffs who, for handsome sums of money, aided and abetted the lords.[16]

Like justices in the courts, the deputies of the Office were plagued by potential suitors who hoped to obtain favourable judgement on land valuations. On 15 November 1593, Anthony Bacon, a relative of Burghley but a member of Essex's clique, thanked the antiquary for the many kind favours he had already extended to his lady and mother and then pleaded that his land be rated at as 'easy a composition as you may'.[17] No reply to this letter has been discovered but there is no doubt that Lambarde had the authority, if he chose to use it, to compound with Bacon for a low land value.

The antiquary faithfully performed his duties in the Office from the time of his appointment until his death. Because he was conscientious and dedicated, he appeared term after term from Michaelmas, 1589 to Trinity, 1601 even at times when he was ill, but it is also true that he would probably have been present in London during term time even if he held no central appointment. In January 1588 he had written to his good friend, Ralph Rokeby, to ask him to 'essoigne' his absence during that Hilary Term, the first that he had missed in 30 years. It was probably the only one he missed between 1559 and 1601.[18]

Despite his conscientious efforts all did not always go smoothly for him in the Office, as two letters of his bear witness. On 13 December 1590, a little more than a year after his appointment, he explained to Burghley's personal secretary, Sir Michael Hicks, why he had left London contrary to his lordship's orders. He had waited, he explained, 15 days after the term even though his poor horses' heads were swollen from the dearth of hay and even though half of his own poor family was ill, and since, he continued, he had seen that the receiver disbursed the revenues according to custom and since the business for which his attendance had been requested was more for 'shewe of duetie, than for any special service', he believed that he could depart with impunity. He asked Hicks to give his apologies to Burghley, when he returned to London, for he himself, was 'not willing to trouble London tyll the next Terme'.[19]

In the second letter, written on 14 July 1596, he apologised to Lord Burghley for his error regarding an entailed estate and admitted that even though it had occurred during a multiplicity of business, he still should have been more careful. Confessing that he was particularly saddened by his oversight because by 'imputation' it might be blamed on his lordship, he besought him 'upon the knees of [his] harte' not to withdraw his favourable opinion of him which he held 'more pretious than the judgement of any person upon the Earthe, [his] Sovereign excepted'. Burghley undoubtedly accepted these apologies especially since he knew that Lambarde, always conscientious, was then co-operating with Lord Keeper Egerton in a reform of the Court of Chancery.[20]

First emerging in the Middle Ages as a secretariat, the Court of Chancery by the 16th century had acquired an independent legal jurisdiction based on the equitable or prerogative powers of the council. One kind of legal device which had brought both a growing business and increased powers to the court, particularly in the 15th century, was the frequently-used trust since the common law courts had refused to protect the interests of the individual for whom the trust was created. Besides having the right to enforce the dictates of conscience in cases where Common Law had no remedy, the Lord Chancellor, the supreme official in the court, possessed the authority to direct suitors to the common law courts by the issuance of writs and as Lord Keeper of the Great Seal had ministerial duties which were delegated to a secretariat that wrote, sealed and recorded all documents that were sent out under the Great Seal.

The court, which sat at the southeast corner of Westminster Hall, has been called a 'conglomeration' held together by the Lord Chancellor, the Great Seal, and the Master of the Rolls, who was second in status only to the Lord Chancellor, but who had no judicial authority of his own. In charge of the Rolls Chapel, the Master had vast powers of appointment with the authority to name the six clerks in charge of enrolments, the three clerks of the Petty Bag, the two examiners who questioned witnesses and examined the writs, and the seven clerks of the Chapel. The Master of the Rolls, of course, had been selected by Lambarde to act as President of his almshouse.[21]

Usually regarded as one of the 12 Masters in Chancery, the Master of the Rolls had greater authority than they although his daily routine was largely indistinguishable from theirs. The duties of the ordinary masters, each of whom had three clerks to assist him, included hearing and investigating cases delegated to them by the Lord Chancellor, handling interlocutory matters, and performing other administrative duties, such as the receiving of the acknowledgment of writs, the taking of affidavits, and the giving of oaths. In the 16th century, since much of the judicial work was delegated to them, the formal decrees of Chancery were largely based on their investigations and opinions.[22]

The individual responsible for the appointment of the antiquary as a Master in Chancery was Sir John Puckering, the newly-named Lord Keeper of the Great Seal, who had probably first become acquainted with Lambarde at Lincoln's Inn where they were called to the bar at the same moot and who must have been aware of his great knowledge of the courts. It is not unlikely that he had seen the presentation copy of the *Archeion* which had been sent to Cecil. By custom a Master in Chancery was inaugurated by the placing of a symbolic cap upon his head and by the taking of a traditional oath with no formal registration as such, although after the appointment of Sir Thomas Egerton as Lord Keeper in 1596, orders were given that a record of appointments was to be kept. On 22 June 1592, only two months after his own elevation, Puckering named Lambarde one of his masters and placed the symbolic cap upon his head.[23]

Since Puckering died on 30 April 1596, he was Lord Keeper of England for only four years but even during that period of time he relied upon Lambarde's legal ability and judgement. In 1594 he asked him how to pass an *innotescimus* on a deed and in 1595 wrote to his 'verie loving frends', Sir John Leveson and William Lambarde concerning a case then pending in Chancery between his servant and another. Puckering was not the antiquary's only old schoolmate to advance high in court circles, for Sir Thomas Egerton, called to the bar at Lincoln's Inn in 1572, procured appointment as Solicitor-General in 1581, Attorney General in 1592, and Master of the Rolls in 1594. At Puckering's death in 1596 he was named the new Lord Keeper of the Great Seal with permission to retain his position as Master of the Rolls.[24]

Since almost all the orders of Puckering for administrative reform of Chancery were issued after 10 April 1594 when Egerton became Master of Rolls, historians have usually agreed that it was Egerton, not Puckering, who pressed for changes. Indeed, it has been argued that Egerton was permitted to retain the position of Master of the Rolls in 1596 at his advancement to the post of Lord Keeper because the Queen and her advisors realised that only a man with the 'power, prestige, and patronage' of both offices would effect the desired reforms.[25] Apparently Egerton relied heavily upon Lambarde's legal sagacity in solving many of the court's problems. The antiquary's appointment to the royal commission of 1596 to hear and determine pleas in the court during the absence of the Lord Keeper is evidence of the trust that Egerton had in his ability, for he had not been named to a similar commission of 1593. The following year, on 27 May 1597, further demonstrating his trust in his old friend, the Lord Keeper appointed Lambarde Deputy Keeper of the Rolls.[26]

Paul Ward has argued on the basis of extant copies of 'Chancery Collections' which were gathered by the antiquary and which contain, among many other treatises, 'Ordinances agreed upon by John Puckering and Thomas Egerton in April 1596 touching procedure in court', 'Orders agreed upon by the Six Clerks touching the better government of themselves', 'Orders for the making up of the Rolls of Chancery' (written in 1599), and 'Orders for the restraining of the length of suits in Chancery', that Lambarde was more than just an assistant to Egerton in the reform movement. In his own account of the April 1596 ordinance on court procedure the antiquary reported that he was privy to the agreements made by Puckering and Egerton.[27]

Further, Ward has demonstrated that these reforms were con-

sonant with suggestions for improving the procedure of the court
which Lambarde had already outlined in his *Archeion* and that,
indeed, the central arguments for limiting the equitable jurisdiction of Chancery which Egerton, a common lawyer, championed
as Lord Keeper had already been set forth in that work on the
central courts. Not only was he an author of reforms, but he
also helped to implement them. After it was discovered that oaths
had not been given regularly to the underclerks of the six clerks,
Egerton asked Lambarde and Dr. Matthew Carew, also a Master
in Chancery, to give them on 7 July 1596, and when the original
decree for the making up of the rolls of Chancery was signed by
the Lord Keeper in 1599, he handed it to Lambarde, his deputy,
for execution.[28]

Apparently the antiquary was interested in the history of the
Court of Chancery long before his appointment as a master, and
included in his 'Collections on Chancery', a discourse on that
court dated March 1577, the year after the *Perambulation* was
printed and two years before the *Archeion* was begun. In the form
of a letter the treatise told the inquirer about the court of its
various fees and of its ancient history, tracing its origins, and
those of other central courts to the Anglo-Saxon heptarchy.[29]

Among the 'Collections on Chancery' can also be found a treatise on the fees of the masters which the antiquary wrote in 1597.
At the beginning of this discourse he explained that twice a year
a master received money from the Hanaper for robes, £3 at Easter
and £3 14s. at Michaelmas. Then he listed the various fees the
master received, among them 2s. for giving the oaths to escheators
and 2s. for taking each recognizance upon bail, and also noted
that formerly the 6s. 8d. fee for cancelling patents belonged to the
masters but that it had since been reserved exclusively for the
Lord Keeper or the Master of the Rolls. At least once, on 19
February 1600, when he certified with Egerton the surrender of a
patent for offices held of the crown, he must have wished that
this fee was still made available to the Masters.[30]

Dissatisfaction with their recompense led them to petition Lord
Keeper Egerton for greater remuneration, and on 26 September
1600, an old friend of Lambarde, John Tyndall, a Master in
Chancery since 1598, wrote to him about their mutual concern for
success in the suit. Expressing pessimism about the response to
the petition, Tyndall complained that even if they were to seek

dead men's shoes, they would probably still have to go barefoot. The need for higher pay was great, he exclaimed, for even though he worked three times as hard in the Court of Chancery as he had formerly in his own private practice, his profits were less than one-third of his previous gain. Whether or not the masters were successful in their suit has not been determined.[31]

As Master in Chancery one of the many duties that Lambarde performed was hearing cases delegated to him by the Lord Keeper. After he had examined the statements of the plaintiff, the defendant, the witnesses, and the other written evidence, it was his responsibility to report his findings and to recommend, whenever he could, a just settlement of the dispute. During the nine years that he served in Chancery, he undoubtedly wrote hundreds of reports, but, unfortunately, many have been lost and still others deteriorate at a touch. Nevertheless, 41 reports which are still legible and which give proof of his painstaking efforts have been discovered at the Public Record Office.

They revealed, first of all, the masters' complete dependence upon the judicial authority of the Lord Keeper. In one case, for example, Lambarde wrote, 'I do think . . . it ought to be decreed by this court . . .'. In others he complained that plaintiffs had requested extensions but that he had not had the authority to grant them, and he prayed the court would agree with him about some suggestions.[32]

Often more than one master was assigned to examine the evidence. Seven reports dated between January 1599 and June 1601 were written by Lambarde with John Tyndall; eight dated between July 1596 and June 1601 were written with Francis Stanhope; and one was written with George Carew, the nephew of Dr. Matthew Carew, also a Master in Chancery. Although no original report written only by the antiquary and Dr. Carew is available, one of the 41 was certified by the two of them in cooperation with John Tyndall. There is evidence that in at least two other instances Lambarde was one of three masters assigned to a case, but this report written by Tyndall, Carew, and him is the only one of its kind to which he was a party that has been found at the Public Record Office.[33]

Two or three masters working together had no more authority than one of them alone had. For example, in one report he wrote with Francis Stanhope, Lambarde concluded that the plaintiff should be dismissed out of court, unless, of course, the Lord Keeper thought otherwise. In another case in which a petition was exhibited against an under-sheriff of Essex, Lambarde and George Carew claimed that a commission granting power to examine the witnesses under oath was necessary before the case could be settled.[34]

Occasionally the Lord Keeper required the masters to hold further proceedings on a case because he was dissatisfied with the results. He had apparently demanded new investigations in the suit of Joe Bott *et. al.* v. Thomas Ware, for example, as Lambarde and Tyndall referred to a report they had both previously written about this controversy. Not always were the same masters ordered to review a case, and on one occasion Lambarde and Francis Stanhope cited a report which had been written by Dr. Stanhope and Dr. Hone about the dispute they were then attempting to settle.[35]

Frequently the plaintiff presented his bill of complaint with the purpose of obtaining arbitration rather than actually proceeding to trial, but often after examining all the evidence, the masters could not recommend a settlement. In one suit Francis Stanhope and the antiquary informed the court that even though they had heard all the evidence they could not agree upon a conclusion to the controversy, and in still another suit they reported that since the differences between the parties were great and the causes many, they could not effect a settlement.[36]

Evidence found in the masters' reports supports Lambarde's statements in the *Archeion* that the Court of Chancery was not so much a competitor of the other central courts as a collaborator for the dispensing of justice. In the case of John Saunders v. William Cotterell, for instance, Francis Stanhope and William Lambarde recommended that the defendant be granted the lands in question until such time as the complainant could recover at Common Law. In another case in which they recommended a settlement, Lambarde and Tyndall warned the plaintiff that if he did not agree to their solution, the case would be dismissed out of Chancery forever and sent to Common Law. In still another controversy, having found that at Common Law the plaintiff was given possession of the land in dispute, Lambarde discovered that the Court of Chancery had subsequently granted his opponent 34 acres of the land. He humbly asked the equity court to explain its action and suggested that until an answer was forthcoming any further proceedings at Common Law should be prevented.[37]

The reports are not the only extant evidence of his efforts in Chancery cases. Among other sources is *Cary's Reports,* a book gathered by George Carew, which was based on cases Lambarde reviewed between 1558 and 1599 and Carew's own collection of cases for the years 1601 to 1605. One case cited by Cary was the suit of Cutting v. the executors of his father-in-law's estate—a significant suit since it further displays both the interaction and conflict among the central courts in Elizabethan England. Cutting had recovered his wife's dowry from the executors at Common Law but the verdict had subsequently been overturned in the Exchequer Chamber. Undaunted by this reversal, he sued in the Court of Chancery where it was discovered that after the debts and legacies of the testator were paid, enough money was left to return the marriage portion. Having made this discovery, Dr. Stanhope and Lambarde recommended that Cutting be satisfied, whereupon the executors exhibited a bill of complaint against Cutting in the Court of Chancery. Somewhat outraged by this action Lambarde excused himself from the dispute because, as he explained, he would be a judge in his own cause, but before he completely withdrew, he recommended the censure of the executors and the execution of his former suggestion, which recommendation was followed by the Lord Keeper.[38]

The other case Cary cited in which Lambarde was a judge involved a controversy between Sir Arthur Capell and Nicholas Mym over the division of some lands. Lambarde's original report, still extant at the Public Record Office, is also significant for its insight into the relationship of the central courts. After studying the evidence for over a year, he reported in October 1599 that because both parties had writings and evidence which seemed contradictory and which had not been made public, he believed that any Chancery decision would be followed by many suits at Common Law. He was, therefore, recommending that all the evidence in his custody and all the witnesses be made available to examination by the counsel on both sides so that a final determination of the cause could be reached in Chancery and the common law suits could be avoided.[39]

Another source of evidence about Lambarde's activities in Chancery is Cecil Monro's *Acta Cancellaria.* Of the five Lambarde cases he cited, two are of special interest, but the one between Charles Cornwallis and William Legrice is significant not because of the legal dispute but because of the attitude of the two masters assigned to hear it. On 26 April 1597, Lambarde and Henry Hobarte petitioned the court to assign the suit to some other fit persons 'with good eyes' who planned to remain in London after the Easter Term was over. Since, they confessed, they had no time for the case during that session and since they had already remained in London after Hilary Term to examine the pertinent evidence, they were determined not to devote any more time to it between terms. Their request was granted, but as Monro explained, it would have sounded rather odd in his age, the 19th century, for a master to petition to have one of his cases transferred to someone else because he wished to discontinue his work on it.[40]

Although the relationship among the central courts was good during the reign of Queen Elizabeth, the attitude of Chancery officials toward provincial equity courts was hostile. Following the direction set by both Sir John Puckering and Sir Thomas Egerton in their attempts to limit the authority of the local courts, Lambarde and Dr. Carew came down heavily against a provincial court in their report of 4 December 1595 on the case of Cheyney v. Godfrey, the other case of special interest cited by Monro. When they discovered that the defendants alleged that as inhabitants of the Cinque Ports they could be impleaded only in the Court of St. James at Dover, the masters argued against that extension of jurisdiction because equity was a royal prerogative which could be delegated only by express royal grant. Ultimately under the leadership of Egerton a compromise was effected between the courts at Dover and London in which equity cases involving parties and premises all inhabitants or all located in the Cinque Ports could be impleaded at Dover. During the course of time, however, partly because of the pressure of equity business at London, this compromise gave rise to the legal fiction that all lands of some estates were located in the Cinque Ports so that the Court of St. James at Dover could handle cases in which they were involved.[41]

Many parties to the cases pending in Chancery wrote letters to Lambarde to request his special attention and favour in their suits. 10 of those letters, which referred to nine different Chancery cases between 1595 and 1600, are at the Folger Shakespeare Library in Washington, D.C. One of the most celebrated cases to which one of the letters referred was the dispute of Dr. Nicholas Steward and Dr. Thomas Byng over a chamber in Doctors' Commons of London, and a copy of the report relevant to this case, which was written by Lambarde and George Carew, is available at the library of Trinity Hall, Cambridge University.[42]

While a chamber within a house in London called Doctors' Commons, then in possession of Dr. Steward, was being claimed at Common Law by Dr. Byng, a Master in Chancery, Dr. Steward entered a bill of complaint into Chancery in which he hoped to prove that the original lease to the house was made in trust for the benefit of the Society of Doctors' Commons which had thereby the sole authority to dispose of its chambers. The defendant, Byng, based his claim to the room at Common Law upon an understanding with the masters, fellows, and scholars of Trinity Hall, upon an original lease of the house made to Trinity Hall by the Dean and Chapter of the Cathedral of St. Paul's and upon another lease in reversion.

Somewhat aggrieved in June 1599, Dr. Steward wrote to the three masters assigned to the case, Dr. Matthew Carew, Thomas Legge, and William Lambarde to complain about one of their preliminary decisions. He stated that his opponent, Dr. Byng, had shown him their written order to examine all witnesses in the case on the next Monday at 2.00 p.m, and he admitted to persons not familiar with the suit the order might appear as indifferent to him as it was to Dr. Byng, but actually, he continued, it was prejudicial to his cause since he, unlike his opponent who relied upon leases already in his possession, had to arrange for witnesses to be in London on that day. (Dr. Steward was undoubtedly also angry that his opponent, a Master in Chancery, had seen the order first.) It is possible that the date of examination was postponed, for his witnesses did appear to give their testimony.[43]

Evidently early in the progress of the suit three masters had been assigned to examine the evidence but when the report was completed in November of that year, only two masters, one of them Lambarde, certified that the case was settled. There is some confusion about the date on which the report was written and about who actually wrote it. Dr. Thomas Byng, the defendant in Chancery, died in December 1599, but the report dated in November referred to him as deceased. Furthermore, along with Lambarde, George Carew endorsed the findings which were, of course, dated in November, but he was not appointed a master until 21 December 1599 when he replaced the deceased Dr. Byng. It is likely that Lambarde began writing the report in November and finished it in December after the death of Byng and the appointment of George Carew.[44]

Having examined the leases and having heard the witnesses, among them Alexander Nowell, Dean of St. Paul's, Lambarde reported that the plaintiff, Dr. Steward, had not proved the existence of a trust. While Trinity Hall had expended a large sum of money to obtain the lease and to repair the house, the Society of Doctors' Commons, he asserted, had never received any rental money for the rooms nor displayed that it had in any way any authority over the chambers. To him it seemed clear that the plaintiff had no case in equity and the defendant, then Dr. Byng's heir, could gain possession of the chamber at Common Law.[45]

Altogether the available Chancery evidence has revealed information about 64 Lambarde cases. They can be catalogued as follows: six concerning fines on lands, two about the custody of deeds, six concerning fraud, seven dealing with land ownership, 10 settlements of estates, four court dismissals, three disputed jurisdictions, nine about leases and rents, three concerning copyhold tenure, two about the profits of a parsonage, two concerning trusts, two concerning recognizances, one controversy over a marriage portion, and finally, seven in which no legal problem could be isolated. These 64 cases are fragmentary records of Lambarde's activity and should not be looked upon as representing proportionately the kinds of disputes that he heard.[46]

For not quite a decade the antiquary served as a Master in Chancery, performing routine business as well as effecting administrative reforms in association with Egerton. Whatever the service, he always attempted to organise and reform the systems in operation. Just shortly before his appointment to Chancery, for example, he had been delighted to learn that the Privy Council had ordered the revision of the commission of the peace, a reformation he had first requested in 1579 of Sir Thomas Bromley, then Lord Chancellor of England. While performing the required duties of his various posts, this dedicated royal servant attempted to organise, to analyse, and to clarify the existing procedures, methods, and goals, with the ultimate desire to have justice as well as law and order in the kingdom.

# The Experienced Justice

DURING the years that Lambarde was journeying to London to perform his duties as a Master in Chancery and as an Alienations' Office deputy, he was fulfilling his responsibilities as a Kentish justice of the peace. Defence remained a chief problem of the county officials in the 1590s since the destruction of the Armada had not ended the Spanish threat to invade Protestant England and since there was the possibility that the Spaniards might succeed in establishing a naval base on the Breton and Picardy coast, a fear that led the Queen to send military expeditions to France. Ireland, too, had to be closely watched particularly after 1596 when Philip II of Spain promised support to the Earl of Tyrone in his rebellion there. Lambarde's effort to maintain the county in a state of military readiness continued under the direction of Lord Cobham, the lord lieutenant, and his deputy, Sir John Leveson.

In January 1590 the lords of the Privy Council, among them Lord Cobham, reminded Leveson, Lambarde and others that as part of the defence preparations, defects in armour had to be repaired and proper provisions of powder and match had to be stored in the customary towns. Two months later these justices were required to hold a general muster and in September to draw up regulations setting the number of artulaturs to be raised from each hundred in the lathe of Aylesford.[1]

From September 1590 to March 1592 Lambarde either did not perform any military duties or all evidence of that activity has been destroyed. A letter written in March 1592 by John Richers to Roger Twysden, in which he said that he had stopped at the home of Leveson where he found Lambarde waiting to accompany his host to view the muster at Rochester, once more revealed the antiquary's involvement in defence. Apparently Lambarde was not only known as a close friend of Leveson but was also viewed as a peacemaker by the others on the commission. In another letter also written about the Rochester muster that March, Robert Bing revealed that Lambarde, who was arbitrating his dispute with John Richers, had wanted permission to ask Leveson's assistance with the mediation.[2]

It was not until July 1594 that more evidence of Lambarde and Leveson co-operating on military service was discovered. That month they informed the constables in their area that they would have to raise enough money to furnish the 300 soldiers that Lord Cobham had demanded for overseas duty and suggested that a rate of 2d. on each pound sterling of goods and 3d. on each pound sterling of land be levied. Almost a year later, on 13 June 1595, when Lord Cobham required five light horses and riders for Ireland where a rebellion was then in progress, he informed the local officials, perhaps to quash all complaints that the government was impoverishing the shire, that the original allotment of six for Kent had been graciously reduced by her Majesty. The antiquary conferred with Leveson and other justices in Maidstone where it was decided to charge each lathe £30 for the cost of the horsemen. Lambarde, himself, was assessed for £22 worth of land and Leveson for £30 at the rate of 5d. per pound sterling.[3]

Pursuant to the orders of Lord Cobham in April of 1596 Sir John Leveson and the justices of Kent impressed 2,000 men who were sent to Dover for transport to Calais where they were to be put under the command of the Earl of Essex. Since the French battle for Calais against the Cardinal Archduke Albert of Austria, Governor of the Netherlands, was lost before the Kentish troops reached Dover, they were immediately discharged and ordered home to save the county the further expense of providing food and shelter for them. But even though the men had not actually participated in the Calais war, the shire still had to raise £89 3s. 1d. for the cost of impressing them. All in the subsidy book were to be charged 5d. on each pound sterling in goods and 8d. on each pound sterling in lands, and Lambarde paid 14s. 8d. while Leveson paid 20s.[4]

In September 1597 Lambarde and Leveson demanded that the

constables and borsholders of their area raise enough money to cover the charges of £61 12d. for impressing three levies of men in their division during the previous year, and in July 1598, the last surviving evidence of the antiquary's military activities, they required the constables to raise £27 1s. 8d. to send four horses to Ireland where English forces were in serious trouble. It may well be that after this date the antiquary ceased to assist Leveson in his military duties for when his lease expired to Halling Palace in September of that year, he moved his family to Greenwich.[5]

Besides sending men abroad to meet the Spanish threat, the justices also attempted to provide care for disabled veterans, who were residents of Kent, and kept records of the parish assessments required by an Act of Parliament of 1593. One assessment record kept by Lambarde was entitled 'A Weeklye Agreement of the parishes within the Northern Division of the Lathe of Aylesford towardes the Gaole Money, renewed at Maydstone 13 July 1593 and towardes the relief of Mayhemed and disabled soldiers, rated at the Midsomer Quarter Sessions, holden at Canterbury, 1593', and provided that each parish be assessed weekly two or three pence for gaol upkeep and one or two pence for the injured soldiers. Following a summary of the rates for his own lathe, Lambarde listed those for the other four lathes of Kent and calculated that the county paid a total of 58s. 8d. weekly for the maimed soldiers.[6]

Because the Spanish threats were directed in great part against English Protestantism, inquiry after Catholics, who were thought to be Spanish spies, was deemed an essential part of the overall defence program. In the 1590s this search seemed particularly important because Englishmen were being trained as priests at special seminaries on the continent for the purposes of returning to their homes to reconvert the Queen's subjects to Catholicism. Prior to this decade only one reference to Lambarde's personal involvement in discovering the identity of recusants can be found and that on 6 March 1587 when the Privy Council ordered him to assist the bailiffs of Maidstone in sending abroad all foreigners who refused to attend church.[7]

On 15 January 1592 the government appointed to a commission of recusancy 32 persons of Kent, many of them justices of the peace, Sir Thomas Scott, Sir John Leveson, Sir Thomas Fludd, Roger Twysden, and William Lambarde as well as the prominent churchmen of the county and Lord Cobham, Lord-Lieutenant, who were instructed to discover the identity of those who were attempting to seduce the people from their allegiance to the Queen and to make special inquiries about those who had come into the country from abroad. Annexed to the commission were several articles with detailed instructions for the commissioners. First, for purposes of organisation they were to divide the county among them and to assemble every 40 days throughout the year to report their findings to the Privy Council. Second, they were cautioned not to ask anyone 'to answeare to any questions of his conscience', but rather to ask him merely if he usually attended church. Only after an individual was proved to be a wilful recusant was he to answer questions about his devotion to the Pope. Third, the Kentish officials were to forward any information they uncovered about recusancy in other counties to the proper authorities there. By these measures the Privy Council hoped to obtain religious conformity in the kingdom without disturbing a man's conscience.[8]

Following the Council's directive, Lambarde, Leveson, and Twysden requested 14 suspicious persons to appear for private questioning at Malling on 23 March 1592 and authorised the bailiff of Malling to direct known recusants to them on the same day. They explained that they did not intend to hold a public hearing until it had been ascertained that the accused were recusants. Lord Burghley wrote to his 'verie lovinge frendes Sir John Leveson and Mr. William Lambarde' requesting them to stay their proceedings against one of those required to appear at Malling, a Thomas Wotton of Addington, gentleman, since it was believed that mild treatment and a conference with a learned minister would convince him to attend church. A few months later, however, because he could not be persuaded to conform, Robert Bing, John Richers, and William Lambarde witnessed the seizure of his pistols and coat of armour as a confirmed recusant. The last evidence of the commissioners' activity has survived in a document which certified that Fludd, Leveson, Twysden, and Lambarde had held a public meeting on 14 September 1592 in Rochester where eight recusants had been commanded to appear. Since the sheriff reported that five no longer lived in the county and that one was so aged he could not travel, only two presented themselves in Rochester, where one of them actually agreed to conform, but the other was placed under a £200 bond to appear at the next Quarter Sessions where his case would be heard.[9]

In the midst of these proceedings against recusants the Privy Council discovered that some justices of the peace had not taken the oath of supremacy to the Queen and ordered trusted individuals in each county, among them Lord Cobham, Sir Thomas Scott, Sir John Leveson, and William Lambarde in Kent, to hold a special session before 20 November 1592 where all on the commission of the peace could take that oath. Any justice who was not sworn in at the session was to forbear from acting in his capacity on the commission until the oath was administered to him by the Lord Keeper of the Great Seal. Since it had also been discovered, the Council continued, that many justices had refused to attend church, all who were recusants or who permitted their wives, sons, or heirs to be recusants were immediately to cease exercising their authority as a member of the commission of the peace. On 14 November 1592 the special session was held in Kent where 46 members swore the oath of supremacy but Lambarde, one of the 24 who was absent, was attending to his duties in London at Chancery and in the Alienations' Office and apparently was given the oath by his friend, Puckering, who had just appointed him Master in Chancery.[10]

In 1592 the Privy Council exerted great efforts not only to learn the names of all recusants and Papists in the kingdom but also to weed them out of the commission of the peace. During that year Lambarde, also greatly concerned about the refusal of some to obey the religious laws of the kingdom, had stressed in his charge to the jury at the regular quarter sessions held on 4 April 1592 that those who believed in the 'superstition of the Roman antichrist' were wicked and evil men and had warned that because the jurors so often closed their eyes to the crimes of wilful recusants who lived among them, it would be their fault if the 'wolvish generation of priests who bear the name of Jesuits' gathered root in the kingdom.[11]

Defence preparations and combating recusancy were not the only problems which Lambarde encountered in his position on the commission of the peace since the dearth of corn, a constant problem of the last half of Queen Elizabeth's reign, became severe again in Kent in the middle of the 1590s to some extent because of ex-soldiers roaming the countryside eating grain that would have been consumed by the indigenous poor. On 18 December 1594 Lambarde gave a charge to a special jury, impounded by a November order of the Privy Council to inquire about corn growers and buyers in Kent, in which he reminded the jurors that providing for a good and happy life for its subjects was one of the weighty burdens of government and exhorted them to use all diligence in their investigations because the information that they obtained would benefit not the wealthy of the county but those of low and middle incomes like themselves.[12]

Continuing in their efforts to obey the government decree which had commanded the justices to do all they could to stay the dearth of corn, Lambarde and Leveson in December 1594 asked the vicars in their area to preach about the virtue of selling grain at charitable prices. The following January Lambarde travelled with William Sedley and John Richers to Malling where they questioned farmers and corn growers about how much grain they could spare for the poor. That some who were questioned were less than eager to sell grain at charitable prices was, of course, one obstacle to enforcing the regulations. One 'obstinate' farmer from Wrotham by the name of Richard Lee informed them when the questioning began that he did not intend to aid the poor because he knew of men a hundred times richer than he who had not done so and that he thought her Majesty's orders were most unreasonable. Lambarde responded to this effrontery with the statement that 'the simplest man . . . would not have said that these orders made by the wisedome of the whole realme were voyd of reason', and that Lee, himself, admitted 'nothing for reason but that which pleaseth [his] owne foolysh braine and therein shewe [himself] to be a foole'. The farmer replied in heat that the justices were fools. No further record of this dispute has survived but despite his obstinacy, Lee probably was forced to capitulate to their demands.[13]

John Richers and William Sedley also interviewed a gentleman who refused to answer their questions about his crops, and on 15 January 1595 they reported the incident to Lambarde and Leveson to ask for some assistance. This gentleman, they wrote, informed them, even though he could produce no licence of exemption, that he did not have to answer their questions because the Lord Keeper and the Lord Chamberlain had exempted him from inquiry, and he maintained that men's goods should not be disposed of at prices decreed by others. Like the incident at Malling this interview proved that not all of her Majesty's subjects were subservient to the wishes of her government.[14]

Other measures taken during this dearth were similar to the emergency ones of 1587. Once again alehouses were suppressed and corn growers were forced to sell their grain in the open market at prices fixed by justices. A census was also taken of all the members of the commission to discover if any of them was either a corn seller or grower, and for the lathe of Aylesford it was noted that Sir Thomas Fludd, Sir John Leveson, William Lambarde, William Sedley, and John Richers, among others, were neither sellers nor growers of grain.[15]

Pursuant to orders of January 1595 of the Privy Council requiring them to discover why the price of corn had risen in Kent, Lambarde and Leveson ordered the constables of the hundreds to make inquiries about the grain crop and attended a special session in October at Maidstone to determine from the evidence the causes of the dearth and of the high prices. Sir John Leveson, Peter Manwood, and William Lambarde as well as six others, reported on 9 October that prices had risen even though the harvest of corn had been of a greater yield than the previous year because the bad weather in the spring had caused it to be of a poorer quality and because of the great exportation of grain out of the shire. Furthermore, they insisted, since butter and cheese were also exported there tended to be a general price rise. Not persuaded by this report and others that the justices were taking all possible measures to avert the crisis, the Privy Council informed them that the Queen had learned that, despite the 'seasonable harvest' with which they had been blessed, the prices of corn and of meat had risen greatly in the county, that her Majesty was convinced that the prices would fall if they performed their duties diligently, and that they should contribute to the poor to serve as examples to others.[16]

Lambarde continued to perform services to assuage the effects of the dearth. In 1596 he was active on the corn subsidy and in 1597 he joined Sir John Leveson, William Sedley, and others in questioning all corn engrossers in the kingdom and binding them to appear at court on 9 October. Despite his efforts and those of the other justices the price of corn continued to rise, and undaunted by the enormity of the task and by past failures, the Privy

Council continued to demand that the justices solve the problem by more dedicated efforts.[17]

Always a difficult problem, feeding the poor was a special concern during periods of the dearth of grain, and at the beginning of 1594, the Privy Council, concerned about the severity of the famine, ordered that housing and care for the Kentish poor be investigated by a special jury. On 17 January 1594 Lambarde gave the charge to the jurors who were admonished to bring to the attention of the justices any embezzlement of funds intended for the poor not only because the Queen, herself, had given special commandment that this fraud be punished but also because God's laws demanded that the citizenry see to the honest and efficient relief of the poor. When they were not well taken care of but were permitted to become vagabonds and beggars, he reminded the jury, they spread pilfery, drunkenness, and whoredom wherever they went.[18]

There is extant a manuscript entitled 'A Presentment for the Lower Division of Sutton At Hone 25 May 1594 for Hospitalls Collected' which, because it was written and presented to the justices of the peace in May after this special session was called in January, was probably part of the jurors' response to Lambarde's charge. One inquiry, that in the town of Dartford, provided an excellent example of how the charge was carried out. On 10 March the jurors questioned the churchwardens and inhabitants of the town about lands which had been given for the maintenance of the poor and gathered information about the various endowments, their administrators, and the almspeople. One Dartford endowment described by them was the Spitelhouse founded by John Beer, esquire, in the reign of King Henry VI, which they noted was honestly administered: 'All the which premises the provits whereof the power have had and now have'.[19]

Early in April 1598 the Privy Council, still concerned about the welfare of the poor, reminded the sheriffs and justices in the kingdom that they were responsible for the execution of statutes for the relief of the poor, the care of maimed soldiers, and the punishment of vagabonds. To the end that they might see that the statutes were diligently enforced, the Council required them first to assemble together after the Easter Sessions to confer upon a uniform course to take for the execution of these laws and next to meet in their several divisions to question constables and other under officials about the enforcement of the poor relief statutes.[20]

These statutes set up provisions for elected collectors of the poor to collect compulsory assessments for the relief of the disabled and sick poor, provided care for illegitimate children as well as for children who could not be supported by their parents, authorised the whipping of vagabonds, erected houses of correction to provide labour for the able-bodied vagabonds and permitted the justices of the peace to appoint overseers of the poor in each parish to administer these laws. It has been suggested that of all the provisions of the Elizabethan poor laws, the first concerning relief of the impotent poor was the most successfully implemented and this seems to be true from the evidence available for Kent. These varying aspects of the poor laws were finally organised together with some elaborations into statutes in 1598 and 1601 to establish the thrust of poor relief in the kingdom until the 19th century[21]

Apparently obeying the orders of the Privy Council, Leveson and Lambarde began inquiring into the enforcement of these statutes in various parishes in their division. The most well-documented inquiry they made was at Shorne on 17 April 1598 where they asked the churchwardens and the overseers of the poor who the poor were, what the assessment for their relief was, who defaulted in paying the rates, who the apprentices were, where the dwelling houses for the poor were, and who were licensed to beg. Until 1608 similar examinations were made in the parish of Shorne and at least once more, in April 1601, Lambarde joined Leveson in questioning the officials there.[22]

In April 1598 Lambarde and Leveson also made similar inquiries at other parishes in their division: Chetham, Cliff, Gillingham, Stroode, Halling, and later in June, Frindsbury. Both the justices, themselves, lived in the parish of Halling where the antiquary was assessed 6s. and Leveson 7s. 4d. for relief of the poor on 24 April 1598; the total collected from the parish amounted to £4 5s. 8d. In Halling at that time were five aged women, four young girls and one young boy who were set to work spinning hemp, and three others who were not able to work and who received 4d. weekly for relief, but in Gillingham there were many more who needed assistance, for besides nine aged or disabled adults, there were 17 children who had to be supported by the parish.[23]

Another activity of the justices in which Lambarde must have been particularly interested since he was a deputy in the Alienations' Office from 1589 was discovering concealed lands held of the Queen in chief. He gave charges at three special sessions convened to discover who was concealing lands that were held of that ancient feudal tenure to avoid paying the various exactions to the crown on each alienation and descent. At the sessions held in April 1595, in November 1596, and in May 1600, he implored the juries in his prologues to be diligent in their inquiries both for conscience's sake and for testimony of their gratitude to the Queen for the benefits of her government. Admitting that there was widespread dislike of the impositions, he reminded them that the service was legally due the Queen and that 'We must . . . not reckon that well gotten to the subject which is wrongfully withdrawn from the prince'.[24]

He gave the charge to the jury at one other special session which was convened because of a 'Riotous Affray at Town Malling, which happened 1 August 1592'. Although the offence, he reminded the jurors, might seem inconsequential since it involved only a few harmless men brawling in the street during fair time, it still should be treated with seriousness because it could have resulted in great havoc and destruction. The overriding consideration to him was the consistent enforcement of the law to ensure peace and order in the kingdom.[25]

Ever concerned about enforcing the law, he had given an even more meaningful reason for punishing lawbreakers in his charge to the jury at the regular Michaelmas Quarter Sessions in 1591 when he had warned that 'unreverent and careless handling' of the laws could result in the greatest peril of all—that of the loss of the right to use juries to investigate crimes. To demonstrate that this was not an idle threat but a real and present danger, he reminded them that no juries were ever used in the Court of Star Chamber and that Parliament was more and more inclined to order that offences be handled at the discretion of the justices rather than by inquiry by a jury because of the negligence of the presentments. Begging them not to be seduced by corruption or the evil examples of other juries he exclaimed, 'Stand fast therefore stand fast, I say in this liberty whereunto you are born and be inheritable'.[26]

Altogether nine exhortations to the regular quarter sessions, dated September 1591 to April 1600 which were apparently delivered by Lambarde in his second decade as a justice of the peace have survived, but between Easter, 1590 and Easter, 1601, 23 regular quarter sessions which he was expected to attend were held. If he was present only at the assemblies where he gave the extant prologues he was absent from about two-thirds of the regular meetings, and it is possible that his added responsibilities in the Alienations' Office and in the Court of Chancery caused this increased number of absences, but it is also possible that he either gave exhortations that have been lost or destroyed or that he attended some sessions without giving them. Indeed, there is evidence to prove that he attended the Michaelmas quarter sessions in 1592 although the only extant exhortation for that year was delivered at Easter.[27]

Since he continued to encourage the juries to make diligent inquiries and complete presentments, these speeches of the 1590s were similar to those given in the 1580s, often appearing to be monotonous repetitions of each other in their emphasis upon local problems of law and order. In April 1593, for example, he told the jurors that one of the greatest problems of the county, the unpunished swarms of rogues, could be solved only if the jurors would 'make our lawful assemblies . . . not for show but for service'.[28] On 17 April 1599 he returned to the theme of service when he lamented :

> I have, not without grief of mind, observed after some long experience, that these our sessions of the peace be only formal and for fashion's sake, that our presentments also be not many and the same cold and without any zeal of justice, as being undertaken rather for private revenge than for any public good.[29]

In the last prologue that he delivered, dated 1 April 1600, he continued to solicit excellent performance from the jurors and complained that disobedience to the law 'creepeth not in corners but marcheth in the open market'. Using history to prove that crime has to be punished, he warned that iniquities on the home fronts were the prelude to the destruction of all great nations, and begged them to awaken from their 'sleep of security' to perform their duties for the honour of God and the Queen.[30]

The earliest extant calendar of the quarter sessions held at Maidstone began with the assembly of 1 April 1600 when Lambarde gave his last charge. That for almost two decades he had been giving these charges to the juries at Maidstone did not indicate that he was the most important justice of the peace in Kent, which after all, was divided into two divisions, with two quarter sessions held in the eastern division at Canterbury that he did not normally attend. Since he was never knighted, he was also socially inferior to Sir John Leveson and other knights on the commission, but still his own importance must have been recognised in the western division at Maidstone in April 1600 when the clerk of the peace listed his name first among the names of those gentlemen present at this session.[31]

There were 17 men in the jury that Lambarde charged to inquire after crimes and they presented evidence in over 31 cases. Among the crimes reported were more than 16 assaults and batteries, one begging offence, one gaming infraction, two trespasses, two thefts, one neglected beacon watch, two decayed highways, four decayed bridges, and two unlicensed tippling houses. Keeping the peace evidently was not an easy task since well over half the crimes investigated involved assault and battery.

Evidence of the duty of the justices to oversee roads and bridges can be found at this session where it was recorded that three bridges and two highways were in need of repair because those responsible for their upkeep had neglected their duty. It was further noted that a bridge of wood and planks on the highway at Waterlane in Hedcorn was in a ruinous state because William Wallett, who was fined 6d. for his offence, had taken so many planks from the bridge that it would no longer be crossed.

Administrative work was also accomplished. Besides ordering the construction of a house of correction, which was apparently to be similar in organisation to the one erected more than a decade earlier at Maidstone, the justices elected Samuel Lennard, esquire, Treasurer for the maimed soldiers of the lathes of Aylesford and Sutton-at-Hone and the Seven Hundreds of Scray.

Although the records for only one quarter session that the antiquary attended have survived, there is extant a Gaol Delivery Roll which revealed his presence at three of the gaol deliveries held between January 1597 and September 1598. These assemblies were not held to coincide with the regular assizes but were held in Maidstone, often at dates coinciding with the Quarter Sessions, and although supposed to be the concern of the justices of the assizes were handled by the ordinary members of the commission of the peace. At them the cases handled were mainly larceny as for example, at the January 1597 session where there were four cases of theft. Of the many defendants who pleaded not guilty most were freed by jury trial and of those convicted, of course, the statutes permitted them to plead benefit of womb and benefit of clergy.[32]

In addition to the regular gaol sessions, there is evidence that the antiquary attended at least one assize in the 1590s where part of the business was also to deliver the gaols. At the Strafford Archives Office is a manuscript on which was listed over 100 names, among them Sir John Leveson and William Lambarde, of those who attended the assize in Rochester on 4 March 1594.[33]

Throughout his career, Lambarde received letters requesting his aid in cases pending before him or asking for leniency for friends of those accused of crimes. On 26 October 1595 the Controller of the Navy asked Leveson and him for mercy for a poor man of Chatham who had rented beds to workers of her Majesty's ship-yards and had, at their request, kept beer in the house to sell to them. After furnishing beer to his boarders, the poor man proceeded to retail it to his neighbours, also at their request, and had thereby maintained a tippling house without a licence. The Controller assured them that the man realised the great crime that he had committed, had asked for pardon, and had promised never to violate the law again. No evidence of any action taken by the two justices has survived, but it is likely that once confronted with a confession of guilt, an earnest promise to refrain from breaking the law in the future, and a letter of intercession written by her Majesty's Controller of the Navy, that they simply bound the landlord to keep his word.[34]

From a review of the evidence available, it is readily apparent that the government considered the justices suitable for any service. Often the whole commission of the peace, or at least a great part of it, was appointed to various other services, such as inquiring after recusants and aiding maimed soldiers. Whenever the Crown needed money it called upon them, and thus Lambarde could be found raising funds for military purposes and for poor relief. In the 1590s he was also appointed to at least three parliamentary subsidy commissions, in 1591, in 1593, and 1595.[35]

The whole fabric of Tudor England rested on the shoulders of the commission of the peace and there is ample evidence that the Kentish justices, at least, rose to that challenge. It is true that they were not always successful even by their own standards, but most of them performed their duties in a highly commendable fashion. Whenever there was a crisis in the county, evidence of Lambarde's leadership in seeking solutions could be found, particularly in caring for the needs of the impotent poor, a special concern of this 'proctor for the poor' and of the county of Kent in the 16th century.

## II

# Family and Friends in Later Life

WHILE he was master of Halling Palace William took a third wife, Margaret Reader of Boughton Monchelsey co. Kent, who, seven years younger than him, was 48 years old on their wedding day, 18 April 1592. The overriding factor in his decision to remarry was, no doubt, the welfare of his children, but he still chose his bride carefully, marrying for the second time a widow with property. Margaret, the youngest of four children born to John Payne of Frittenden, yeoman, and his wife, Jane, the daughter of a clothier, had already been married twice, first to John Meryam and then to Richard Reader, both of Boughton Monchelsey. Of the first husband little is known except that he was the eldest of three children born to a mason of that parish and that his sister, Juliana, married John Reader, the elder brother of Richard. Consequently, Margaret may have been introduced to her second husband, Richard, by Juliana, the sister of her first husband.[1]

Lambarde had been acquainted with the Reader family since 1582 when he noted in his 'Ephemeris' that, along with Thomas Randolph, he had bound Richard and Walter Reader, yeomen, in £100 for their good behaviour and required them to appear at the next Easter Sessions unless they were released from their bonds prior to that time.[2] Two years before this incident, Richard had drawn up a will in which he had named his wife, Margaret the executrix, and had left most of his property to any children they might have, and in default of legally-begotten heirs, to his brother, Walter. The residue of the estate was bequeathed to his wife. Evidently Richard died between 25 September 1582, the date he was bound to good behaviour by Lambarde, and 10 October 1582, the date the will was proved, leaving his wife childless and a widow for the second time. She remained unmarried for almost 10 years until her union with Lambarde in April 1592 and, of course, was widowed for a third time at his death in August 1601. Although she was not a wealthy heiress, Margaret did have an independent income including rents of £54 10s. on lands she held for life and annuities of £12 as well as a debt of £60 paid to her in September 1592 and money and gold in her possession worth £34. Because she was the executrix of her second husband's will, the antiquary gained control of that estate, paying at least two of its bequests as late as 1596.[3]

Not only did he increase his annual income during the 1590s but he also continued to invest in real property. In 1593 he purchased Hollands Farm in Cranbrook and Hawkhurst for £500 and Wheatfield Farm for £15; in 1594 he obtained Hall Lands for £370 and in 1596 Balden House with its 30 acres in Hedcorn for £225. The last piece of property he purchased was the Farm of Clarks in Leigh and Tunbridge for £650 in May 1597. During slightly more than a four-year period in the middle of this decade he had spent £1,760 for property, a large sum of money, indeed, indicating that his marriage and other activities had brought an increase in funds which could be invested.

Besides purchasing land outright he also obtained leases of property. In February 1590 he bought a 21-year lease to a house in the parish of St. Peter the Poor of London for £100 and an annual rent of £5. After the mother of his second wife, Mrs. Dean, had paid him half of the purchase price, he assigned the house to her and spent more than £13 improving it, but two years later she surrendered the lease and obtained the return of her £50. In 1595 after he had sold the lease of that house, the antiquary purchased still another lease to a house in that parish for £200 and an annual rent of £5 from the Drapers' Company. He also held leases to lands in Kent, his rent and receipt book indicating that he held lands in West Malling for £3 6s. 8d. and obtained the lease of the demesne of Otford Manor from George Multon the younger.

In the October before his third marriage he had reckoned his worth in cash and goods at only £380 but in October 1592, six months after Margaret became his wife and four months after his appointment as a Master in Chancery, he reckoned himself worth £719, in addition to his leases, household stuff, rents, books, cattle, the lands of his ward, and the annuity of £7. The primary difference between the two estimates was the amount of the debts and ready cash on hand. In 1591 there were only £78 in debts and £180 in cash but by 1592 these figures had increased to £265 and £337 respectively. After his third marriage he never reckoned his worth in cash and goods at less than £484 and that in October 1596 after he had purchased property worth almost £600. At the end of this decade he reckoned his worth at £808.

The amount of ready cash he had on hand was frequently increased by the sale of timber from his lands. In August 1592, for example, he noted that he earned £5 from the sale of timber from the Lilly lands and that he had returned 13s. 4d. of that amount to his tenant, Thomas Russell, who had felled the trees, as a gift for his namesake and godson, Lambard Russell. In 1595 he received £22 4s. 9d. from the sale of timber from lands his wife held.

According to his personal records, he continued to lend money to the same people who had been borrowing from him for almost two decades. In early 1591 he noted that both Margery and Humphrey Windham owed him £5. Many others, including George Bing and Thomas Wyckyn continued to be in debt to him, and if he charged any of them interest on the loans, there is no record of it in his receipt books.

In October 1593 he described his plate, listing silver bowls of all sizes, spoons, cups, pots, and salt holders with covers. In all he claimed that he owned 433 ounces of silver, which when computed at 5d. per ounce was worth £108 and of that amount he confessed that £72 had belonged to his second wife. Three years later, on 26 March 1596, he made another inventory of his plate, estimating that it was then worth £125 and claiming that his jewels, including Margaret's gold chain and rings, were worth £40.

That Lambarde took a third wife in April of 1592 can be attributed in part to the concern that he felt for the welfare of his children, a concern that was manifested in other ways as well. On the first page of his family diary he wrote in 1589 that it contained the dates of marriages, births, and deaths of his relatives and that he wished it to remain with his lands to be inherited by his children, 'one after an other, according to their priorities of Byrthe, and woorthyness of Bloode, being of no moment to any other persons'. Those heirs, of course, were requested to keep the diary up to date by entering the important family events.[4]

Evidence of his concern for the future of his children was also discovered in a will, dated in 1595, of his friend, George Roberts of Brenchley, who named him executor and entrusted to him the education of Margaret, his sole daughter and heiress. Roberts confessed that for the 'especial love and entire favour' he had long borne the antiquary and for the assurance of a home for his child, he was bequeathing all of his estate to her and her future husband, Multon Lambarde, but if Multon did not marry her by his 20th birthday, it was to descend to his second choice for her husband, Gore, the elder Lambarde twin. If she obstinately refused to marry both of these Lambarde boys, her inheritance would first descend to Multon, and if he died without heirs, then to Gore and his heirs. Until the marriage of Margaret, the antiquary was to collect all the rents from her lands. Evidently written with his approval, the existence of this will proves that at a time when his sons were less than 12 years old, he was already seeking suitable wives for them.[5]

Arrangements for the supervision of his children's education were of particular importance to the antiquary, who, in his will drafted in 1597, gave Sir John Leveson £20 to oversee the education of Multon, his heir, and of Francis Tresse, his ward, and in November 1599 paid 53s. 4d. to Lincoln's Inn for permission for his heir to enter his chamber there. The next year he noted that he paid the treasurer of the society all reckonings due for Multon and Francis between July and December 1600. In his will he also bequeathed £20 each to John Tyndall, barrister of Lincoln's Inn and later Master in Chancery, and George Bing, justice of the peace of Kent, for supervising the education of his twin sons, Gore and Fane, respectively. Tyndall was also permitted to purchase his enamelled spectacles for 5s.[6]

Although his daughter's training was not so grave a concern as that of the sons, he willed his wife a 20-mark stipend to supervise her education and required that she win the approval of Lady Mary Abergavenny, Lady Christian Leveson, his own wife, Margaret, Margery Windham, and Audrey Multon if she desired to

marry between the ages of 18 and 21. If they approved of her intended, she would receive £800 in money, his best bedstead, some
chests and other furniture, and her mother's marriage ring of
gold, a generous dowry, indeed, but if she was unmarried at her
21st birthday, these gifts would then be hers. Both his daughter
and his wife were bequeathed the right to buy some of his clothing, and his wife was also granted £100 in gold, several pieces of
silver plate, the gelding of her choice with the best saddle, bed-
ding and other household goods she had brought to the marriage,
and her jewellery, including a chain of gold and some rings. For
her lifetime the house he had leased from the Drapers' in London
and the Manor of Westcombe were to be hers, but after her death,
they were to descend to his heir, Multon.

All three sons were devised a featherbed with three sheets
while most of the London property was to be divided between the
twins. Multon, as the heir, was to obtain all the property in Kent,
except for the college lands, and like his sister, was given the right
to purchase some of his father's clothing. The antiquary further
stipulated that one of his felt black hats was to be given to his
stepson, Maximilian Dalison.

Others were provided for in his will. The overseers were each
bequeathed £5 for a cup of silver while Leveson, in addition,
was given all the evidences and deeds of Cobham College then in
Lambarde's possession.[7] Sir Thomas Egerton, the Lord Keeper of
England, was given three old rose nobles of gold, a gold ring that
had once belonged to the mother of King Henry VII, and the
books and records of Ralph Rokeby. The college at Greenwich
was not forgotten as Thomas Kitchell of Clifford's Inn was asked
to collect the rents and the Drapers' Company was begged to continue leasing the lands to his descendants at the rents then pre-
vailing. Finally, he left bequests to his servants and to the poor
in the parish where he died.

He had his will witnessed by a Master in Chancery, Sir Edward
Stanhope, and then published twice, first in the presence of four
people, including Thomas Fortescue of the Alienations' Office,
in February 1598 and second in the presence of four people,
including Sir Peter Manwood, justice of the peace of Kent,
and Thomas Lowe, the future father-in-law of Multon Lambarde in April 1601. Two days after the last publication he
added a codicil leaving an additional £30 to his wife and £10 to

Lincoln's Inn to be employed in plate by his dear friend, John Tyndall.[8]

Apparently he had a strong affection for his two stepchildren, who, along with their maternal grandmother, continued to live with him at Halling Palace after their mother's death, although Sylvestre, the stepdaughter, moved to Lincolnshire in September 1591 to reside with her Dalison uncles. It is possible that he failed to leave Sylvestre a gift and bequeathed Maximilian only one of his hats because their own father, William Dalison, had already provided for them in his will of 1581. The dowry Dalison left his daughter amounted to £300, a rather paltry sum when compared to the more than £800 dowry of Margaret Lambarde, and the problems he bequeathed his son by requiring that he wait until his 24th birthday to gain control of his inheritance were ultimately resolved only by legal action.

At his 21st birthday in 1597 Maximilian, with scarcely any pocket money, had insufficient funds even to sue out his livery and to pay the appropriate fines to her Majesty as a court ward in the custody of his stepfather, William Lambarde. He, therefore, was forced to petition the Court of Wards to compel his uncles to loan him £1,000 of his rent money to sue out his livery. At Michaelmas Term the Court ordered the uncles to account for the rent money, but only Thomas Dalison complied while the other uncle, Robert, was imprisoned in the Fleet for obstinately refusing to obey the court decree and was still there in June 1598 as Maximilian complained 'solacing himself with play and good cheere'. Ultimately the nephew sent a petition to the Queen, which was probably written by the antiquary, to ask her Majesty to force Robert to show his accounts and to furnish him with funds to sue out his livery.[9] After some difficulty, Maximilian did obtain the necessary money and even his stepfather gave him a gift in April 1600 'ingratitude to his son Dalyson towardes his livery suit'.[10]

He was forced to continue to rely upon the charity of his stepfather because his uncles were reluctant to part with the rents that they had been collecting since 1581 and which they could keep if he died before he reached his 24th birthday. Thus, in January 1601, after he became 24 years old, he obtained his inheritance only after he had entered a bill of complaint in the Court of Requests, an action similar to the one his stepfather had taken more than 40 years earlier, giving further proof that in the 16th century, at least, an heir's minority often gave opportunity to even the most trusted friends and relatives to appropriate his inheritance.[11]

The decade of the 1590s was memorable not only because of Lambarde's grave illness in 1596 which probably prompted him to write his will but also because of the deaths of so many friends and relatives. Early in the decade he lost his first two mothers-in-law, Agnes Multon on 23 September 1591 and Mrs. Dean on 9 November 1594. On 4 June 1596, his friend, Ralph Rokeby, died, leaving a will in which he and Sir Thomas Egerton were named the executors, and one year later, on 26 June 1597, his banker cousin, Thomas Gore, after whom he had named one of his twins, died, leaving him with the responsibility for overseeing his estate and bequeathing him £40. Less than one year before Gore's death, on 6 August 1596, Lambarde had written a letter to Egerton about his progress in administering the Rokeby estate and explained that 'The Chest (I doubt not) is in sure handes, wheather Mr. Gore lyve or dye, such is myne interest both in him and his heire or follower'. In addition to acting as the antiquary's banker, his cousin Gore may well have been the custodian of the Rokeby funds.[12]

Early in the 1590s he was asked to arbitrate a dispute between Thomas Fane and his sister-in-law, Lady Mary Abergavenny, the widow of Sir Thomas Fane, the namesake of the other Lambarde twin. The controversy developed over a trust which Sir Thomas had administered, until his death in 1589, for the daughter of Thomas Fisher of Swanford. According to a memorandum drafted by Lambarde, the brother, Thomas, agreed to administer the Fisher trust, following arrangements Fisher had made with Sir Thomas and at his own expense, if his sister-in-law, Lady Mary, would deliver all of Fisher's plate and goods to him. When Thomas failed to keep this promise because Lady Mary had neglected to deliver the effects to him a suit was brought against her on behalf of Fisher's daughter in the Court of Wards. Evidently preferring not to have her family quarrel become the subject of a public trial, Lady Mary wrote to her 'verye lovinge frende Mr. Lambarde, esquire' on 7 February 1591 to entreat him 'to make an ende' between her brother Fane and herself in all matters concerning the trust. Later the antiquary, apparently resolving the dispute, wrote in a note that Lady Mary would soon deliver all the plate and goods to Fane.[13]

His friendship with Lord Burghley, his patron who died in 1598, seems to have continued during this decade, and in 1593, four years after he became a deputy in the Alienations' Office, Lambarde asked his lordship via a letter to his secretary, Sir Michael Hicks, to grant the escheatorship of Kent and Middlesex to his own servant, Mr. Kitchell, who was well qualified for the post because of his 'long education and practice' and because of his 'marriage with a landed wife'.[14] Evidently the request was not an unexpected manifestation of their relationship because the post of Latin Secretary was offered to him in 1596 but he refused it, perhaps because he believed that the addition of that lesser office, during a year when he, himself, was gravely ill, would be too burdensome.[15]

Another important patron of Lambarde to die in this decade was Sir William Brooke, Lord Cobham, who, preceding Burghley by one and a half years, died on 6 March 1597. A trusted member of Queen Elizabeth's government, Lord Cobham had been appointed Lord Warden of the Cinque Ports in 1558 and held that position until his death 38 years later. He had also served as a member of the Privy Council since 1585, Keeper of Eltham Palace since 1590, and Lord Chamberlain since 1596. At various times he had held the office of Lord Lieutenant of Kent, probably from 1559 to 1561, in 1569, and from 1587 to 1597, the year of his death, when his son, Sir Henry, succeeded him in his title and that office. His close association with the Queen's government had been furthered in 1589 when his daughter, Elizabeth, married Sir Robert Cecil, the son of the Lord Treasurer.[16]

When the antiquary first became closely associated with the Cobham family of Kent is not known, but he must have been acquainted with Lord Cobham in 1568 when he was appointed to a commission of sewers for the western division of Kent along with his lordship and other dignitaries of the shire. A little over a decade later, in October 1579, he handled the sale of some property to Robert Bing of Wrotham for Lord Cobham's brother, Sir Henry Brooke, during his term as ambassador to France. At that time, Lambarde who lived at Ightham, only 10 miles from Rochester, was probably a friend of his lordship as well and surely after his move to Halling Palace in 1583, where he lived within walking distance of Cobham Hall, a closer relationship developed.[17]

Indeed, on 15 November 1587, when Lord Cobham appointed Lambarde and Walter Wood of Rochester his lawful attorneys to collect and disburse his rents according to his direction while he was on her Majesty's business in Flanders, he gave proof of his respect for the antiquary's honesty and ability. On his return from Flanders in October 1588, Lord Cobham acquitted them of their duties, giving evidence that they had followed his orders and had performed competently. It was in 1587, of course, that his lordship also drew upon the antiquary's historical knowledge of beacons by referring the dispute over the watch at Denge Marsh to him.[18]

From that time forward the Cobham family's trust in his abilities remained constant. In 1594 his lordship's youngest son, George Brooke, placed his deed to the rectory on the Island of Greane in his custody. Since this property was a gift from his father, the safekeeping of the deed was of unusual interest to George, who one day might have to prove his ownership of the rectory to his brothers, and by choosing the antiquary to assist him, he gave evidence of his belief in his honesty.[19]

As steward of the manor of Gravesend in June 1595, Lambarde drew up an agreement for Lord Cobham between the Lord Mayor and the Court of Aldermen of London and the portreeve and inhabitants of Gravesend and Milton about the ferrying of passengers to and from London and Gravesend. Among the stipulations of the agreement were orders concerning the common barge, called the Gravesend Barge, which was required to serve the inhabitants at every tide. The owner of the barge, furthermore, was authorised to collect two pence 'and no more' from each passenger and admonished not to deny passage to those 'contented to goo with' him.[20]

Of course, throughout the years he lived at Halling Palace, he assisted the Lord Lieutenant and his deputies in preparing Kent against a Spanish invasion and in whatever service his lordship required. Lord Cobham was responsible for escorting foreign diplomats safely from their ports of debarkation in Kent to the Queen's court, and on at least one occasion, in August 1596, he required Lambarde and about 25 other Kentish knights and gentlemen to escort the French Duc de Bouillon to Greenwich.

Since in one 15-day period, Lambarde wrote one letter, Leveson four, and Lord Cobham four concerning this journey through Kent, arranging for the escort of foreign dignitaries was not an easy task.[21]

The month after the Duke's journey it was rumoured at court that Lord Cobham was sick with ague and evidently he did not regain his health, for he died in London the following March and was buried in April. In his will, dated 24 February 1597, he named his cousin, Sir Edward Wotton, Sir John Leveson, Thomas Fane, and William Lambarde executors and appointed Sir Robert Cecil, his son-in-law, and the Lord Treasurer his overseers. For their pains the executors were each given £40 plus recompense for any expenses incurred during the performance of their duties, and Cecil was bequeathed Cobham's best silver basin while the Lord Treasurer was to have £50 and a cup of gold. In addition to providing for the estate of his three sons (Sir Henry, William, and George) and his grandchildren, Lord Cobham also arranged for the endowment of an almshouse.[22]

A college for the poor had been founded near Cobham Hall by Sir John Cobham in 1362 and after its dissolution in the reign of King Henry VIII, George Brooke, Lord Cobham, who had been granted the right to purchase its lands, gained parliamentary confirmation of his title in 1537. 60 years later, the old college still lay in ruins, but his heir, William, Lord Cobham, made plans to replace it with a new structure.[23]

Information about the drafting of Lord Cobham's will during the winter of 1597 has survived in letters written by William Lambarde who attended his lordship in London. On 12 February 1597 he informed his friend, Leveson, who was then in Kent that he had discussed with his lordship the difficulties that might arise if Sir Henry, his heir, attempted to thwart the endowment of an almshouse and disclosed that he had made two pertinent suggestions: first that his lordship reveal his plans to his heir immediately so that he could not be offended by secrecy and second that before his death his lordship deliver to his executors the funds necessary to construct the college.

Another problem of administering the estate was treated in this letter. Since none of the then proposed executors resided near Cobham Hall during most of the year, it would be impossible for them to maintain the needed surveillance of the almshouse. One executor, Thomas Fane, the Lieutenant of Dover Castle, was frequently at the seaside; another, Sir Edward Wotton, was often required at court; and the antiquary, himself, was in London during every term and would soon have to move from Halling to Greenwich. To solve this problem Lord Cobham had suggested that Leveson be named an executor since he lived and worked near Cobham Hall, and Lambarde admitted that he liked the appointment, but he warned his friend that if he accepted the responsibility and if Sir Henry were offended by the endowment, Leveson would have the unhappy prospect of living near a hostile Lord Cobham.[24]

Shortly after Leveson agreed to the appointment, Cobham drew up a will, leaving the executors all the edifices and grounds with their appurtenances that had been the property and site of the old college, 100,000 burned bricks and 40 tons of timber. To support the inmates he left his leases, rents, and interests in lands in Canterbury, Chalk, and various other parishes of Sussex and Kent, and some plate and jewels. Finally, he asked his son, Sir Henry, to permit the execution of his will without interference or disturbance according to the secret trust that he had reposed in his executors.[25]

On 6 March 1597 the date of Cobham's death, Lambarde and Leveson had initiated preparations for carrying out that trust even before they learned the news of his death. They wrote to Thomas Fane at Dover Castle, informing him of the 'weake and dangerous estate' of his lordship's health and requesting his presence in London with all possible speed to begin his duties as executor. Almost one week later, then at Lincoln's Inn, the antiquary explained in a letter to Lord Burghley, one of the overseers, what Cobham's secret trust involved.[26]

According to Lambarde's explanation, Cobham had depended solely upon the integrity of his executors, whom he entrusted with £5,600 and some rich furniture, to see that his property was used as he wished. He had requested them to spend £2,000 to build a new college, to use £2,000 to free his second son from debt, and to spend £1,600 to procure a life interest in a suitable dwelling for his third son and to provide for the estate of his daughter's children by Sir Edward Becker. The rich furniture, worth £2,000, was to be delivered to the son that married first. Finally, the antiquary was pleased to inform Burghley that the three sons had accepted the provisions of their father's will and were most kind and courteous to each other.

Letters surviving from the following year indicate that the early acceptance of the will had given way to family quarrelling. On 2 January 1598 the new Lord Cobham demanded the presence of Leveson and Lambarde at court where he wished to discuss the will, but on the following day the antiquary informed his friend, Leveson, that he was determined not to comply with his lordship's wishes. Instead, he had written to Lord Cobham and to his brother, George, 'moving them to compound the Question', and suggesting that they should refer their dispute to the two overseers of the will, Lord Burghley and his son, Sir Robert. For his own part, Lambarde continued, he would rather displease both of them by refusing to become involved in the controversy than strive to please either one of them. This dispute and others indicate that the antiquary's suggestion to William, Lord Cobham, that the funds necessary for the construction of the college be entrusted to the executors before his death was sound advice, but that his lordship agreed to this recommendation was astonishing in an age when guardians and trustees often had to be compelled by court order to account for their wards' funds and was a shining testimony to Cobham's trust in Lambarde's honesty and judgement.[27]

Much energy was obviously expended in performing all of the tasks required by Cobham's will and secret trust. On 22 May 1597, Lambarde, then at Westcombe, wrote to Leveson at Halling to thank him for the great care that he had taken in overseeing the construction of the new college building which he hoped would be slated by winter so that the first inmates could be admitted in the spring of 1598. Thomas Fane, he informed Leveson, had already arranged for the collection of the college rents and the estate of Sir Edward Becker's children.[28]

Inscribed on one wall of the new college structure, a neat quadrangular building of small squared stones, was the message that the building had been completed in September 1598 and that the college had been founded by Sir William Brooke, Lord Cobham, who died on 6 March 1597. Even though the building was completed in 1598, it did not hold 20 almsmen until May 1599. In the 'Booke of Entrye of the monethelie payment of the pensions', it was noted that on 1 April 1599 only two inmates were paid the pension of 6s. 8d. and that on 1 May 1599 20 received that stipend.[29]

Since the rules for the college were almost identical to the ones for Queen Elizabeth's college at Greenwich, the antiquary was obviously the chief author of them. The almshouse was incorporated by the Crown and placed under the control of the wardens of Rochester Bridge who were authorised by the Letters Patent to be the presidents. To emphasise that the new almshouse was a secular and not a religious endowment, the old seal of the college which had depicted the Virgin Mary holding a lily with the Christ Child and a kneeling figure was changed to one representing Rochester Bridge with a lion from the Brooke crest.

The internal organisations of the Greenwich and Cobham almshouses were almost identical, each having 20 poor with two of them serving as warden and sub-warden, but at Cobham instead of the poor people selecting the two officers, Lord Cobham and the presidents had that authority. The candidates had to be godly, be residents in the parishes selecting them, and know the prescribed prayers and articles of faith. As inmates they had to wear identifying badges, obey rules such as no tippling or swearing, and undertake responsibilities like ringing the handbell and learning the college morning and evening prayers.

The inscription crediting Lord Cobham with the founding of the almshouse is natural since it was his endowment that made its construction possible. However, it should be noted that Lambarde received no formal credit even though it was his suggestion that permitted Lord Cobham to secrete the necessary funds from his heirs, that it was his legal drafting that gave the college its framework and form, that it was Lambarde's and Leveson's efforts and negotiations that transformed the funds into a building, and that it was they who served as its first presidents. The best testimony to the importance of their efforts is that the endowment left by Lord Cobham to found a college for the poor resulted in an institution still existing and still serving that purpose today.

Lambarde and Leveson served as presidents of the college by virtue of their positions in the Rochester Bridge Corporation which supervised the upkeep of the stone bridge on the Medway River that linked the road between Stroode and Rochester. The bridge, apparently built by Sir John Cobham in the 14th century to replace an ancient wooden structure of the pre-Conquest period, was about 560 feet long and 14 feet wide. At the time it was rebuilt it was incorporated with two appointed wardens, then Sir John Cobham and Sir John Knollys, and 12 assistants who were elected annually by the tenants of the lands contributing money for its upkeep.[30]

Since the upkeep of the bridge had grown lax by the 16th century partly because the wardens were powerless to raise assessments on the contributory lands, a royal survey was made and then the corporation was updated by a statute of 1575 which required the election of the wardens as well as the assistants and distributed the monetary support of the nine arches among the tenants of the contributory lands. An extant document, undated and signed by Lambarde, Leveson and four others, indicated which lands according to the statute of 1575 were responsible for which arches. The document was probably drafted in 1585 the year the antiquary was first elected warden, and it is likely that he, along with the other warden of that year, Sir Peter Manwood, supported the enactment of a statute passed in 1585 which further strengthened the corporation by authorising the wardens to raise assessments on the lands, by charging tenants who did not appear at Rochester Castle for the election of the wardens and the assistants 10s., and by ordering the wardens at the end of their terms to permit the examination of their accounts by auditors.[31]

The first dated evidence of the antiquary's association with the bridge was his election, along with Sir Peter Manwood, as warden in April 1585. Although he had not previously served on its court of assistants, he was not ignorant of the aims and functions of the corporation since his father-in-law, George Multon of Ightham, had served with Sir Roger Manwood as warden in 1579. Lambarde's term began, according to tradition, on Thursday of Pentecost, which fell on 13 June in 1585, and ended on 25 May 1586. Both Lord Cobham and Lord Abergavenny as well as Sir Thomas Fane and his brother, Thomas, were elected to the court of assistants in 1585.[32]

Three more times in the next 15 years he was elected warden : on 9 April 1589 with Sir Thomas Fludd, on 10 April 1594 again with Fludd, and finally on 27 April 1598 with Sir John Leveson when the two of them together also assumed the duties of presidents of Cobham College. During the years that he did not serve as warden, he held other positions on the corporation : from 1586 through 1601 he was annually elected as an assistant and from 1586 through 1596 as an auditor as well. He served as an assistant after 1598 even though he no longer lived in the Rochester area and was even elected to that position in 1601, when he was not present at Rochester Castle for the elections; but except for that one absence, he attended the other Easter Sessions and many Pentecost Thursday assemblies especially when as auditor it was his duty to certify the accounts of the out-going wardens.

In 1586 as his first term as warden was ending, he certified with Sir Peter Manwood that Richard Harlow, the paymaster, had received his annual stipend of £8 and delivered the ready money on hand, £58 15s. 6d., and his accounts to the newly-elected wardens, Henry Cutte and John Leveson. He also recorded that he had loaned £40 to the corporation, and in subsequent years, especially after Philip Symonson became paymaster, he often noted the negotiations of these short-term loans, which were repaid presumably when the assessments from the contributory lands were collected.

Evidence of those transactions with Symonson for the years between 1593 and 1598 has survived in the antiquary's rent and receipt books where he noted in December of 1593 that Symonson had paid him £7 4s. for 24 tons of timber, and the next year, when he was elected warden for the third time, that he made two loans of £20 to the paymaster, which were repaid in October but which had to be extended to the corporation again the next spring. At the end of this term as warden in 1595, he certified with Sir Thomas Fludd that Symonson had received his £10 annual stipend, £2 more than the previous paymaster had been paid. Even when he was not serving as warden, Lambarde made loans to the paymaster, but their relationship soon advanced beyond that of two gentlemen administering the funds of a corporation, for it was in 1596 that Lambarde asked Symonson, who had great talent in map drafting, for a map of Kent to be included in his new edition of the *Perambulation*. Because in 1598, Symonson, who had been elected Mayor of Rochester, joined the list of his close friends who died in this decade, Lambarde sadly noted that the accounts from his last term as warden had to be certified in 1599 by Widow Symonson.[33]

During this last term as warden the antiquary's lease to Halling Palace expired, but his move from there first to London and then to Greenwich, did not cause him to lose interest in the bridge, and he continued to perform the duties of a member of the court of assistants from 1599 to 1601. In a letter written on 26 July 1599 to his friend, Leveson, he discussed the difficulties of fortifying the walls of Rochester Castle against the erosion and decay of the river and commented, 'in which respect (though I bee not amongest you a dweller, yet for the good of the Bridge to which you would hold me an assit.) I pray you let me yet reckon one your neighbour.'[34] This letter, as well as the one written to Leveson in 1600 about the weirs on the Medway, demonstrated the concern and love he had for Rochester and his friends who lived there.

Although in those years he was occupied with national and local problems and with responsibilities to deceased friends, he did not neglect his scholarship. It was in the middle of the 1590s, probably 1594, that he wrote a treatise on the Court of Admiralty[35] and in 1596 that he prepared a second edition of the *Perambulation*. The treatise on the Alienations' Office, of course, was penned in 1590 and notations in the book of Sir Julius Caesar about the Court of Requests were made in 1598, while he was continuing to redraft his manuscript of the *Archeion* and to re-edit his handbooks on justices of the peace and the constables.

In this period of his life he added still more books to his library. The *Biblia Sacra* which was edited by F. Junius, *Queen Elizabeth's Prayer Book* which was published in 1590, and R. Percyvall's *Bibliotheca Hispanica* which was enlarged by Thomas Doyley all belonged to him and remained a part of the family library until the 20th century.[36] One interesting volume in his possession was a manuscript written by John de Beauchesve in 1597 and entitled 'A Booke, containing the true portraiture and attires of the King of England'. Like the other Lambarde works, this volume, with its many marginal notes, some of them from Holinshed, demonstrated not only that he treasured his books and manuscripts but also that neither poor eyesight nor official duties could force him to neglect his reading.[37]

This was a momentous decade for him. He became quite prosperous, adding lands in Kent worth over £1,700 to his estate, and won new friends, some of them relatives of his third wife, but it was a time of sadness, too, as he lost many of his long-time associates. Seriously ill, himself, in 1596, he must have become even more aware of the precarious hold one has on life when his intimate friend, Ralph Rokeby, died in that year, followed in 1597 by Lord Cobham and Cousin Gore, and in 1598 by Lord Burghley and Philip Symonson. It is no wonder that his thoughts turned to the future of his house, and that he provided financial security for his children in a will drawn up in 1597, but despite the many occasions he had to dwell upon death and the afterlife in this decade when he passed his 60th year, he did not lose his hold on reality: the poor still had to be fed; the criminals had to be brought to justice; the Spanish and Catholics were still on the attack and had to be defeated to the glory of God and the Queen. Wealthier in material riches and in intellectual achievements, but sadder from the losses of friends and relatives, his vigilance for law and order and his concern for justice did not abate.

## 12

# Progenitor and Pioneer

SADDENED by the expiration of his lease to Halling Palace in September 1598, William Lambarde wrote in his diary that after living there for 15 years he was going to London where he had taken his first breath to breathe his last. It is possible that he was in poor health at the time of his entry. Indeed, two years earlier he had written in a new edition of the *Perambulation* that he was "drawing on the last scaene of his life" and had informed Sir Thomas Egerton in a letter that he had heard the bells toll thrice for him, but since there is no corroborative evidence of a grave illness in 1598, it was probably only his way of expressing his great sorrow at losing his 'halcyon days' on the Medway.[1]

Although it seems unlikely, especially since he had arranged to have 20 quarters of wheat and barley delivered on each of three days, 3 February 1599, 3 February 1600, and 3 February 1601, at the common bridge in Greenwich for his use at Westcombe, he may have remained with his family in London from the autumn of 1598 to the late summer of 1599. The evidence for that conjecture is a letter written on 1 September 1599 to Sir John Leveson in which he stated that he had 'spent one moneth upon barrein Blackheath, wheare [his] wife and [he were] (for a few weekes) now begynners of a poore housekeeping'.[2]

In anticipation of the expiration of his lease to Halling Palace in 1598, he had begun making improvements at Westcombe Manor, expending £24 on plumbing, £16 on a walk in the garden, and £240 on a wall and stable there in 1596 and disbursing over £400 for repairs to the manor house in 1598. Despite a total outlay of over £900 by October 1599, he still recorded in his rent

and receipt book that two wings of the manor house needed reno-
vating, a sad state of affairs which had probably led him to refer
to his 'poore housekeeping' in the letter to Leveson that autumn.
Despite these enormous expenditures he was still a prosperous
gentleman and could reckon his worth in cash and goods in
October 1600 at £972—£332 of that amount in gold and £355 of
it in silver.[3]

After his move to Greenwich Lambarde neither lost contact
with the problems of the Rochester area nor forsook his long-
standing friendship with Sir John Leveson. At least as early as
August 1596 he had written to him from London about court
rumours and news, a practice he continued after his departure
from Halling Palace. On 20 October 1598, for example, he informed Leveson that no one had yet been appointed to replace
Lord Burghley as Lord Treasurer or Master of the Court of
Wards and that the choice seemed to lie between the Earl of
Essex and Sir Thomas Fortescue. The next year he discussed the
rumours of war and complained that the ghost of Sir Francis
Walsingham 'groaned to see Ingland Baron of a serviceable in-
telligence'.[4]

A month after this last letter was written he took advantage of
their friendship to seek assistance for a Greenwich neighbour
whose dogs had been stolen and sold to people throughout the
county. Since Jackson, the neighbour, had been willing to com-
pensate the victims of the fraud for the money they had paid for
the dogs, he had succeeded in recovering all of them except for
those that had been sold to an obstinate waterman of Gravesend.
The favour that Lambarde asked was for Leveson to accompany
Jackson (who delivered the letter of request) in yet another
attempt to regain his pets from the waterman.[5]

Even though he had been reluctant to leave his friends at Halling, many of his London acquaintances and others not resident in
Kent clearly associated him with Greenwich where besides own-
ing a manor and endowing an almshouse, he occasionally performed business for the Crown. In 1592, along with Admiral Sir
John Hawkins, he was appointed to a special commission of the
Court of Exchequer to survey land there which was claimed
both by Thomas Hazelwood and the Queen, and, of course, he
served on the commissions of sewers for the Greenwich Marsh as
well as handling judicial inquires there as a justice of the peace

of Kent. Besides his growing eminence in local Kentish matters, both in Rochester and Greenwich, he also advanced in stature in Lincoln's Inn where he was elected a bencher in 1597 and was asked to serve on various important committees in 1599 and 1600.[6]

The number of honours bestowed upon him clearly did not diminish as he grew older. On 21 January 1601, after summoning him to a royal audience and praising him for his excellent endeavours in her behalf, Queen Elizabeth appointed him the Keeper of the Records in the Tower of London, only three days after a courtier, Fulke Greville, offered his assistance to Sir Michael Hicks, former secretary to Lord Burghley, in obtaining the position. It is possible that Hicks was not interested but it is also possible that Sir Thomas Egerton, Lord Keeper of England, intervened on behalf of the antiquary who was admirably qualified for the appointment since he knew well the chancery records stored there.[7]

Shortly after he assumed this position, Lambarde prepared a catalogue of all the documents in the Tower and attempted to send it to Queen Elizabeth via the Countess of Warwick, but her Majesty decided to grant him a private audience in her privy chamber at East Greenwich on 4 August 1601 where he could personally present the 'Pandecta Rotulorum'. At least feigning interest in the manuscript, she asked him questions about the various entries and then paused as she approached the notes on the records of King Richard II. With the recent Essex conspiracy and the frequent playing of the drama, 'King Richard II', in London still fresh on her mind, she exclaimed, 'I am Richard II know ye not that?'. When he responded that the evil scheme had been plotted by a 'most unkind gentleman Essex the most adorned creature that ever her Majestie made', she continued her examination of his 'Pandecta' for a while, but once again returned to the subject, asking him if he had ever seen a true picture of that King. Upon discovering that he had not, she promised to show him a likeness that was stored at Westminster and then commented: 'In those days force and arms did prevail: but now the wit of the fox is everywhere on foot so hardly a faithful and vertuous man may be found'. In Lambarde, an old and sick gentleman with only two weeks more to live, she had a faithful and honourable subject and she knew it: After praising his work she closed the audience by calling him her 'good and Honest

Lambarde'. He must have written his account of the meeting with great joy and pride particularly since she had forbidden him 'from first to last to fall upon [his] knees before her'.[8]

After the antiquary's death, P. E. Proby, a clerk at the Tower of London, petitioned for the position of Keeper of the Records, offering to relinquish his £40 pension and to pay Widow Lambarde £100 for the catalogue and complaining that Lambarde had not been to the Tower since 10 July and had only appeared there infrequently since his appointment, an absence undoubtedly caused by his grave illness that year which even prevented the faithful recording of his private transactions in his rent and receipt book. Five days after the interview with the Queen he sent to his friend, Leveson, a letter which was not written by his own hand, thanking him for inquiring about his health and stating : 'I have not found it lower thanking God and depending upon his divine pleasure whatever he have determined the continuance of this myne earthely webbe'. 10 days later, on 19 August 1601, he died, but not unprepared, since he had drawn up his will in 1597 and had paid 40s. to Giles de Witte of Cobham, mason, for his tombstone in 1599, a rather paltry sum when compared to the £6 10s. bequest that Ralph Rokeby left for his monument.[9]

Named after Saint Alphege, the parish church of East Greenwich, where his monument was placed against the south wall of the south aisle, was built on the site where tradition claimed the saint was murdered in 1011 by the Danes. The monument was inscribed with the following eulogy :

> William Lambarde of Lincoln's Inn, sometime master in Chancery, Keeper of the rolls and records within the Tower, of the Office of Alienations to Queen Elizabeth, founded the College of the Poor of Greenwich and endowed it. Obiit 1601, August 19, at Westcomb in East Greenwich.

Shortly after one of the pillars of the nave arcade collapsed on 28 November 1710, causing the church roof to fall in, Lambarde's descendants removed the tombstone and placed it in the north aisle of St. Nicholas' Church at Sevenoaks where it has since reposed.[10]

After his death the officials of the Drapers' Company supervised the college as required by its statutes and had custody of the

rents of his lands during the minority of his heirs. The officials
were not particularly pleased with the section of the Lambarde
will in which Margaret, the daughter, was bequeathed £800 that
was to be left in their custody until she married or reached the age
of 21. They had been authorised by the antiquary to loan that
money to poor drapers but if any of them defaulted, the Company
was to be held liable. Despite their hesitancy in the matter, the
Company officials did accept the bequest money and ultimately
delivered it to Margaret intact.[11]

On 5 May 1609 at the age of 23 Margaret married Thomas
Godfrey, also 23 years of age and the second son of Thomas Godfrey of Lydd, in St. Catherine's Church by the Tower of London.
Their marriage was of short duration since she died on 29 June
1611, possibly from complications arising from the birth of her
only child, a son named Lambard after his maternal grandfather.
Lambard Godfrey, the first grandson of the antiquary, sided with
the Roundheads during the civil wars of the 17th century, representing in Parliament the county of Kent in 1654 and the town
of New Romney in 1659.[12]

Lambarde's heir, Multon, was admitted to Lincoln's Inn on 18
October 1599, called to the bar on 26 November 1606, and obtained permission to travel abroad for three years in 1607 without
losing or forfeiting his chamber there, but whether or not he
actually took the Grand Tour is not known, since he was certainly in England on 11 February 1608, when he wrote: 'It
pleased his Majestie to bestowe ye honnoure of knighthood upon
mee at Whitehall as he passed through the gallery to ye Chapell'.
At the age of 27, shortly after the death of his stepmother, Sir
Multon married Jane, the daughter of Sir Thomas Lowe, alderman of London, who bore him four children during their 21-
year marriage.[13]

Unlike the son of Margaret Lambarde Godfrey, Thomas, the
heir of Sir Multon, remained loyal to the Crown during the civil
wars of the 17th century. Born in 1615, he lived to be 60 years of
age and to see not only the execution of King Charles I but also
the restoration of the Stuart line. Because of financial problems
during the turmoil of that century, Thomas was forced to sell
the manor at Westcombe, subsequently purchasing property at
Sevenoaks which became the home of the Lambarde family. Particularly interested in his grandfather's manuscripts, he had a re-

vised edition of the *Archeion* printed in 1635 to replace an inferior edition of that work.

According to at least one pedigree, the Lambarde twins died in 1590, but, of course, that date is incorrect since their father devised property to them both in his will of 1597. Since no references to their deaths have been found in the family diary, it is likely that they survived their father, dying in the early 17th century before their nephew, Thomas, compensating for the carelessness of his father, Sir Multon, began to enter important family dates in the diary.[14]

The Lambarde family with its library full of manuscripts and books survived into the 20th century, but because of financial problems, William Gore Lambarde, the last male descendant of the antiquary, was forced to sell many of the manuscripts in 1924. He had only two daughters, neither of whom bore any offspring, and only one of them, Debora Sylvestre Campbell (Mrs. S. F. Campbell), survives. She has attempted to retain in her possession some of her ancestor's manuscripts, such as the diary, the book of purchases, and the rent and receipt books, and she also owns an original oil painting of the antiquary, which shows him wearing a black coat with scalloped collar and a black cap with a small bill and striking a serious but handsome pose in the 16th-century tradition.

In his memory Mrs. Campbell has erected a window in the parish church of Sevenoaks with the following inscription :

In memory of William Lambarde Keeper of the records in the Tower to Queen Elizabeth 1st and founder of the Queen Elizabeth almshouse of Greenwich, and of his descendants who lived and owned land in West Kent, since his time and have resided in the parish of Sevenoaks since 1654. This window is erected by Debora Campbell daughter of William Gore Lambarde 1954.

Thus the antiquary has neither been forgotten by his last living descendant nor by modern scholars, and although it is true that general histories of England and often even more serious studies do not refer to his works, those who study 16th century poor relief, legal institutions, jurisprudence, topography, or the history of Kent must know Lambarde.

He was, after all, a great founder—a pioneer as it were—in many fields. First, because he wrote and published the *Archaionomia*, he was a pioneer in Anglo-Saxon studies—a fame he deserves even if he had assistance in the gathering of the research for the book. In the area of local history he was also an outstanding contributor, writing the first history of the county of Kent and having the honour of being the first to write a history of any English county. Furthermore, he encouraged others to write topographical histories and had thoughts of expanding his 'Description' into a national history when the appearance of Camden's masterpiece caused the abandonment of that project.

As an author of works which described the institutions of the 16th century, he can hardly be equalled. Not only did he write handbooks for justices of the peace and other local officials, but he also described the English court system in the *Archeion*, a work which has been so highly esteemed by modern legal historians that two of them, Charles McIlwain and Paul Ward, have had another edition of it published. His writings and decisions about Equity and Common Law are of great value for the modern world because they were written on the threshold of an era when the two realms of justice were to undergo a bitter struggle. Although trained in Common Law, he foresaw no inevitable clash between them and could and did praise the system of Equity in the Courts of Chancery and Star Chamber because it was based upon the conscience of the Queen who was the earthly source of all English justice.

In addition to these scholastic successes, he founded an almshouse, not the first after the Reformation, but certainly a valuable contribution to English social life that has endured for nearly four centuries. He was also successful in continuing the Lambarde line, although it will die out in the 20th century, but that it has lasted so long is in itself remarkable. Few gentle houses today can trace their ancestry beyond the 16th century.

There is no doubt that he was trusted and respected by his contemporaries. The great number of wills in which he was named executor, the public demand for his books, the requests for his impartial intercession, the gifts presented to him, and the positions of responsibility that those like Sir Thomas Egerton and Lord Burghley gave him are all evidence of his ability and integrity. Even the Queen, in bidding him adieu at the end of the audience at East Greenwich, called him 'good and Honest' at a time when she was much troubled by the duplicity of other subjects.

For all his accomplishments he deserves great tribute, but his importance should not be exaggerated. He was not a unique Elizabethan. As an administrator and dispenser of justice, he was only one of many whose combined efforts effected good government in England, and, like most of his associates on the commission of the peace for Kent, he performed his duties faithfully with only an occasional complaint about heavy taxes and the many burdens of the office. But ever concerned about obedience to the law then existing, he never seriously questioned the authority of the Queen or the order of society and reacted with anger when anyone disputed the wisdom of her Majesty's government.

Lambarde's great efforts were, themselves, a testimony to the wisdom of the Queen's style of government. As an administrator he was underpaid for his vast efforts when paid a stipend at all and he could not place any great hope on social advancement since he served under a Queen who was disinclined to bestow titles or knighthood even on those who had served her long and well. What better opportunity could her Majesty have had to knight Lambarde, than at the audience at East Greenwich when before her stood a loyal and dedicated subject who had devoted long years to her service and to the furtherance of scholarship and who, in his old age, was presenting her with his last work of love, the 'Pandecta Rotulorum'. But knighthood was not his reward.

Seven years later his son, Sir Multon, was knighted by King James I, perhaps because he was the antiquary's son and surely because he was willing to pay for that honour with gold. It could be argued that William, too, had purchased the right to knighthood by his charitable gifts, by his contributions to scholarship, and by his service to her Majesty, but his only reward was the royal interview. For him, however, it was sufficient. This, then, was the greatness of Elizabethan England that many 'of inferior note and station', like William Lambarde, were willing to devote their talents and energies to the royal government without hope of great monetary gain or great social elevation simply because the Queen was Elizabeth.[15]

# Notes

## Chapter One

[1]Brigadier-General Fane Lambarde, 'William Lambarde's Pedigree Notes', *Archaeologia Cantiana* (1927), XXXIX, 131. There may have been other children lost in infancy whose existence was unknown to the antiquary when he drew up his family tree; Percival Boyd, 'Manuscript Notes on Pedigrees', 1952, Drapers' Hall.

[2]Percival Boyd, 'Notes on Pedigrees'; W. Archer-Thomson, *Drapers' Company. History of the Company's Properties and Trusts* (London, 1943), I, 30.

[3]Rep. 7(3), ff. 783–84, Drapers' Minute Books; Percival Boyd, 'Notes on Pedigrees'.

[4]Lambarde Diary, p. 56, p. 157, and p. 305. This manuscript belongs to Mrs. S. F. Campbell of London. A brief fragment of it was published by Multon Lambarde in *Miscellanea Genealogica* (1876), II, 99–114.

[5]William Brigg, ed., *The Register Book of the Parish of St. Nicholas Acon, London, 1539–1812* (Leeds, 1890), p. 1 and p. 83; Lambarde Diary, p. 275; W. W. Jenkinson, *London Churches Before the Fire* (London, 1917), pp. 136–37.

[6]Booke of Purchases and Buyldings of John Lambarde, Campbell manuscript; Rent and Receipt Book, 1557–1574, Campbell manuscript. Microfilm copies of all rent and receipt books are available at the local library at St. John's Park, Blackheath; E 318/678–79, Court of Augmentations.

[7]Fane Lambarde, 'William Lambarde's Pedigree Notes'. p. 131; See C 1/1138, No. 2 and C 1/1242, No. 12, Chancery Proceedings for cases about other Ledbury lands.

[8]John G. Nichols, ed., *Diary of Henry Machyn, Citizen and Merchant Taylor of London, 1550–63* (London, 1848), p. 67; A. H. Johnson, *The History of the Worshipful Company of the Drapers of London* (Oxford, 1915), II, 177. Johnson has claimed that the wealth from joint-stock and regulated companies helped the livery companies to survive to modern times.

[9]Woodthorpe Brandon, *An Inquiry into the Freedom of the City of London in Connection with Trade* (London, 1850), p. 12; Percy A. Harris, *London and its government* (London, 1933), p. 17.

[10]Rep. 7(3), f. 428, f. 429, and f. 878; Rep. A, f. 82, f. 155, f. 192, f. 206, and f. 209; Rep. B, f. 34.

¹¹Rep. A, f. 143 and f. 183.

¹²William Lambarde, *The Perambulation of Kent* (London, 1596), pp. 12–13.

¹³Edward Hasted, ed., Henry H. Drake, *History of Kent* (London, 1886), I, 47–51. Hasted believed that after the conviction of Nicholas Ballard, Westcombe descended to the heirs of Nicholas and that they sold the manor to the Lambardes. His belief, however, seems to be disproved by a note William, the antiquary, made in his rent and receipt book. He stated there that he possessed the conveyance from Nicholas to John for Westcombe.

¹⁴John Philipott, 'The Visitation of the County of Kent', *Archaeologia Cantiana* (1863), V, 123–256; The original grant of the coat of arms is possessed by Mrs. Campbell.

¹⁵A. H. Johnson, *Company of Drapers*, II, 106.

¹⁶Rep. B, f. 31 and ff. 54–55; Thomas Girtin, *The Triple Crowns*, pp. 130 ff.

¹⁷Lambarde Diary, p. 227 and p. 235; John G. Nichols, *Diary of Henry Machyn*, p. 67; John Stow, *Survey of England* (Oxford, 1908), I, 297–98.

¹⁸Rep. B, f. 86; W. W. Jenkinson, *London Churches*, p. 177.

¹⁹31 More, Somerset House.

²⁰George S. Fry, ed., *Abstracts of Inquisitions Post Mortem* (London, 1896), I, 132–33; 6 More, Somerset House.

## Chapter Two

¹*Patent Rolls*, Queen Mary I, Vol. II, p. 75, and Vol. IV, p. 79; George Fry, *Inquisitions*, II, 153; He later acquired the right to bear the White and Dean coats of arms through his marriage to Sylvestre Dalison. They descended to her son, Maximilian Dalison, at her death in 1587.

²*Patent Rolls*, Elizabeth I, Vol. V, p. 144; William noted in his book of purchases that he had sold Heddington and other Wiltshire property for £1,560. In 1588 he was a witness in the case of Partridge v. Jenkins concerning this manor. See C/2 Elizabeth P. 1, No. 37, Chancery Proceedings; For more information about the dyehouse see Kent Ms. U962, T84, Kent Archives Office.

³For information about this custom and how it affected inheritance in Kent, see Elizabeth Melling, 'Aspects of Agriculture and Industry', *Kentish Sources*, (Maidstone, 1961), III, 2–5; Charles Elton, *The Tenures of Kent* (London, 1867), p. 2ff, pp. 39–41, and p. 285; William Lambarde, *The Perambulation*, pp. 563 ff.

⁴C 3/114/13, ff. 1–5, Chancery proceedings. Two decrees have been found. See C 33/36, f. 40b and C 33/35 f. 120b, Chancery Decree Books.

⁵This deed belongs to Mrs. Campbell.

⁶Charles Elton, *Tenures*, p. 7; Felix Hull, 'The Custumal of Kent', *Archaeologia Cantiana* (1959), LXXII, 148–59; William Lambarde, *Perambulation*, p. 546; Woodhall 63, Somerset House.

⁷H. F. Fear, 'Westcombe', *Transactions of the Greenwich and Lewisham Antiquarian Society* (1964), VII, 8–14; George F. Bosworth, *Kent*

(Cambridge, 1909), p. 124; William Lambarde, *Perambulation*, pp. 429–31.

[8]Elizabeth Melling, *Kent Sources*, III, 1–20.

[9]Edward Hasted, *History of Kent*, 51–53. Hasted claimed that Robert Cecil, Earl of Salisbury, revenged himself upon some neighbors who refused to sell land to him by urging the king to enlarge and wall in the royal land in East Greenwich.

[10]Star Chamber 5, Bundles III, VII, VIII, XI, XVI, and XXXII.

[11]Percival Boyd, 'Pedigree Notes'; John Philipott, 'Visitation of Kent', p. 252; George Fry, *Inquisitions*, I, 133 and II, 62; Uncle John Horne who died in March of 1601 was probably a relative of William's mother, but not a brother as she was the sole heiress to her father. Jasper Nicholson was the son of Christian Goodrich Nicholson and John Nicholson of London, currier. Margaret Bond was the daughter of Elizabeth Lambarde Bond.

## Chapter Three

[1]William Lambarde, *Description of England* (London, 1730), p. 64 and p. 254.

[2]In the 1570s Lambarde recorded in his receipt book that he loaned money to various people at Cambridge, one at Peter House. Later in the 1590s he recorded that he had sent his son, then a student at Lincoln's Inn, to Cambridge. He did not indicate that he actually attended the university. There was a student on scholarship in 1549 at Jesus College, Cambridge by the name of William Lambert. Because of his wealthy background and the statements in the *Description*, the antiquary was probably not that student. See John and J. A. Venn, *Book of Matriculation of Cambridge* (Cambridge, 1913), p. 409; The register of Oxford does indicate that a William Lambert was admitted in 1553, received his B.A. in 1561, and his M.A. in 1565, but it also indicates that this 'Lambarde' came from Buckinghamshire. See Charles Boase and Andrew Clark, *Register of Oxford, 1449–1662* (Oxford, 1884), I, 223.

[3]In his diary, written in 1589, William noted that he had been admitted to the Inn on 12 April, 1556. He may have meant that he received official permission to enter at that time; *The Records of the Honorable Society of Lincoln's Inn, Registry of Admission* (London, 1896), I, 62; *Black Books*, I, v–viii; Robert Pearce, *A Guide to the Inns of Court and Chancery* (London, 1855), p. 384; William Holden Spilsbury, *Lincoln's Inn, Its Ancient and Modern Buildings* (London, 1873), pp. 18–21; J. Douglas Walker, *Short Notes of Lincoln's Inn* (London, 1912), p. 159.

[4]D. Plunkett Barton, Charles Benham, and Francis Watt, *The Story of Our Inns of Court* (London, 1942), p. 265, pp. 275–77, and p. 280; *Black Books*, I, 318 and 337; *Acts of the Privy Council*, VIII, 246.

[5]*Black Books*, I, 350, 356, 387–99.

[6]*Ibid.*, 412.

[7]*Ibid.*, II, 51.

[8]*Ibid.*, II, 58 and 63 ff.

[9]Both, of course, helped to advance Lambarde's career.

¹⁰*Acts of the Privy Council*, XVIII, 303, XVII, 207–08, and XXX, 27–31; *State Papers Domestic*, Elizabeth I, Vol. V, p. 163.

¹¹*Journals of the House of Commons* (London, 1803), I, 76.

¹²Norah M. Fuidge, 'The Personnel of the House of Commons, 1563–7', M.A. thesis at the University of London, 1950, p. 87 and p. 202; J. E. Neale, *Elizabeth I and her Parliaments 1559–1581* (New York, 1958), pp. 90ff; J. E. Neale, *The Elizabethan House of Commons* (New Haven, 1950), p. 245 and p. 363; The arguments discussed in this section were debated at the history seminar conducted by Sir John Neale at the Institute of Historical Research, University of London, June and July, 1966.

¹³Add. Ms. 5123, British Museum; There are several 17th-century copies there as well: Harleian Mss. 4619 and 2234; Lansdowne Ms. 489; Two 17th-century copies are at the University of Dublin, G. 31 Ms. ff. 29–35b and at the Bodleian Library, Rawlinson Ms. A. 78, ff. 136–41; It has been published in the *Harleian Miscellany* (London, 1809), IV, 559–71.

¹⁴Lambarde did possess one manuscript about parliament which was not listed in the bibliography. It was entitled 'De Gradibus Parliamenti qui sex in numero'. See Rawlinson Ms. D. 1228, F946, Bodleian Library; William Lambarde, eds. Charles McIlwain and Paul L. Ward, *Archeion* (Cambridge, Mass., 1957).

¹⁵Catherine Strateman, *The Liverpool Tractate* (New York, 1937), p. xli.

¹⁶William Lambarde, *Archeion*, pp. 145–48.

¹⁷Catherine Strateman, *The Liverpool Tractate*, p. xli; Conyers Read, ed., *William Lambarde and Local Government* (Ithaca, New York, 1962), p. 9 and p. 46; Ms. X.d. 121 (2), Letter of William Lambarde to Ralph Rokeby on 20 January, 1587–8, Folger Shakespeare Library. In this letter Lambarde explained that Hilary Term, 1588 was the first he had missed in 30 years.

¹⁸William Lambarde, *Description*, p. 4, p. 331, p. 12, and p. 209.

¹⁹William Lambarde, *Description*, p. 55; William Lambarde, *Archaionomia* (London, 1568), pp. Ala-Blb.

²⁰Lambarde Diary, p. 174 and p. 296. During the second session of that Parliament William Thornton of Lincoln's Inn was imprisoned for instigating some of the other students there to discuss the question of the succession. To meddle with high politics even on this low level endangered a man's position in the kingdom. See Mortimer Levine, *The Early Elizabethan Succession Question 1558–68* (Stanford, California, 1960), p. 71.

²¹William Lambarde, *Description*, p. 220; For the Proctor Book, see British Museum shelfmark C. 55a 27.

²²William Lambarde, *Description*, p. 369.

²³*Calendar of Patent Rolls*, Elizabeth I, Vol. V, No. 698, p. 89.

²⁴30 Rutland, Somerset House; *Calendar of Patent Rolls*, Elizabeth I, Vol. III, No. 2732, p. 490; In February of 1570, still another Lambert,

this one of Norfolk, was sued in the Court of Requests for enclosing a common. See Court of Requests 2, Bundle 159/12 f. 1.

²⁵John Nichols, *Bibliotheca Topographica Britannica*, I, 527–29; Add. Ms. 33,923, f. 9; Conyers Read, *Local Government*, p. 96.

²⁶Julius Ms. C. V. 9, f. 25, British Museum; Conyers Read, *Local Government*, p. 10; John Nichols, *Bibliotheca Topographica Britannica*, I, 525–56.

## Chapter Four

¹Ralph Churton, *The Life of Alexander Nowell, Dean of St. Paul's*, Oxford, 1809; Evidence that he was not the Dean of Lichfield is to appear in my article, 'Notes on a Court of Requests Case of 1571', *English Language Notes* (Boulder, Colorado, 1973); See, for example, Requests 2, 45/13, ff. 1–16.

²Lambarde Diary, p. 88 and p. 291; William Lambarde, *Archaionomia* (London, 1568), pp. Ala–Blb. Louis Mennuti of Arizona State University Graduate School helped with the translation of the letter of introduction.

³Anthony A. Wood, *Athenae Oxonienses* (London, 1813), I, 246; Conyers Read, *Local Government*, p. 6, n. 9.

⁴William Lambarde, *Archaionomia*, pp. AIIIa–AIIIb.

⁵Wilbur Dunkel, *William Lambarde, Elizabethan jurist* (New Brunswick, New Jersey, 1965), pp. 33–34.

⁶Had either Cordell or Nowell done the major part of the work, it would have been insulting for Lambarde to have criticised the workmanship; In 1644 the book was printed again, this time by Abraham Wheelock in a volume with Bede's *Ecclesiastical History*.

⁷Conyers Read, *Local Government*, pp. 95–96 and p. 100; F. S. Fusner, *The Historical Revolution* (New York, 1962), pp. 98 ff.

⁸Sir William Holdsworth, *A History of the English Law* (Boston, 1937), V, 403; Virgil B. Heltzel, 'Notes: Sir Thomas Egerton and William Lambard', *The Huntington Library Quarterly* (1948), XI, 201–03. Among the scholars who read it were William Bradbridge, Dean of Salisbury and John Fox, author of the *Acts and Monuments*; William Shakespeare may also have had a copy. See Ms. V. a. 230, Folger Shakespeare Library.

⁹William Lambarde, *Description*, p. 178 and p. 264.

¹⁰William Lambarde, *Description*, p. 410; There is an unprinted manuscript at the Kent Archives Office which is dated 1577 and which may have been intended as a part of the *Description*. See Wilbur Dunkel, *William Lambarde*, p. 56; William Lambarde, *The Perambulation*, p. A2b; For the letter to Camden, see Julius Ms. C. V. 9, f. 25a.

¹¹William Lambarde, *Description*, p. 319, p. 171, p. 182, p. 202, p. 90 and p. 198.

¹²*Ibid.*, p. 288; The British Museum has Lambarde's copies of Leland.

¹³William Lambarde, *Description*, p. 203, p. 127, and p. 402; See Selden Supra Ms. 63, p. 1, Bodleian Library for a list of books which Lambarde thought should be read to understand the historical development of English.

¹⁴William Lambarde, *Description*, p. 67 and pp. 314–15.

¹⁵William Lambarde, *Perambulation*, p. A2; Robin Flower, 'Laurence Nowell and the Discovery of England in Tudor Times', *Proceedings of the British Academy* (1935), XXI, 58.

¹⁶For sources of Lambarde's books and manuscripts, see John Nichols, *Bibliotheca*, I, 510–12; *Hodgson's Catalogue* (London, 1924); Francis Edwards, *The Lambarde Catalogue of Early Printed Books* (London, 1909).

¹⁷Nowell's copy of the Cambrensis is Add. Ms. 34,762 and Lambarde's copy at the Bodleian Library is B471; Nowell's copy of the Peterborough Chronicle is Add. Ms. 43,704. See Selden Supra Ms. 63, f. 1 at the Bodleian Library; For the translation of Bede, see Otho Ms. B XI, British Museum; Lambarde wrote on the Arundel book that Parker had loaned it to him. See John Nichols, *Bibliotheca*, I, 511 and John Strype, *The Life and Acts of Matthew Parker* (Oxford, 1821), II, 518.

¹⁸Requests 2, 45/13, ff. 1–6; For other information about Nowell's disappearance, see my article soon to be published.

¹⁹William Lambarde, *Perambulation*, p. A1 and p. 74; Francis Edwards, *Catalogue of Lambarde Books*, no. 184.

²⁰William Lambarde, *Perambulation*, p. 261 and *Description*, p. 318.

²¹William Lambarde, *Perambulation*, p. 246 and *Description*, p. 372.

²²William Lambarde, *Perambulation*, p. 296.

²³*Ibid.*, pp. 319–20.

²⁴*Ibid.*, pp. 12–13. In the chapter on the estate of Kent, he spoke of wealthy people from London settling in Kent, but this description may only have been valid for western parts of the county. See W. K. Jordan, 'Social Institutions in Kent', *Archaeologia Cantiana* (1961), LXXV, p. 1a; and A. M. Everitt, 'The County Committee of Kent in the Civil War', University College of Leicester, *Occasional Papers* (1957), IX, 8.

²⁵One historian thought he had discovered the 1576 map but that was later disproved. See Edward G. Box, 'Lambarde's Carde of this Shrye', *Archaeologia Cantiana* (1926) XXXVIII, 89; Grevile M. Levitt, 'Early Kent Maps (Sixteenth Century), *Archaeologia Cantiana* (1938), XLIX, 251–77; William Lambarde, *Perambulation*, p. 220.

²⁶William Lambarde, *Perambulation*, pp. 68–70.

²⁷George E. Eland, ed., *Thomas Wotton's Letter Book* (London, 1960), p. xviii.

²⁸William Lambarde, *Perambulation*, p. 383 and *Description*, p. 289 and p. 441.

²⁹John Strype, *Parker*, III, 276 and 439.

³⁰For information about the 'Textus' see Dr. F. Liebermann, 'Notes on the Textus Roffensis', *Archaeologia Cantiana* (1898), XXIII, 96–109; William Lambarde, *Perambulation*, p. A5, p. 293, pp. 385–91, and p. 531; John Strype, *Parker*, II, 508 and 518; For discussion of a verse attributed to Lambarde erroneously, see M. R. James, *Descriptive Catalogue of the Manuscripts at Corpus Christi College, Cambridge* (Cambridge, 1909–1913), II, 419–21; Paul R. Ward, 'William Lambarde's Collections on Chancery', *Harvard Library Bulletin* (1953), VII, 272–73.

³¹In the 1570s the antiquary acquired some works from Parker that were not cited in the county history. In 1574 he obtained 'Chronicon

Gallice' which is Dounce Ms. CXXVIII, Bodleian Library and Ms. 301, Christ Church, Canterbury; In 1571 he obtained a copy of *Du Gaignage Des Terres* by Walter of Henley which belonged to Parker. See The Revd. Professor W. Cunningham, 'Walter of Henley', *Transactions of the Royal Historical Society* (1895), IX, N.S., 216; Add. Ms. 20,709. For the French transcript, see Ms. B471, f. 16, Bodleian Library.

³²William Lambarde, *Perambulation*, pp. A4–5; Lambarde Diary, p. 144.

³³William Lambarde, *Perambulation*, p. 252, p. 317, and p. 407; R. F. Jessup, 'Excavation of a Roman Barrow at Holborough, Snodland', *Archaeologia Cantiana* (1955), LXVIII, 4; In the section on Hakington he added a note about a tilt which had been copied for him by Francis Thynne. Thynne was admitted to Lincoln's Inn in 1561 and assisted with the edition of *Holinshed* edited by John Hooker in 1587.

³⁴William Lambarde, *Perambulation*, p. 9, p. 113, p. 324, and pp. 526–27.

³⁵Thomas Kendrick, *British Antiquity* (London, 1950), p. 119; William Camden, *Britain*, trans. Philemon Holland (London, 1610), p. 323.

³⁶G. S. Thomson, 'The Twysden Lieutenancy Papers, 1583–1668', *Kent Records* (Ashford, Kent, 1926), X, 72. See Chapter 7 for an explanation of the Captain's practical use of Lambarde's knowledge of the beacons.

³⁷W. A. Scott Robertson, 'Romney, Old and New', *Archaeologia Cantiana* (1880), XIII, 361–62.

³⁸William Lambarde, *The Perambulation of Kent* (London, 1826), p. 124; F. S. Fusner, *The Historical Revolution*, pp. 98–99.

³⁹Thomas Kendrick, *Antiquity*, pp. 4–5, p. 72, p. 99 and pp. 140 ff; In the *Archaionomia* Lambarde had earlier credited the story that King Arthur subdued Norway. See Richard Hakluyt, *The Principal Navigations, voyages, traffigues and discoveries of the English nation* . . . (Glasgow, 1903–05), I, 312.

⁴⁰Felix Hull, 'Kentish Historiography', *Archaeologia Cantiana* (1957), LXX, 223–34; The second edition was the last one printed by Lambarde but there were three new ones in the 17th-century and a new one in the 19th-century.

## Chapter Five

¹He may have read the following while a student: STC 9278, Copy 2, *Magna Carta*, Folger Shakespeare Library; B471, ff. 43A–52B, 'Preceptes and Practizes for the writing and making of deeds or muniments in Lawe', Bodleian Library; Harleian Ms. 5141, Law Cases of William Dalison, British Museum; He was also overseer of a Kentish will. See Add. Charter 54,239; Edward Hasted, *History of Kent*, pp. 109–11.

²*Calendar of the Patent Rolls*, Elizabeth I, Vol. V, no. 1867, p. 220; Elizabeth Melling, 'Some Roads and Bridges', *Kent Records* (Maidstone, 1959), I, 25.

³D593/S/4/14/16, Stafford Archives Office; For other references see D593/S/4/37/8 and Conyers Read, *Local Government*, p. 16; Information about the Greenwich Marsh was communicated to me by Mrs. David

Burkitts, local history librarian, St. John's Park, Blackheath and about the sewer commissions by Elizabeth Melling, Kent Archives Office, Maidstone.

⁴Add. Ms. 34,218, f. 44.

⁵F. J. Bennett, Ightham (London, 1907), pp. 91–93; Lambarde Diary, p. 140, p. 305, p. 369; W. Bruce Bannerman, ed., *The Visitations of Kent*, Harleian Society (London, 1924), LXXV, 11.

⁶These lands were held of East Parkham Manor. See Lambarde Muniments, f. 19b, Campbell Manuscript; Add. Ms. 33,923, f. 366.

⁷Captain C. Hesketh, 'The Manor House and Great Park of the Archbishop of Canterbury at Otford', *Archaeologia Cantiana* (1915), XXXI, 3–22.

⁸Lambarde probably hoped to be appointed to the Commission of the Peace. He owned a book called *The Justice of the Peace*, now at the British Museum and in 1574 he sent a manuscript to Bromley, who as Lord Chancellor appointed the justices. See the Atcheson L. Hinch Collection at the University of Virginia.

⁹Lambarde Diary, p. 276; Sir Edward Harrison, 'The Court Rolls . . . of the Manor of Ightham . . .', *Archaeologia Cantiana* (1936), XLVIII, 217.

¹⁰William Lambarde, *The Perambulation* (1596), p. 569; After Multon's death he obtained Melchior Kling's *In Quatuor Institutionum Juris Principis Justiniani Libros Enarrationes Lugdune*, possibly from the library of his father-in-law since his name was on the title page. See Francis Edwards, *The Lambarde Catalogue*, No. 181; Lambarde Diary p. 302.

¹¹W. K. Jordan, 'Social Institutions in Kent', pp. 1–3.

¹²The Revd. A. G. L'Estrange, *The Palace and the Hospital* (London, 1886), I, 359; W. H. Mandy, 'Notes from the Assize Rolls and Other Documents', *Greenwich Antiquarian Society* (1914), I, 311.

¹³Thomas Dugdale, *Curiosities of Great Britain, England and Wales Delineated* (London, 1854–60), V, 857–94; E. E. Ratcliffe, *The Royal Maundy* (London, 1952), pp. 1–2; Wilbur Dunkel, *William Lambarde*, pp. 44–45.

¹⁴John Nichols, *Progresses of Queen Elizabeth* (London, 1828), I, 325–36; 'The Order of the Maundy', *Archaeologia* (1779), I, 7–9; Add. Ms. 6183, f. 73; Add. Ms. 32,097, f. 70; There is an account of the performance of the Maundy by Queen Mary in the Venetian Calendar; A rough-draft copy of the Maundy was penned by Lambarde in a volume entitled, 'Coronation Ceremonies, Historical Tracts, etc.', which was given to him in 1571 by Richard Atkins of Lincoln's Inn. He also wrote some notes on the Charter of the Forest in this volume. See Add. Ms. 32,097, f. 2, and ff. 166b–170.

¹⁵These books were listed by Francis Edwards in *The Lambarde Catalogue*. The following were also in the library: William Terrien, *Commentaire de Droit Civil tant Public que Prive, Observe au Pays de Normandie*; George Buchanan, *Basilia Rauracorum Guarinus Nerveus*; Launcelot Brown's copy of *Palladii Institutionum Veterum Scripta Recte Intelligenta Mire Utiles*. Another inventory of the Lambarde library can be found in *Hodgson's Catalogue*, June 1924. The Bodleian Library and the British Musenm

also have books and manuscripts that belonged to Lambarde; For the cycle see Julius Ms. IX, f. 105, British Museum.

¹⁶Add. Ms. 33,923, f. 365; See Chapter 12 for more information about the Cobham family; X.d. 121 (2), Letter from William Lambarde to Ralph Rokeby, 20 January 1587–88, Folger Shakespeare Library. In this letter Lambarde revealed his presence in London during those terms.

¹⁷For more information about the sale of the houses, see Kent Ms. U962, T84 and 'Lambarde Muniments', p. 25b; It was probably in 1574 that he obtained the lease of the parsonage of Ferring in the county of Suffolk for £46 13s. 4d. No other information is available about this lease. All other property purchased in the 1570s was granted to his almshouse.

¹⁸Conyers Read, *Local Government*, p. 15; 'Survey of College Lands', ff. 4b–5a.

¹⁹X.d. 121(1), Letter of William Lambarde to Ralph Rokeby, December, 1577, Folger Shakespeare Library. This was a note of thanks to Rokeby for a horse as a Christmas present.

## Chapter Six

¹Edmund Chapman was a benevolent friend to the poor and to prisoners. See Edward Hasted, *History of Kent*, p. 89.

²The property for income was: Beltring Farm purchased for £520 and rented for £20 and two capons. Brenchley Manor alias Criel's and other lands including Curtey's Farm purchased for £900 and rented for £40; Brattel's Messuage and Chelmill Tenement purchased for £600 and rented for £23 6s. 8d. See 'Survey of the College Lands', Drapers' Hall; The Statutes of the College indicated that the revenue was only £80 19s. 8d. of which £72 were pensions. Of the remaining £8 19s. 8d. the Master of the Rolls was to receive a pair of gloves worth 3s. 4d., the Upper Wardens 20s. for *ipocras*, the Steward for keeping the Court Barons 3s. 4d., the paymaster 3s. 4d., the Keeper of the Records of the Rolls for keeping the college chest 2s. 6d., the minister at Greenwich 10s., and the constable 5s. The remaining income was to be set aside for repairs to the building. See William Bristow, *Schemes Relating to the Charities in the Parish of Greenwich* (Greenwich, 1890), pp. 192–212; Another estimate of the revenues was £86 8s. ¼d. See the *Calendar of the Manuscripts of the Marquis of Salisbury preserved at Hatfield House, Hertfordshire* (London, 1883–1940), XIII, 123.

³Another estimate of the cost of the founding of the college can be found in the 'Survey of College Lands', at Drapers' Hall. It came to £2,642 8s. 6d., broken down as follows: Letters Patent £20, purchase of the college close £70, bricklayers . . . £297, repair of the eves, crest and windows £4 6s. 8d., carpenter for oak timber and workmanship £120, for posts, gates and other items £50, for four tons of Lambarde's own elm timber £13, the freemason and three stones with inscriptions £34, the smith for labour and locks £5, the plumber for gutters and pump 26s., the pump rest and elm trunk 45s., the glasser . . . £6 6s. 6d., the

labourers for hedging and ditching the close £10, the sealing of the house of prayer with deal board and the table and prayer forms £4, the two parts of the silver seal for the corporation 57s., the paving and flint for the skirt of the court and gutters £5 8s. 4d., two chests with locks £4 10s., Brenchley Manor £905, Brattels and Chelmill £605, Hicson's Grove £16, more tiling in 1579 25s. and other unspecified sums to the carpenter. He gave slightly higher purchase prices for the lands in the estimate than in the book of purchases. Another estimate at the Drapers' Hall listed the total cost at £2,702 6s. 6d.

⁴Conditions were attached to the conveyance. If ever the offices of Master of the Rolls or of the upper wardens should be altered or its holders should neglect to maintain the house in good order, or if it should not be lawful to say the prayer prescribed, the public bargain would be void and the lands returned to the Lambardes; John Nichols, *Bibliotheca*, I, 515.

⁵The places within Blackheath Hundred were as follows: The High Steward of East Greenwich was to choose one and the upper wardens another from three selected by the parish of East Greenwich; then one was to be elected from Deptford, three from Lewisham, one from Lee, three from Eltham, one from Charlton and Kidbrook, one from Woolwich, and finally six from East Greenwich.

⁶Rent and Receipt Book, 1575–95.

⁷Rep. F, f. 293; 'Volume of Queen Elizabeth's College', ff. 41–41b.

⁸W. K. Jordan, 'Social Institutions in Kent', p. 16, p. 37, and pp. 133–34; Mildred Philipps left a bequest to found an almshouse in Maidstone in 1558.

⁹Louis B. Wright, *Middle-Class Culture in Elizabethan England* (Chapel Hill, North Carolina, 1935), p. 2 and p. 20.

¹⁰Rep. F, f. 102b and f. 106; 'The Lambarde Cup', *Archaeologia Cantiana* (1927), XXIX, 131–37. The Company had a plinth made for the cup from verdite stone. Since the only verdite mine in the world was one closed down in the Transvaal, the Company negotiated to have a 90-pound specimen dug from the garden of the former mine owner's estate. Professor R. Y. Goodden of the Royal College of Art designed the plinth which was produced from the verdite. See M. A. Greenwood, *The Company's Ancient Plate* (London, 1930), p. 13.

¹¹'Volume of Queen Elizabeth's College', f. 41b; 63 Woodhall; Since Lambarde administered the college while he lived, there were few entries in the Company's minute books. On 30 September 1590 it was noted that they questioned a candidate for admission.

¹²Rep. H, ff. 249–50 and ff. 274–75; The antiquary probably corresponded with Egerton frequently about the college after he became Master of the Rolls. See Add. Ms. 41,340, f. 139.

¹³W. Archer-Thomson, *Drapers' Company*, p. 194.

¹⁴Actually Mrs. Tallis left this rent charge because she was required to do so by contract. In 1586 Lambarde sold two houses to her for 100 marks and a 10s. fee to the college. These messuages had reverted to him at the death of Thomas Bury. See Edward Hasted, *History of Kent*, p. 90.

[15]X.d. 121(1), Folger Shakespeare Library.

[16]X.d. 121(3) and X.d. 121(2), Folger Shakespeare Library. On at least one occasion the two friends co-operated on a case. In May 1587 the Privy Council asked them to give justice to Dorothy Kelke, an orphan. See *Acts of the Privy Council*, XIV, 99.

[17]Rep. H, ff. 14a–16a and f. 231b; In 1595 about a year before Rokeby's death Lambarde paid £180 to the Company for a 30-year lease to one of their houses in St. Peter the Poor in London and agreed to pay £5 in rent each year until the lease terminated.

[18]J. Payne Collier, ed., *The Egerton Papers*, Camden Society (London, 1830), p. 228 and p. 308.

[19]Add. Ms. 12,503, f. 274. The £100 to which he referred was probably intended for the Marshalsey prisoners. The other recipients were Christ's Church, St. Catherine's Parish, scholars at Oxford and Cambridge, debtors at Ludgate prison, the Fleet, the King's Bench, Newgate and the White Lion.

[20]The book is now at the British Museum. Caesar may have expected an entirely different response. In the antiquary's early draft of the *Archeion* he discussed the exalted position of the Court of Requests but in later drafts omitted that erroneous contention. See William Lambarde, *Archeion* (1957), p. vii and pp. 167–70.

[21]Lansdowne Ms. 162, f. 22, Add. Ms. 12,504, f. 7a, Add. Ms. 12,497, f. 201, and Lansdowne Ms. 162, f. 12, British Museum.

[22]The Revd. Daniel Lysons, *The Environs of London* (London, 1748), IV, 485; Edward Hasted, *The History of Kent*, p. 90.

## Chapter Seven

[1]Conyers Read, *Local Government*, p. 15; T. G. Barnes and A. Hassell, 'Justices of the Peace from 1558 to 1688—A Revised List of Sources; *Bulletin of the Institute of Historical Research* (1959), XXXII, 223–32' Bertha Putnam, ed., 'Kent Keepers of the Peace, 1316–17', *Kent Records* (Ashford, 1933), XIII, xv; The Atcheson L. Finch Collection at the University of Virginia has a manuscript written in 1574 by Lambarde which he presented to Sir Thomas Bromley, Lord Chancellor.

[2]Conyers Read, *Local Government*, p. 15.

[3]Conyers Read, *Local Government*, p. 16; Lambarde ceased to work with Multon when he moved to Halling Palace in 1583 at the time of his second marriage.

[4]'Orders for the Musters, 15 March 1590', *Calendar of the Manuscripts of the Marquis of Salisbury*, V, 16–18; Add. Ms. 33,923, f. 215; G. S. Thomson, 'The Origin and Growth of the Office of Deputy Lieutenant', *Transactions of the Royal Historical Society* (1922), 4th series, V,152.

[5]G. S. Thomson, 'The Origin and Growth', pp. 158–60.

[6]G. S. Thomson, 'The Twysden Lieutenancy Papers', pp. 66–67.

[7]D593/S/4/12/7.

[8]D593/S/4/13/2 and D593/S/4/14/16. On 23 September he wrote a letter to Leveson requesting his signature on some purchase warrants for military provisions.

⁹D593/S/4/11/1–2 and D593/S/4/13/1; Conyers Read, *Local Government,* p. 47.

¹⁰Henry Abell, *History of Kent,* pp. 184–86; D593/S/4/11/1; Add. Ms. 33,923, f. 223, Letter of John Leveson to Roger Twysden and George Rivers on 26 July 1588.

¹¹*Acts of the Privy Council,* XVII, 11–12; D593/S/4/12/4–5, D593/S/4/ 12/18, and D593/S/4/11/1–5. These manuscripts indicated that Lambarde also witnessed the swearing in of James Fuller as a gunner on 15 June 1589; one of the justices, William Sedley, was a member of Lincoln's Inn.

¹²Add. Ms. 33,923, f. 218; Sir John Twysden, *The Family of Twysden or Twisdon,* comp. C. H. Dudley Ward (London, 1939), pp. 103–04.

¹³*Acts of the Privy Council,* XIV, 246 and XXIII, 264–65; *The Manuscripts of the Right Honourable F. J. Savile Foljambe of Osberton,* Historical Manuscripts Commission (London, 1897), 15th Report, Appendix V, p. 18.

¹⁴W. J. Lightfoot, 'Documents Relating to a Dispute between the Seven Hundreds and Lydd concerning the Watch at Denge Marsh', *Archaeologia Cantiana* (1872), VIII, 299–310; *Acts of the Privy Council,* XVIII, 243 and 411–12; 'Calendar of the Quarter Sessions', Kent Ms. Z/SR1, f. 13, no. 7, Kent Archives Office.

¹⁵G. S. Thomson, 'The Twysden Lieutenancy Papers', p. 72; See also Chapter 4 for his opinion about Lambarde's scholarship.

¹⁶D593/S/4/11/1; *Acts of the Privy Council,* XXI, 133–34, XXII, 160.

¹⁷*Acts of the Privy Council,* XV, 255 and XVI, 336–37; On 1 October 1582 Lambarde noted in his receipt book that Alford owed him £10.

¹⁸Conyers Read, *Local Government,* pp. 28–29. A copy of this rate schedule is in Add. Ms. 41,137 ff. 180–81.

¹⁹Bertha H. Putnam, 'The Earliest form of Lambard's *Eirenarcha* and a Kent Wage Assessment', *English Historical Review* (1926), XLI, 261–62; J. B. Black, *The Reign of Elizabeth* (Oxford, 1959), p. 266.

²⁰Conyers Read, *Local Government,* p. 32, p. 35, and p. 39.

²¹Conyers Read, *Local Government,* p. 25 and p. 29. It is possible that the house of correction was not in use until after the second session as well.

²²Conyers Read, *Local Government,* pp. 56–8; Although the *Custos Rotulorum* gave the charge in Wiltshire, it is not certain that he did so in Kent. Further, there is no evidence that Wotton held that office before 1584. Lambarde's first charge was given in 1582.

²³Conyers Read, *Local Government,* pp. 56–8; William Lambarde, *Eirenarcha* (London, 1610), pp. 404–05; Francis Thynne, a close friend of Lambarde, lived with his cousin at Longleat. They may have collaborated on the prologues.

²⁴Conyers Read, *Local Government,* p. 58 and p. 138.

²⁵*Ibid.,* pp. 168–76.

²⁶D593/S/4/62.

²⁷Conyers Read, *Local Government,* pp. 161–65.

²⁸D593/S/4/10/12–14 and D593/S/4/60/9.

[29]D593/S/4/18/7; *Acts of the Privy Council*, XIV 319–20 and 359–60.

[30]Conyers Read, *Local Government*, p. 28 and pp. 39–40; D593/S/4/11/1, D593/S/4/37/8, and D593/S/4/66/10. Even though this chapter is primarily about Lambarde's activities as a justice of the peace between 1579 and 1589 the few references to his purveyance duties in the 1590s have been included here.

[31]Conyers Read, *Local Government*, p. 50; D593/S/4/10/19, D593/S/4/10/11, D593/S/4/10/13; Leveson was knighted in late 1589 or early 1590

[32]D593/S/4/14/16; Conyers Read, *Local Government*, p. 50, n. 48.

[33]D593/S/4/11/1 and D593/S/4/10/16.

[34]Add. Ms. 41, 137, 'Rates of Wages', ff. 171–74; B. H. Putnam, 'The Earliest Form of Lambard's *Eirenarcha*', p. 262.

[35]*Acts of the Privy Council*, XIII, 123, XVI, 168, and XIV, 187.

[36]Conyers Read, *Local Government*, p. 27 and p. 29.

[37]For criminal investigations not included, see *Acts of the Privy Council*, XV, 123 and X.d. 121(4), Folger Shakespeare Library.

[38]There was only one entry for March and one for April of 1581 but neither referred to the Quarter Sessions. The other two sessions in Kent were held at Canterbury in the eastern division.

[39]Conyers Read, *Local Government*, p. 85.

[40]*Ibid.*, pp. 88–90.

[41]*Ibid.*, pp. 94–96.

[42]*Ibid.*, pp. 78–79.

[43]*Ibid.*, pp. 153–57; X.d. 123, Folger Shakespeare Library; Since Culpeper was a recusant, it has been suggested that the attack was motivated by fear of his religion. See Wilbur Dunkel, *William Lambarde*, p. 71.

[44]Conyers Read, *Local Government*, p. 47, pp. 24–25, and p. 32. In the notebook he called the Maidstone assize both a gaol delivery and an assize and later referred to the Justice of the Assize at the gaol delivery in Rochester. He used the two words interchangeably.

[45]Conyers Read, *Local Government*, p. 28 and p. 32; William Blackstone, *Commentaries on the Laws of England*, ed. William G. Hammond (San Francisco, 1890), VI, 1270–71.

[46]Lambarde Diary, p. 30 and p. 229; B. H. Putnam, 'The Earliest Form of the *Eirenarcha*', p. 362; Conyers Read, *Local Government*, p. 7; Apparently there were three printings of the first edition. The British Museum possesses one dated 1581/82, and two different others simply dated 1582. The Short-Title Catalogue also lists three separate printings.

[47]The 1581 printing was actually done in January 1582 but because of the Elizabethan calendar differences, it is dated 1581. Lambarde Diary, p. 30; There was a dispute over the second printing of the first edition. See Wilbur Dunkel, *William Lambarde*, p. 192, n. 5; Virgil B. Heltzel, 'Notes: Sir Thomas Egerton and William Lambard', *The Huntington Library Quarterly* (1948) XI, 201; A dispute over publication rights to the 1594 edition is printed in Cecil Monro, ed., *Acta Cancellaria* (London, 1847), pp. 649–51; Add. Ms. 41,137, f. 1, 'Eirenarcha', British Museum.

[48]B. H. Putnam, 'The Earliest Form of the *Eirenarcha*', p. 263; Wilbur Dunkel, *William Lambarde*, p. 68; John Strype, *Annals of the Reformation* (Oxford, 1824), III–1, 108–09; Tyndall was willed a pair of spectacles by Lambarde. See 63 Woodhall.

[49]B. H. Putnam, 'Early Treatise on the Practice of the Justices of the Peace', *Oxford Studies in Social and Legal History* (Oxford, 1924), VIII, 112, 215–18, and 235; Dutton's *County Justice* and Burn's *Justice of the Peace* were based on his work.

[50]William Lambarde, *Eirenarcha* (1619), pp. 1–3, p. 7, p. 54, p. 66, and p. 336; E. P. Cheyney, *History of England* (London, 1948), II, 314.

[51]At the Harvard Law School is Ms. 81, written by John Goldwell of Gray's Inn. Apparently it did not meet the standards of the printer either, for it was refused for publication. In 1584 Lambarde owned a copy of Richard Crompton's revision of Fitzherbert which is now at the British Museum.

[52]Conyers Read, *Local Government*, p. 20 and pp. 75–59; A Tithing was formed by 10 men who were sworn to arrest any one of their group who committed a crime. The borsholder was the spokesman of the tithing but by the 16th century was no more than a petty constable.

## Chapter Eight

[1]13 Bakon, Will of Robert Dean; 40 Darcy, Will of William Dalison; Dalison was the son of Sir William Dalison, justice of the Queen's Bench.

[2]Conyers Read, *Local Government*, p. 28; Lambarde Diary, p. 77 and p. 315.

[3]Lambarde Diary, p. 302, p. 9, and p. 239; It has been suggested that Gore was named after Sir John Gore of Lincoln's Inn, but there is no reference to this knight in Lambarde's personal records. See Wilbur Dunkel, *William Lambarde*, p. 104; Fane may have been named after the brother of Sir Thomas, also named Thomas. According to the 'Ephemeris' Lambarde occasionally worked with the younger Thomas on the commission of the peace. See Conyers Read, *Local Government*, p. 16 and p. 46.

[4]Lambarde Diary, p. 315 and p. 265.

[5]Add. Ms. 8836, f. 120, 'W. Alexander's Collections'; John Thorpe of Bexley, 'Antiquities of Kent', *Bibliotheca Topographica Britannica* (London, 1790), I, 28; For sketches of the palace in ruins see Add. Ms. 32,365, f. 7, F. W. L. Stockdale, 'Ruins of Halling Palace'.

[6]Lambarde Diary, p. 275; John Strype, *Annals of the Reformation*, III–1, 723; Add. Ms. 33,923, f. 332, Streatfeild Papers.

[7]He also had the lease of sundry houses and lands in Halling for £30 15s. 4d. and the lease of a 100-acre parcel of land in East Guildford Marsh, Sussex for £10 which were to expire on 15 January 1599; In 1581 before his marriage he spent £40 on repairs at Westcombe.

[8]D593/S/4/14/16.

⁹Tilghman was given the duty in his will of collecting the college rents if others named failed to do so; 63 Woodhall; D593/S/4/16/16–17.

¹⁰In 1581 John Nicholson, the husband of Christian Goodrich, had agreed to give him a £7 annuity for 28 years on a house in Allhallows by London Wall in lieu of a £60 debt then due.

¹¹He did not explain why the houses escheated to him at the death of Thomas Bury, and he sold them to Bury's widow then the wife of Thomas Tallis.

¹²D593/S/4/14/18. A letter, probably addressed to Lord Cobham, was left unsigned, but in it the author, probably Leveson, pleaded to go abroad as a captain in the army.

¹³D593/S/4/14/16.

¹⁴Joan Evans, *A History of the Society of Antiquaries* (London, 1956), pp. 10–11; John Stow, *Survey of London* (Oxford, 1908), I, preface; see Chapter 4 for more information about Camden.

¹⁵John Strype, *Annals of the Reformation*, III–1, 415–16; William Lambarde, *Description*, p. 181 and p. 328.

¹⁶'Note about William Lambarde', *Notes and Queries* (1926), CL, 330. Reference is made here to Holinshed; For record of Osorio and Chopin see Francis Edwards, *The Lambarde Catalogue*, no. 173 and no. 186; *Hodgson's Catalogue* and W. Cunningham and Elizabeth Lamond, eds., *A discourse of the Common Weal of this Realm of England* (Cambridge, 1893) discuss the Hale book; Both the Hale and Beurhusius books are at the British Museum; He also had two manuscripts about the mint. See B198 Ms. ff. 81–93, Bodleian Library and Lansdowne Ms. 171, ff. 298–404, British Museum.

¹⁷D593/S/4/24/4; *Acts of the Privy Council*, XII, 39.

¹⁸Lansdowne Ms. 43, art. 76; J. B. Black, *The Reign of Elizabeth*, p. 350; His revised act did not take effect. See Frederick Seaton Siebert, *Freedom of the Press in England 1476–1776* (Urbana, Illinois, 1952), pp. 59–60.

¹⁹*Acts of the Privy Council*, XVI, 416–17.

²⁰F. William Cock, 'Additional Notes on the Horne and Chute Families of Appledore', *Archaeologia Cantiana* (1938), XLIX, 160; For information about the subsidy see D593/S/4/14/10 and John Strype, *Annals of the Reformation*, III–1, 723–24. The evidence does not indicate when he was first appointed to the commission but it was probably in 1585 when the subsidy was first collected.

²¹The Cromer evidence is in a Campbell manuscript; For the Sprinte case see State Papers Domestic 12, Vol. 189, No. 20, f. 52A; Other inquiries the Privy Council ordered him to make can be found in *Acts of the Privy Council*, XIV, 99 and XVII, 13–14, and X.d. 121(2), Folger Shakespeare Library.

²²For the Pelsant manuscript see Kent Ms. U47/11 T485, Kent Archives Office; for the wills see State Papers Domestic 12, Vol. 223, No. 39; 12 Drury, Will of Robert Rudston.

## Chapter Nine

[1]Faith Thompson, *Magna Carta, Its Role in the Making of the English Constitution* (Minneapolis, 1948), p. 188.

[2]William Lambarde, *Archeion* (1957), p. 146.

[3]*Ibid.*, pp. 145–46; Tanner Ms. 435, 'Archeion, 1579', Bodleian Library; Folger Ms. 511121.1, 'Star Chamber', Folger Shakespeare Library; Harvard Ms. 68, 'Archeion', Harvard Law School.

[4]William Lambarde, *Archeion* (1957), pp. 9–10, pp. 45–46; Faith Thompson, *Magna Carta*, p. 188.

[5]William Lambarde, *Archeion* (1957), p. 81.

[6]*Ibid.*, pp. viii–ix.

[7]William Lambarde, *Archeion* (1957), pp. 139–40; for a list of the Lord Chancellors see X.d. 122(1), Folger Shakespeare Library.

[8]William Lambarde, *Archeion* (1957), pp. A3–A4; Wilbur Dunkel, *William Lambarde*, p. 130; For information about Egerton and Lambarde, see Virgil B. Heltzel, 'Notes: Sir Thomas Egerton and William Lambard', pp. 201–02; Lambarde had owned a copy of Fitz-Neal since 1574. See John Nichols, *Bibliotheca Topographica Britannica*, I, 511.

[9]V.a. 208, William Lambarde, 'A Declaration of the yerely profites, raysed by the Sundrye Deputies in this Office . . .', Folger Shakespeare Library. Burghley may have shared his lease with the Under Treasurer of the Exchequer although Lambarde did not relate that fact in his treatise on the office. Furthermore, his lordship apparently appointed Lambarde on his own authority. See M. S. Giuseppi, *Guide to the Public Records* (London, 1963), I, 258.

[10]Lansdowne Ms. 61, art. 60, f. 163, British Museum; John Strype, *Annals of the Reformation*, III–ii, 501–02; For the mint manuscripts see B191, ff. 81–93, Bodleian Library and Lansdowne 171, art. 186, ff. 398–404.

[11]M. S. Giuseppi, *Guide to the Public Records*, I, 258; V.a. 208, William Lambarde, 'Of the Service called the Office of Compositions for Alienations', and 'A Declaration of the yerely profites . . .', Folger Shakespeare Library. For many years these were attributed to Sir Francis Bacon.

[12]Index 9976, 'Entries of Licences and Pardons for Alienations', f. 297, Public Record Office.

[13]*Ibid.*, f. 332; A. 7, nos. 7–14, 'Writs of Covenant'; A. 9 no. 1, 'Writs of Entry in Recoveries'; For other evidence of Lambarde's activity see *Calendar of the Manuscripts of Major-General Lord Sackville . . . preserved at Knole, Sevenoaks, Kent, Historical Manuscripts Commission* (London, 1940), I, 238.

[14]For a receiver's report, see *Calendar of the Manuscripts of the Marquis of Salisbury*, XIII, 503. This document was erroneously attributed to the Court of Wards; The farmer paid rents to the Hanaper and sent all his profits to the Exchequer at the end of the term. See M. S. Giuseppi, *Guide to the Public Records*, I, 258; For the report of profits, see *State Papers Domestic*, Elizabeth I, Vol. IV, p. 246; Lambarde kept a personal

record of the profits, see V.a. 208, Folger Shakespeare Library.

¹⁵Titus B. IV, ff. 217–19, British Museum. Another treatise is bound with the 'Appolligie' which praises her Majesty for placing writs of entry in recoveries not held in chief under the authority of this Office. See ff. 219A–B.

¹⁶Titus B. IV, ff. 20B–21B, British Museum.

¹⁷Add. Ms. 4111, no. 146, f. 103.

¹⁸X.d. 121(2), Folger Shakespeare Library.

¹⁹Lansdowne Ms. 65, art. 70, f. 191; There is a third letter concerning a suitor who paid £10 into the Office. See Lansdowne Ms. 77, art. 46, f. 131.

²⁰Lansdowne Ms. 82, art. 71, f. 165.

²¹E. P. Cheney, *History of England*, I, 125; William J. Jones, 'The Elizabethan Chancery, Some Legal and Other Aspects', Ph.D. thesis, London University College, 1958, p. 5 and p. 30.

²²B471 Ms., f. 39, Bodleian Codices Rawlinsoniani, William Lambarde, 'Notes on the Officers of the Court of Chancery'; William Jones, 'The Elizabethan Chancery', pp. 17–18, pp. 85–87, and p. 231; Often more than 12 masters were appointed and were known as Masters Extraordinary but were not given the robes of the ordinary masters.

²³E. P. Cheney, *History of England*, I, 133; Lambarde Diary, p. 181; Harley Ms. 6996, no. 63, f. 122, British Museum.

²⁴D593/S/4/37/18.

²⁵William Jones, 'The Elizabethan Chancery', p. 59 and p. 80.

²⁶Paul Ward, 'William Lambarde's Collections on Chancery', p. 275; Lambarde Diary, p. 154.

²⁷Harvard Law Ms. 1034; For other copies of this collection copied out by Thomas Powys in the 17th century, see Stowe Ms. 415 and Harley Ms. 2207, British Museum, and Hale Ms. 44, Lincoln's Inn Library, London.

²⁸Paul Ward, 'William Lambarde's Collections on Chancery', p. 281 and pp. 285–86; Harvard Law Ms. 1034, ff. 59B–62.

²⁹Harvard Law Ms. 1034, ff. 1–13; The *Archeion* and the 'Collections' are not the only discourses written on the Court of Chancery. Deposited at the Bodleian Library is a manuscript entitled 'Notes of the Officers of the Court of Chancery', see B471 Ms. ff. 39A–42B.

³⁰*Calendar of Patent Rolls*, Elizabeth I, Vol. III, no. 868, pp. 169–70; Harvard Law Ms. 1034, ff. 55–56. Evidence that Lambarde received the money for his robes has survived in his rent and receipt books.

³¹X.d. 121 (14), Folger Shakespeare Library.

³²C/38/3, pt. II, 'Sanderson and Maltby v. Furlonge', f. 660, 'Bynley v. Hartley and Clough', f. 458, and 'Cavell v. Martin', f. 434.

³³There is some confusion about the identity of the Stanhopes. *In his Catalogue of lords Chancellors, Keepers of the Great Seal, masters of the rolls and principal officers of the High Court of Chancery* (London, 184), pp. 88–89, Sir Thomas Hardy failed to list a Stanhope as a Master after April 1598 when Sir Edward Stanhope was replaced by John Tyndall. (According to Sir George Cary, 'Reports or Causes in Chancery', *The English Reports*

(1902), XXI, 4–5, Sir Edward was also a doctor.) A Stanhope was certainly active on the court after 1598 but it was impossible to read his first name on the reports he endorsed. It could have been Francis; For the case of three masters see C/38/3, pt. II, 'Cavell v. Martin', f. 434.

[34]C/38/3, pt. I, 'Bird and Cole v. Chandler and Cole'. f. 54; C/38/4, 'Ponntes and Cuttel v. Williams'.

[35]C/38/3, pt. I, 'Bott and Bott v. Drury and Ware', f. 382, and 'Hunt v. Fitzherbert', f. 182.

[36]C/38/1, 'Cole v. Saveacre, Whitington and Whitington'; C/38/3, pt. I, 'Finche v. Finche', f. 149.

[37]C/38/3, pt. II, 'Saunders v. Cotterell and Cotterell', f. 662; C/38/4, 'Pomrey v. Pomrey and Turpin'.

[38]Paul Ward, 'William Lambarde's Collections on Chancery', pp. 277–78; Sir George Cary, 'Reports or Causes in Chancery', pp. 4–5.

[39]C/38/3, pt. II, 'Capell v. Mym', f. 438; Sir George Cary, 'Reports or Causes in Chancery', p. 9.

[40]Cecil Monro, ed., *Acta Cancellaria* (London, 1847), pp. 13–16.

[41]Cecil Monro, *Acta Cancellaria*, pp. 25–56; *State Papers Domestic*, Elizabeth I, Vol. IV, p. 138; William Jones 'Chancery and the Cinque Ports in the reign of Elizabeth I', *Archaeologia Cantiana* (1961), LXXVI, 144–46.

[42]For a discussion of the letters at Folger Shakespeare Library, see Wilbur Dunkel, *William Lambarde*, pp. 160–180. They are addressed to Lambarde from the following suitors: Michael Moleyns, Lord Mountjoy, George Coppin, Thomas Derdent, Robert Adams, Anne Peckham, Sir Richard Lewkner, Dr. Nicholas Steward, Thomas Baker, and William Sedley.

[43]X.d. 121 (11), Folger Shakespeare Library.

[44]Sir Thomas Hardy, *Catalogue of lords Chancellors*, pp. 88–89; Dr. Byng was Master of Clare from 1571 to 1599 and Dr. Steward held his degrees from Trinity Hall. These biographical data as well as a copy of the report were forwarded to me by C. W. Crawley, librarian, Trinity Hall, Cambridge University.

[45]Trinity Hall Ms. Misc. Vol. IV, no. 134.

[46]One unmentioned source of information about the cases he had is at the Stafford Archives Office. See D593/S/4/14/16 which discusses Lambarde's work on the estate of Sir Francis Willoughby. See also Chapter 8 for a reference to that knight. 11 cases dated from 1592 to 1600 from *Cary's Reports* were included in this reckoning although only two of them have been definitely attributed to Lambarde.

## *Chapter Ten*

[1]G. S. Thomson, 'Twysden Lieutenancy Papers', p. 73; D593/S/4/11/1; Add. Ms. 33,923, Streatfield Papers, f. 228.

[2]Add. Ms. 33,923, f. 242.

[3]D593/S/4/36/3–5; The hundred of Shamele delivered £6 16s. 9d,

Hoo 59s. 3d., and Toltingtroe, £5 19s. 2d. in July; D593/S/4/37/3 and D593/S/4/36/7; G. S. Thomson, 'The Twysden Lieutenancy Papers', pp. 95–97.

⁴G. S. Thomson, 'The Twysden Lieutenancy Papers', pp. 105–06; D593/S/4/40/2 and D593/S/4/46/6. Elizabeth had hoped to regain Calais by sending the relief column, but Henry IV of France would not consent to her terms and lost the town to the Spanish instead.

⁵D593/S/4/46/5–6 and D593/S/4/66/2.

⁶Add. Ms. 41,137, ff. 182–90.

⁷*Acts of the Privy Council*, XIV, 25. He had, of course, investigated the whereabouts of Benedicta Horne but she had already been identified as a recusant.

⁸D593/S/3/6. A Recusancy Commission had been in existence prior to January 1592, but the Privy Council, dissatisfied with its results, issued this new one. Whether or not Lambarde was a member of the old commission is unknown. See D593/S/4/6/15.

⁹Add. Ms. 33,923, f. 243; D593/S/4/6/13–14; D593/S/4/34; D593/S/4/22.

¹⁰*Acts of the Privy Council*, XXIII, 253–56; D593/S/4/22; Lambarde was at the Alienations' Office on 11, 15, and 18 November 1592. See A. 7 'Extracts from Writs of Covenant on which fines were paid', f. 445 ff. and A. 4, Index 9977, 'Entries for Licenses and Pardons for Alienations', 48b ff.

¹¹Conyers Read, *Local Government*, pp. 110–11.

¹²*Ibid.*, pp. 165–68 and p. 183.

¹³D593/S/4/36/1.

¹⁴D593/S/4/16/16.

¹⁵D593/S/4/36/1.

¹⁶D593/S/4/13/18; D593/S/4/38/15; Lansdowne Ms. 78, art. 61, ff. 173A–B; *Acts of the Privy Council*, XXV, 25–27.

¹⁷D593/S/4/10/32; D593/S/4/14/16; D593/S/4/67/4; J. Payne Collier, *The Egerton Papers*, p. 228; *Acts of the Privy Council*, XXVIII, 29–31 and XXX, 733–35.

¹⁸Conyers Read, *Local Government*, pp. 179–84.

¹⁹Major F. Lambarde, 'Some Kentish Charities, 1594', *Archaeologia Cantiana* (1915), XXXI, 189–202; Campbell manuscript.

²⁰*Acts of the Privy Council*, XXVIII, 388–89.

²¹Elizabeth Melling, 'The Poor', *Kentish Sources* (Maidstone, 1964), IV, xv.

²²A. F. Allen, 'An Early Poor Law Account', *Archaeologia Cantiana* (1951), LXIV, 74–80; Kent Ms. P336/12/1/1 Kent Archives Office.

²³D593/S/4/55/1; D593/S/4/23/14.

²⁴Conyers Read, *Local Government*, pp. 176–179 and pp. 185–89. The last charge is much shorter than the others and, according to Read, had no terminal punctuation.

²⁵*Ibid.*, pp. 158–61.

²⁶*Ibid.*, pp. 103–08.

²⁷*Ibid.*, pp. 145–49. The charge prepared for the Easter Sessions, 1601,

was not delivered because Lambarde was not present. See Kent Calendar Ms. Q/SR2, m. 3, p. 12. The nine extant charges which were delivered are dated Easter, 1592, 1593, 1596, 1598, and Michaelmas, 1591, 1595, 1596, 1599, and 1600. In the Streatfeild Collection there is a reference to a charge which is no longer extant. See Add. Ms. 33,923, f. 407; Lambarde did attend the quarter session of Michaelmas, 1592. See D593/S/4/10/19.

²⁸Conyers Read, *Local Government*, pp. 113–16.

²⁹*Ibid.*, p. 138.

³⁰*Ibid.*, pp. 140–45.

³¹Kent Ms. Q/SR1, 'Calendar of the Quarter Sessions', p. 11, Kent Archives Office.

³²Kent Ms. Q/SRg, 'Calendar of the Gaol Delivery Roll, 1596–1605,' Kent Archives Office. See also D593/S/4/14/16 for Lambarde's reference to the gaol delivery in January of 1597.

³³D593/S/4/10/25.

³⁴D593/S/4/37/14.

³⁵D593/S/4/6/22; D593/S/4/6/25; D593/S/4/38/16; These manuscripts give evidence of Lambarde's activities as a subsidy commissioner.

## Chapter Eleven

¹Lambarde Diary, p. 108; Margaret's second husband also had a brother named Walter who wed the daughter of Margaret's brother, Robert, thus drawing the Paynes of Frittenden and the Readers of Boughton Monchelsey even closer through family alliances. See Brigadier-General Fane Lambarde, 'William Lambarde's Pedigree Notes', pp. 132–33.

²Conyers Read, *Local Government*, p. 26.

³Lambarde Muniments, p. 46A.

⁴Lambarde Diary, p. 1. This journal still remains in the possession of Lambarde's descendant, Mrs. S. F. Campbell.

⁵Lambarde Muniments, pp. 34A–35B. Roberts borrowed £20 from him in 1596 and was named a possible college rent collector in Lambarde's will.

⁶Thomas Lambarde entered the date of 1600 in the family diary for the entrance of Multon to the Inn, but the antiquary clearly marked the date of 1599 in his receipt book. The Inn records also gave the date of 18 October 1599 for his admission. See *Registry of Admissions*, I, 128; In the summer of 1601 Tresse and Multon went to Cambridge but the purpose of the trip was not explained.

⁷See the last part of this chapter for a discussion of Cobham College.

⁸Woodhall 63; John Philipott, 'The Visitation of the County of Kent', pp. 253–56.

⁹D593/S/4/24/13, Draft Petition, probably written by Lambarde.

¹⁰Rent and Receipt Book, 1596–1601.

¹¹Requests 2, 'Maximilian Dalison v. Robert and Thomas Dalison'.

¹²Cobham 5, Will of Thomas Gore; J. Collier Payne, *The Egerton Papers*, p. 228.

[13]D593/S/4/10/6; He was also named a trustee in the will of Robert Oliver the elder of Laybourne. See Lambarde Muniments, p. 23A.

[14]Lansdowne Ms. 75, art. 62, f. 134; Kitchell was probably the same servant who was asked to collect the college lands in Lambarde's will. See Woodhall 63.

[15]*Calendar of the Manuscripts of the Marquis of Salisbury*, VI, 92–93, 248, and 432–33; For his illness see J. Payne Collier, *The Egerton Papers*, p. 228 and p. 308; The evidence for the Latin Secretary offer does not clearly specify that it was Lambarde of Lincoln's Inn who refused the office.

[16]Lambarde Diary, p. 342 and p. 69; G. S. Thomson, 'The Twysden Lieutenancy Papers', pp. 7–8.

[17]Add. Ms. 33,923, f. 365, Streatfeild Collection; Lambarde Muniments, p. 27B.

[18]Kent Ms. U962, E18, Kent Archives Office.

[19]X.d. 121 (5), Folger Shakespeare Library; *State Papers Domestic*, Elizabeth I, Vol. IV, pp. 363–64.

[20]Kent Ms. U565, m. 6, Kent Archives office. Miss Melling sent additional information about Lambarde's activities here.

[21]D593/S/4/10/28. Information about the Duc de Bouillon was supplied by Mrs. Valerie Hill of the Stafford Archives Office.

[22]*Report on the Manuscripts of Lord De L'Isle and Dudley*, Historical Manuscripts Commission (London, 1925–62), II, 259 and 278; W. A. Scott Robertson, 'Six Wills Relating to Cobham Hall', *Archaeologia Cantiana* (1877), XI, 209–14; Lansdowne Ms. 830, f. 249; Cobham 45, Will of Lord Cobham; *State Papers Domestic*, Elizabeth I, Vol. IV, pp. 363–64.

[23]*Statutes of the Realm* (London, 1817), III, 738; A. A. Arnold, 'Cobham College', *Archaeologia Cantiana* (1905), XXVII, 64–71.

[24]D593/S/4/14/16.

[25]Cobham 45, Will of Lord Cobham.

[26]A. A. Arnold, 'Cobham College', pp. 79–80; John Strype, *Annals of the Reformation*, IV, 376–78; Lansdowne Ms. 83, art. 43; D593/S/4/14/16.

[27]D593/S/4/19/34; D593/S/4/66/17; For information about Lambarde's activities in buying land for Cobham College, see Rochester Ms. CC, E62–E68, Rochester Bridge.

[28]D593/S/4/14/16.

[29]John Thorpe, 'Antiquities of Kent', *Bibliotheca Topographica Britannica* (1780), I 3; James Dugdale, *The New British Traveler* (London, 1819), III, 1; J. G. Waller, 'The Lords of Cobham', *Archaeologia Cantiana* (1878), XII, 155; A. A. Arnold, 'Cobham College', p. 81; Rochester Ms. CC. A.D. 1; Antiquaries Ms. 176, Society of Antiquaries, London; D593/S/4/66/15.

[30]T. Fisher, *History and Antiquities of Rochester* (London, 1772), 107; Edith Scoggs, *Archives* (1954), II, 183–84; A. A. Arnold, 'Rochester Bridge in A.D. 1561', *Archaeologia Cantiana* (1887), XVII, 212–14; Add. Ms. 28, 648; 'Records of the Wardens and Assistants of Rochester

Bridge', *Historical Manuscripts Commission, Ninth Report* (London, 1883–84), p. 285.

[31]T. Fisher, *History of Rochester*, p. 56; Add. Ms. 28,648, ff. 18–38; Rochester Ms. A.D. 102; Antiquaries Ms. 174, Sir Roger Manwood, 'A True Discourse of the ancient wooden and present stone bridge at Rochester', Society of Antiquaries.

[32]Rochester Ms. A. C. 91, 'Wardens' Accounts', I, 31.

[33]Rochester Ms. A. D. 101, ff. 46b–47b; Rochester Ms. A.C. 92–93; The Hon. H. Hannen, 'Further Notes on Phil Symonson, Maker of the Map of Kent Dated 1576–1596', *Archaeologia Cantiana* (1915), XXXI, 272.

[34]D593/S/4/10/41.

[35]Lansdowne Ms. 145.

[36]*Hodgson's Catalogue*, nos. 631, 561, and 563; He also possessed *Vocabularium Jures Utrusque* which was given to him by William Sedley. See Francis Edwards, *The Lambarde Catalogue*, no. 188.

[37]Lansdowne Ms. 218.

## Chapter Twelve

[1]Lambarde Diary, p. 275; William Lambarde, *Perambulation* (1596), p. 407; J. Payne Collier, *The Egerton Papers*, p. 228.

[2]D593/S/4/14/16.

[3]This was the last reckoning of his worth. He died before October 1601, the month when these annual accountings were made.

[4]D593/S/4/10/28; D593/S/4/14/16.

[5]D593/S/4/14/16.

[6]Edward Hasted, *History of Kent*, pp. 77–78.

[7]Lambarde Diary, p. 22; Actually he may not have had the grant of the office but only the executing of it. See the Letter of John Chamberlain to Dudley Carleton, *State Papers Domestic*, Elizabeth I, Vol. V, p. 544; Lansdowne Ms. 88, art. 1, f. 2; For a discussion of the Chancery officials' attitude toward this office, see Paul Ward, 'Collections on Chancery', p. 275.

[8]Stowe Ms. 543, 'The Pandecta Rotulorum'; For information about the Countess of Warwick, see Sir John Neale, 'The Elizabethan Political Scene', *Essays in Elizabethan History* (London, 1958), p. 65 and Wilbur Dunkel, *William Lambarde*, p. 177; For the interview see Add. Ms. 15,664, f. 226; John Nichols, *Bibliotheca Topographica Britannica*, I, 525–26; John Britton and E. W. Brayley, *Memoirs of the Tower of London* (London, 1830), p. 338; Frederick Chamberlin, *Sayings of Queen Elizabeth* (London, 1923), pp. 52–55; John Nichols, *Progresses of Queen Elizabeth* (London, 1823), III, 552; John Thorpe, *Custumale Roffense* (London, 1788), p. 89.

[9]For Proby's letter see *Calendar of the Manuscripts of the Marquis of Salisbury*, XI, 350; Coke owned the 'Pandecta', and for a discussion see Catherine Bowen, *The Lion Under the Throne* (Boston, 1956), p. 491 and F. S. Fusner, *The Historical Revolution*, p. 135; For the letter to Leveson, see D593/S/4/14/16; For information about Rokeby see J. Payne Collier, *The Egerton Papers*, pp. 308–12.

[10]Edward Hasted, *History of Kent*, p. 90.

[11]Rep. H, f. 249 and ff. 276–78.

[12]Lansdowne Ms. 235, 'Diary of Thomas Godfrey'; R. H. D'Elbaux, 'Miscellaneous Notes, "An Armorial Lambeth Delf Plate" ', *Archaeologia Cantiana* (1948), XL, 121; John Stokes, 'The Barons of New Romney in Parliament', *Archaeologia Cantiana* (1905), XXVII, 55.

[13]Lambarde Diary, p. 44; John Nichols, *Bibliotheca Britannica Topographica*, I, 530; John Philipott, 'Visitations of Kent', p. 248; *Black Books*, II, 102 and 104.

[14]John Philipott, 'Visitation of Kent', p. 248; As an example of the carelessness of Sir Multon, he forgot to enter the date of his entry into Lincoln's Inn in the diary and his son, Thomas, entered an incorrect date.

[15]John Nichols, *Bibliotheca Topographica Britannica*, I, 493.

# Bibliography

PRIMARY SOURCES

*Volumes with Lambarde Manuscripts*

Bristow, William *Schemes Relating to the Charities in the Parish of Greenwich.* Greenwich (1890).

Cary, Sir George *Reports or Causes in Chancery.* London (1872).

Chamberlin, Frederick *Sayings of Queen Elizabeth.* London (1923).

Edwards, Francis *The Lambarde Catalogue of Early Printed Books.* London (1909).

Hakluyt, Richard *The Principal navigations, voyages, traffiques and discoveries of the English Nation at any time within the compasse of these 1600 years.* 12 v. Glasgow (1903–1905).

*Hodgson's Catalogue.* London (1924).

Lambarde, William *An Alphabetical Description of the Chief Places in England and Wales.* London (1730).

——, *Archaionomia.* London (1568).

——, *Archeion or, a Discourse upon the High Courts of Justice in England.* Charles H. McIlwain and Paul L. Ward, eds. Cambridge, Massachusetts (1957).

——, *The Duties of Constables, Borsholders, Tythingmen, and such other low and lay Ministers of the Peace.* 16th ed. London (1640).

——, *Eirenarcha, or of the Office of the Justices of the Peace.* 12th ed. London (1619).

——, *A Perambulation of Kent.* 2nd ed. London (1596).

Melling, Elizabeth ed., *The Poor* (Kentish Sources, IV). Maidstone (1964).

Monro, Cecil ed., *Acta Cancellaria.* London (1847).

Nichols, John *Progresses of Queen Elizabeth.* 3 v. London (1823).

Read, Conyers ed., *William Lambarde and Local Government.* Ithaca, New York (1962).

Strype, John *Annals of the Reformation,* 4 v. Oxford (1824).

*Periodicals with Lambarde Manuscripts*

Allen, A. F. 'An Early Poor Law Account', *Archaeologia Cantiana,* LXIV (1951), 74–84.

Cary, Sir George 'Reports or Causes in Chancery', *The English Reports,* XXI (1902), 1–65.

Hesketh, Captain C. 'The Manor House and Great Park of the Archbishop of Canterbury at Otford', *Archaeologia Cantiana,* XXXI (1915), 1–24.

Lambarde, Brigadier-General Fane 'William Lambarde's Pedigree Notes', *Archaeologia Cantiana*, XXXIX (1927), 131–133.

Lambarde, Multon 'The Lambarde Diary', *Miscellanea Genealogia et Heraldica*, II (1876), 99–114.

Liebermann, Dr. Felix 'Notes on the Textus Roffensis', *Archaeologia Cantiana*, XXIII (1898), 101–112.

Lightfoot, W. J. 'Documents Relating to a Dispute between the Seven Hundreds and Lydd Concerning the Watch at Denge Marsh', *Archaeologia Cantiana*, VIII (1872), 299–310.

'Migrations of Historical Manuscripts', *Bulletin of the Institute of Historical Research*, II (1924), 61–62.

'Order of the Maundy', *Archaeologia*, I (1779), 7–9.

'The Orders, proceedings, punishments, and privileges of the Commons House of Parliament in England', *The Harleian Miscellany*, IV (1809), 559–571.[1]

Putnam, Bertha Haven 'The Earliest Form of Lambard's *Eirenarcha* and a Kent Wage Assessment of 1563', *English Historical Review*, XLI (1926), 260–273.

Randolph, Dr. John 'Memoirs of William Lambarde', *Bibliotheca Topographica Britannica*, I, John Nichols, ed. (1790), 493–530.

Ward, Paul L. 'William Lambarde's Collections on Chancery', *Harvard Library Bulletin*, VII (1953), 271–298.

*Manuscript Collections*

Calendars of Quarter Sessions and Gaol Deliveries, 16th century. Kent Archives Office, Maidstone co. Kent.

College of Queen Elizabeth Papers, late 1570s, mostly in the handwriting of William Lambarde. Drapers' Hall, London.

Courts of Chancery, Requests, Star Chamber and Wards decrees and cases, 16th century. Public Record Office, London.

Lambarde Family Papers, 16th to 19th centuries, many in the handwriting of William Lambarde. Mrs. S. F. Campbell, London.

Masters' Reports, 16th century, mostly in the handwriting of William Lambarde. Public Record Office, London.

Minutes of the Drapers' Company, 16th century. Drapers' Hall, London.

Office of Alienations papers, 16th century. Public Record Office.

Rochester Bridge and Cobham College Manuscripts, 16th century. Bridge Chamber Rochester, Kent.

Streatfeild Collection, 17th century, mainly in the handwriting of the Revd. Thomas Streatfeild. British Museum, London.

Sutherland Collection, late 16th and early 17th centuries, mostly in the handwriting of Sir John Leveson and William Lambarde. Staffordshire County Council, Stafford.

Wills of the Lambarde family and friends, 16th century. Somerset House, London.

[1]This manuscript, of course, has not been conclusively identified as that of William Lambarde, the antiquary.

*Public Documents*

Briggs, William trans., *The Register Book of the parish of St. Nicholas Acon, London, 1539–1812*. Leeds, 1890.

*Calendar of State Papers, Domestic Series of the Reigns of Edward VI, Mary, Elizabeth, 1547–1580*. 7 v. London, 1856–1871.

*Calendar of State Papers, Domestic Series of the Reigns of Elizabeth and James I Addenda, 1580–1625*. vol. 12. London, 1872.

*Calendar of the Patent Rolls preserved in the Public Record Office. Edward VI*. 5 v. London, 1924–1929.

*Calendar of the Patent Rolls preserved in the Public Record Office. Elizabeth*. 5 v. London, 1939–1964.

*Calendar of the Patent Rolls preserved in the Public Record Office. Philip and Mary*. 4 v. London, 1936–1939.

Chester, Colonel Joseph Lemuel *London Marriage Licences, 1521–1869*. Joseph Foster, ed. London (1887).

Cobbett, William *Parliamentary History of England*. 36 v. London (1806–1820).

Dasent, John Roche ed., *Acts of the Privy Council*. New Series. 32 v. London (1890–1907).

D'Ewes, Simonds *Journals of all the Parliaments . . . of Queen Elizabeth*. London (1682).

Fry, George S. ed., *Abstracts of Inquisitions Post Mortem Relating to the City of London returned into the Court of Chancery*. 3 v. London (1896–1908).

Guiseppi, M. S. *Guide to the Public Records*. 2 v. London (1963).

Hull, Felix *Guide to the Kent County Archives Office*. Maidstone (1958).

*Journals of the House of Commons*. vol. 1. London (1803).

*Letters and Papers, foreign and domestic of the reign of Henry VIII, preserved in the Public Record Office, the British Museum, and elsewhere*. 21 v. London (1862–1910).

Palgrave, Sir Francis *Reports of the Deputy Keeper of the Public Records, Tenth through Sixteenth*. London (1849–1855).

*Parliamentary Papers*. vol. 62. London (1878).

*Statutes of the Realm*. vol. 3. London (1817).

Thomas, F. S. *Handbook to the Public Records*. London, (1853).

Thorpe, John *A Collection of Statutes concerning Rochester Bridge*. London (1733).


*Volumes of Private Documents*

Ball, W. W. Rouse and Venn, J. A. eds., *Admissions to Trinity College, 1546–1900*. 5 v. London (1913–1916).

Bannerman, W. Bruce ed., *The Visitations of Kent Taken in the years 1530–1, Thomas Benolte, and 1574, Robert Cooke* (Harleian Society, LXXIV). London (1923).

——, *The Visitations of Kent Taken in the years 1574 and 1592, Robert Cooke* (Harleian Society, LXXV). London (1924).

Boase, Charles William and Clark, Andrew eds., *Register of the University of Oxford, 1449–1622*. 2 v. Oxford (1884–1889).

Boyd, Percival *Roll of the Drapers' Company of London*. London (1934).

*Calendar of the Manuscripts of Major-General Lord Sackville . . . preserved at Knole, Sevenoaks, Kent*. Historical Manuscripts Commission. London (1940).

*Calendar of the Manuscripts of the Marquis of Salisbury, preserved at Hatfield House, Hertfordshire. Historical Manuscripts Commission*. 18 v. London (1883–1940).

Collier, J. Payne ed., *The Egerton Papers*. Camden Society. London (1840).

Eland, George E. ed., *Thomas Wotton's Letter-Book, 1574–1586*. London (1960).

Ellis, Sir Henry *Original Letters of Eminent Literary Men of the 16th, 17th, and 18th centuries*. Camden Society. London (1843).

Hearne, Thomas ed., *A Collection of Curious Discourses Written by Eminent Antiquaries*. 2 v. London (1773).

James, M. R. *A Descriptive Catalogue of the Manuscripts in the Library of Corpus Christi College, Cambridge*. 2 v. Cambridge (1909–1913).

*The Manuscripts of the Right Honourable F. J. Savile Foljambe of Osberton*. Historical Manuscripts Commission. London (1897).

Nichols, John Gough ed., *The Diary of Henry Machyn, Citizen and Merchant Taylor of London, 1550–63*. Camden Society. London (1848).

Philipott, John *Visitation of Kent Taken in the Days 1619–1621* (Harleian Society, XLII), Robert Hovenden, ed. London (1898).

*The Records of the Honourable Society of Lincoln's Inn, The Black Books*. 4 v. London (1897).

*The Records of the Honourable Society of Lincoln's Inn. Registry of Admission*. 2 v. London (1896).

*Report on the Manuscripts of Lord De L'Isle and Dudley, preserved at Penhurst Place*. 5 v. London (1925–1962).

*The Reports of the Commissioners Appointed in Pursuance of Various Acts of Parliament to Enquire Concerning Charities in England and Wales. Relating to the County of Kent*. 32 reports. London (1819–1837).

Venn, John and Venn, J. A. *Alumni Cantabrigienses*. Cambridge (1922).

Welch, Joseph ed., *A List of Scholars of St. Peter's College, Oxford, admitted to that foundation since 1663*. London (1852).

Williams, Sarah ed., *Letters Written by John Chamberlain*. Camden Society. London (1861).

Wood, Anthony A. *Athenae Oxonienses*. 4 v. London (1813).

*Manuscripts Published in Periodicals*

Ellis, Henry 'Plan projected in 1561 for building a House of Correction in Westminster', *Archaeologia*, XXI (1827), 450–454.

——, 'Queen Elizabeth's remarks on the conduct of those who pressed her to name a successor to the crown in 1566', *Archaeologia*, XVIII (1817), 240–242.

Essex, Mr. 'A Plan of the ancient timber bridge at Rochester collected from two Mss. published in Lambarde's *Perambulation of Kent*', *Bibliotheca Topographica Britannica*, XV, John Nichols, ed. (1784), 395–404.

Harrison, Sir Edward 'Some Records of Ightham Parish', *Archaeologia Cantiana* LIII (1941), 17–28.

——, 'The Court Rolls and other Records of the Manor of Ightham as a Contribution to Local History, *Archaeologia Cantiana*, XLVIII (1936), 169–218.

——, 'The Court Rolls and Other Records of the Manor of Ightham as a Contribution to Local History. Second and Final Part', *Archaeologia Cantiana*, XLIX (1938), 1–95.

Howard, Joseph Jackson 'Annotations to the Heraldic Visitation of London, 1633', *Miscellanea Genealogica et Heraldica*, III (1890), 71–72.

——, 'Dalison Wills', *Miscellanea Genealogica et Heraldica*, V (1894), 246–248 and 269–271.

Kirby, W. J. 'The Churchwardens' Accounts of the Parish of St. Alfege, East Greenwich, 1630–40', *Transactions of the Greenwich and Lewisham Antiquarian Society*, IV (1954), 270–284.

Lambarde, Fane 'Pedigree of Beale', *Miscellanea Genealogica et Heraldica*, V (1923–1925), 240–241.

Lambarde, Major F. 'Some Kentish Charities, 1594', *Archaeologia Cantiana*, XXXI (1915), 189–202.

Mandy, W. H. 'Notes from the Assize Rolls and Other Documents', *Transactions of the Greenwich and Lewisham Antiquarian Society*, I (1914), 282–312.

Nichols, John Gough 'The Domestic Chronicle of Thomas Godfrey, esquire', *The Topographer and Genealogist*, II (1853), 450–467.

Philipott, John 'The Visitation of Kent, Taken in the year 1619, Part II', *Archaeologia Cantiana*, V, John Jackson Howard, ed. (1863), 223–256.

'The Records of the Wardens and Assistants of Rochester Bridge', *Report of the Historical Manuscripts Commission*, IX (1883), 285–286.

Robertson, W. A. Scott 'Six Wills Relating to Cobham Hall', *Archaeologia Cantiana*, XI (1877), 199–304.

*Writers of the Sixteenth and Early Seventeenth Centuries*

Camden, William *Britain*. Philemon Holland, trans. London (1610).

Cunningham, The Revd. William and Lamond, Elizabeth eds., *A Discourse of the Common Weal of this Realm of England*. Cambridge (1893).

Stow, John *A Survey of London*. 2 v. Oxford (1908).

Wheeler, John *Treatise of Commerce*. London (1601).


SECONDARY SOURCES

*Books*

Abell, Henry Francis *History of Kent*. Ashford (1898).

Adams, Henry G. *An Historical and descriptive account of Rochester Bridge in three epochs*. Rochester (1856).

Archer-Thomson, W. *Drapers' Company. History of the Company's Properties and Trusts*. 2 v. London (1943).

Barton, D. Plunkett, Benham, Charles and Watt, Francis *The Story of Our Inns of Court*. London (1942).

Beaven, A. B. *The Aldermen of the City of London*. London (1908).

Beard, Charles A. *The Office of Justice of the Peace in England, Its Origin and Development*. New York (1904).

Bennett, F. J. *Ightham: The Story of a Kentish Village and its Surroundings*. London (1907).

Berry, William *County Genealogies*. London (1830).

Black, J. B. *The Reign of Queen Elizabeth*. Oxford (1959).

Blackstone, Sir William *Commentaries on the Laws of England*. William G. Hammond, ed. 4 v. San Francisco (1890).

Bosworth, George Frederick *Kent*. Cambridge (1909).

Bowen, Catherine *The Lion and the Throne*. Boston (1956).

Brandon, Woodthorpe *An Inquiry into the Freedom of the City of London in Connection with Trade*. London (1850).

Brayley, Edward Wedlake *A Topographical and Historical Description of London and Middlesex*. 5 v. London (1810–1816).

Britton, John *An Essay on Topographical Literature*. London (1843).

Britton John and Brayley, E. W. *Memoirs of the Tower of London, comprising historical and descriptive accounts of that fortress and palace*. London (1830).

Cheyney, E. P. *History of England*. 2 v. London (1948).

Churton, Ralph *The Life of Alexander Nowell, Dean of St. Paul's*. Oxford (1809).

Corbett, Uvedale *An inquiry into the elective franchise of the freeholders of and the rights of election for the corporate counties in England and Wales*. London (1826).

Dearn, T. D. W. *An historical, topographical and descriptive account of the weald of Kent*. Cranbrook (1814).

Douglas, David C. *English Scholars*. London (1939).

Dugdale, James *The New British Traveler*. 3 v. London (1819).

Dugdale, Thomas *Curiosities of Great Britain, England, and Wales Delineated*. 8 v. London (1854–1860).

Dunkel, Wilbur *William Lambarde, Elizabethan Jurist, 1536–1601*. New Brunswick, New Jersey (1965).

Elton, Charles *The Tenures of Kent*. London (1867).

Evans, Joan *A History of the Society of Antiquaries*. London (1956).

Fisher, Thomas *History and Antiquities of Rochester*. London (1772).

——, *The Kentish Traveller's Companion*. 4th ed. Canterbury (1794).

Foss, Edward *Judges of England*. London (1857).

Fry, Edward Alexander *Almanacks for Students of History*. London (1915).

Furley, Robert *A history of the Weald of Kent with an outline of the early history of the county*. 2 v. London (1871–1874).

Fusner, F. S. *The Historical Revolution*. New York (1962).

Girtin, Thomas *The Triple Crowns: a narrative history of the Drapers' Company, 1364–1964*. London (1964).

Hardy, Sir Thomas Duffus *A Catalogue of lords Chancellors, Keepers of the great seal, masters of the rolls and principal officers of the High Court of Chancery*. London (1843).

Harris, Dr. John *The History of Kent*. London (1719).

Harris, Percy A. *London and Its Government*. London (1933).

Harrison, O. B. C. *The practice of the sheriffs' court of the City of London.* London (1860).

Hasted, Edward *History of Kent.* Henry H. Drake, ed. Vol. I. London (1886).

Herbert, William *Antiquities of the Inns of Court and Chancery.* London (1804).

Holdsworth, Sir William *A History of English Law.* 9 v. London (1922–1926).

Hone, William *The every day book and Table Book.* 3 v. London (1835).

Hook, Walter Dean *Lives of Archbishops of Canterbury.* 4 v. New Series. London (1872).

Howarth, William comp., *Some particulars relating to the ancient and royal borough of Greenwich.* Greenwich (1882).

Hurst, Sir Gerald *A Short History of Lincoln's Inn.* London (1941).

Ireland, W. H. *History of the County of Kent.* 4 v. London (1830).

Jenkinson, W. W. *London Churches Before the Fire.* London (1917).

Jesse, John Heneage *Historical and Literary memorials of the City of London.* Boston (1901).

Jessup, Frank W. *A History of Kent.* London (1958).

Johnson, The Revd. A. H. *The History of the Worshipful Company of the Drapers of London.* 5 v. Oxford (1915).

Jordan, W. K. *The Charities of London,* 1480–1660. London (1960).

——, *Social Institutions in Kent* (Archaeologia Cantiana, LXXV). London (1961).

Kendrick, Thomas Downing *British Antiquity.* London (1950).

Kilburne, Richard of Hawkhurst *A Topographie or Survey of the County of Kent.* London (1659).

Kimbell, John *An Account of the Legacies, Gifts, Rents, etc., appertaining to the Church and Poor in the County of Kent.* London (1816).

Leach, Arthur F. *English Schools at the Reformation.* Westminster (1896).

L'Estrange, The Revd. A. G. *The Palace and Hospital.* 2 v. London (1886).

Levine, Mortimer *The Early Elizabethan Succession Question.* Stanford, California (1966).

Lodge, Edmund *Life of Sir Julius Caesar.* London (1827).

Loftie, William John *The Inns of Court and Chancery.* London (1893).

Lysons, Daniel *The Environs of London.* 6 v. London (1746).

Mee, Arthur *Kent: The Gateway of England and Its Great Possessions.* London (1936).

Melling, Elizabeth ed., *Aspects of Agriculture and Industry* (Kentish Sourches, III). Maidstone (1961).

——, *Some Roads and Bridges* (Kentish Sources, I). Maidstone (1959).

Milne, Alexander Taylor *Writings on British History, 1934–1945.* London (1937–1960).

Neale, Sir John E. *Elizabeth I and Her Parliaments, 1559–1601.* 2 v. London (1953).

——, *The Elizabethan House of Commons.* New Haven (1950).

——, *Queen Elizabeth.* London (1934).

Nichols, John Gough *Annals of Antiquities of Lacock Abbey*. London (1835).

Orridge, Benjamin B. *Some account of the citizens of London and their rulers from 1060 to 1867*. London (1867).

Osborne, Bertram *Justices of the Peace, 1361–1848*. Shaftesbury, Dorset (1960).

Page, William ed. *Victoria History of the County of Kent*. 3 v. London (1926).

Pearce, Robert *A Guide to the Inns of Court and Chancery*. London (1855).

Philipott, Thomas esquire *Villare Cantianum*. London (1776).

Phippen, James *Descriptive Sketches of Rochester, Chatham, and their Vicinities*. Rochester (1862).

Putnam, Bertha Haven *Early Treatises on the Practice of the Justices of the Peace in the 15th and 16th Centuries*. Oxford (1926).

——, *Kent Keepers of the Peace, 1316–1317* (Kent Records, XIII). Ashford (1933).

——, *Proceedings before the Justices of the Peace in the Fourteenth and Fifteenth Centuries from Edward III to Richard III*. London (1938).

Ratcliff, E. E. *The Royal Maundy*. London (1952).

Read, Conyers ed., *Bibliography of British History, Tudor Period, 1485–1603*. Oxford (1959).

——, *Mr. Secretary Cecil and Queen Elizabeth*. London (1955).

Richardson, Henry S. *Greenwich: its history, antiquities, improvements, and public buildings*. Greenwich (1834).

Russell, J. M. *The History of Maidstone*. Maidstone (1881).

Siebert, Frederick Seaton *Freedom of the Press in England 1476–1776*. Urbana, Illinois (1952).

Smith, Frederick Francis *A History of Rochester*. London (1928).

Smith, John Russell *Bibliotheca Cantiana*. London (1837).

Spilsbury, William Holden *Lincoln's Inn, its ancient and modern buildings*. London (1873).

Strateman, Catherine *The Liverpool Tractate*. Columbia University Studies. New York (1937).

Strype, John *The Life and Acts of Matthew Parker*. 3 v. London (1821).

Tanner, Thomas *Bibliotheca Britannico-Hibernica*. London (1748).

Thomson, G. S. *The Twysden Lieutenancy Papers, 1583–1668* (Kent Records, X). Ashford, Kent (1926).

Thompson, Faith *Magna Carta, Its role in the making of the English Constitution, 1300–1629*. Minneapolis, Minnesota (1948).

Thorpe, John *Custumale Roffense*. London (1788).

——, *Registrum Roffense*. London (1769).

Twysdon, Sir John *The Family of Twysdon or Twisdon*. C. H. Dudley Ward, comp. London (1939).

Unwin, T. Fisher *Greenwich and Blackheath*. London (1881).

Upcott, William *A Bibliographical account of the principal works relating to English topography*. 3 v. London (1818).

Walker, J. Douglas *Short Notes of Lincoln's Inn*. London (1912).

Ward, A. W. and Waller, A. R. *Cambridge History of English Literature.* 15 v. Cambridge (1908–1927).

Ward, Dr. Gordan *Sevenoaks Essays.* London (1931).

Woodcock, W. *Lives of Illustrious Lord Mayors and Aldermen of London.,* London (1846).

Wright, Louis Booker *Middle-Class Culture in Elizabethan England.* Chapel Hill, North Carolina (1935).

*Periodicals*

Arnold, A. A. 'Cobham College', *Archaeologia Cantiana,* XXVII (1905), 64–109.

——, 'Rochester Bridge in A.D. 1561', *Archaeologia Cantiana,* XVII (1887), 212–240.

Barnes T. G. and Smith, A. Hassell 'Justices of the Peace from 1558 to 1688—A Revised List of Sources', *Bulletin of the Institute of Historical Research,* XXXII (1959), 221–242.

Box, Edward G. 'Lambarde's "Carte of this Shyre" '. *Archaeologia Cantiana,* XXXVIII (1926), 89–96.

——, 'Lambarde's "Carte of this Shrye", Third Issue with Roads Added', *Archaeologia Cantiana,* XXXIX (1927), 141–148.

Cave-Brown, The Revd. J. 'Knights of the Shire for Kent from A.D. 1272 to A.D. 1831', *Archaeologia Cantiana,* XXI (1895), 198–243.

Charrington, John 'Lambarde's *Perambulation*', *Notes and Queries,* CLI (1926), 249.

Chettle, Lieutenant-Colonel H. F. 'Lacock Abbey', *Wiltshire Magazine,* LI (1947), 1–13.

Clark-Maxwell, The Revd. W. G. 'The Customs of Four Manors of the Abbey of Lacock', *Wiltshire Magazine,* XXXII (1902), 311–348.

Cock, F. William 'Lambarde's *Perambulation*', *Notes and Queries,* CLI (1926), 321 and 431.

——, 'Additional Notes on the Horne and Chute Families of Appledore', *Archaeologia Cantiana,* XLIX (1938), 157–166.

Cunningham, The Revd. William 'Walter of Henley', *Transactions of the Royal Historical Society,* IX (1895), 215–222.

D'Elboux, R. H. 'Miscellaneous Notes, "An Armorial Lambeth Delf Plate" ', *Archaeologia Cantiana,* LX (1948), 121–122.

Ducan, Leland L. 'The Church of St. Alfege, Greenwich', *Transactions of the Greenwich and Lewisham Antiquarian Society,* I (1910), 54–60.

Fear, H. J. 'Westcombe', *Transactions of the Greenwich and Lewisham Antiquarian Society,* VII (1964), 8–14.

Flower, Robin 'Laurence Nowell and the Discovery of England in Tudor Times', *Proceedings of the British Academy,* XXI (1935), 47–74.

Gibson, J. P. 'The Homes and Migrations of Historical MSS', *Bulletin of the Institute of Historical Research,* I (1923), 37–44.

Hannen, The Honorable H. 'Further Notes on Phil Symonson, Maker of the Map of Kent Dated 1576–1596', *Archaeologia Cantiana,* XXXI (1915), 271–274.

Harrison, Edward 'Miscellaneous Notes, "A Lambarde Relic"',
  *Archaeologia Cantiana*, LXVIII (1955), 216–217.

Hatton, Ronald G. and Hatton, The Revd. Christopher H. 'Notes
  on the Family of Twysden and Twisden', *Archaeologia Cantiana*,
  LVIII (1946), 43–67.

Heltzel, Virgil B. 'Notes: Sir Thomas Egerton and William Lambard',
  *The Huntington Library Quarterly*, XI (1948), 201–203.

Howard, Joseph Jackson 'Corrections and Additions', *Miscellanea,
  Genealogica, et Heraldica*, V (1923–1925), 312.

Hull, Felix 'The Custumal of Kent', *Archaeologia Cantiana*, LXXII (1959),
  148–159.

——, 'Kentish Historiography', *Archaeologia Cantiana*, LXX (1957),
  221–230.

——, 'The Lathe in the Early Sixteenth Century', *Archaeologia Cantiana*,
  LXVIII (1955), 97–100.

'Introduction: Containing an Historical Account of the Origin and
  Establishment of the Society of Antiquaries', *Archaeologia*, I (1779),
  i–xliii.

Jessup, R. F. 'Excavation of a Roman Barrow at Holborough, Snodland',
  *Archaeologia Cantiana*, LXVIII (1955), 1–61.

——, 'Holborough: A Retrospect', *Archaeologia Cantiana*, LVIII (1946),
  68–72.

Jones, William J. 'Chancery and the Cinque Ports in the Reign of
  Elizabeth I', *Archaeologia Cantiana*, LXXVI (1961), 143–162.

'The Lambarde Cup', *Archaeologia Cantiana*, XXXIX (1927), 135–138.

'Laurence Nowell and a Recovered Anglo-Saxon Poem', *British Museum
  Quarterly*, VIII (1943), 130–132.

Lawson, Tancred, Sir Thomas 'Parliamentary History of Aldborough
  and Boroughbridge', *York Archaeological Journal*, XXVII (1924),
  325–368.

Livett, Grevile M. 'Early Kent Maps (Sixteenth Century)', *Archaeologia
  Cantiana*, XLIX (1938), 247–277.

——, 'Supplementary Note on Early Kent Maps', *Archaeologia Cantiana*, L
  (1939), 140–146.

Matthews, M. C. 'The Charitable Institutions of Greenwich Parish
  One Hundred Years Ago', *Transactions of the Greenwich and Lewisham
  Society*, III (1935), 276–293.

Nichols, John Gough 'Memorials of the Family of Cobham', *Collectanea,
  Topographica and Genealogica*, VII (1841), 320–354.

Pearman, A. J. 'Residences of Bishops of Rochester', *Archaeologia
  Cantiana*, XXXIII (1918), 131–151.

Putnam, Bertha Haven 'Justices of the Peace from 1558 to 1688', *Bulletin
  of the Institute of Historical Research*, IV (1926–1927), 144–156.

Robertson, W. A. Scott 'Romney, Old and New', *Archaeologia Cantiana*,
  XIII (1880), 349–373.

Stokes, John 'The Barons of New Romney in Parliament', *Archaeologia
  Cantiana*, XXVII (1905), 44–63.

Thomson, G. S. 'The Origin and Growth of the Office of Deputy-Lieutenant', *Transactions of the Royal Historical Society*, V (1922), 150–166.

Thorpe, John esquire, 'Antiquities in Kent, hitherto Undescribed', *Bibliotheca Topographica Britannica*, I (1780), 1–28.

Von Roemer, Mary 'Notes on the Lineage of Richard De Combe', *Wiltshire Notes and Queries*, VII (1914), 499–511.

Wadmore, J. F. 'Brenchley, Its Church and Ancient Houses', *Archaeologia Cantiana*, XIII (1880), 127–140.

Waller, J. G. 'The Lords of Cobham', *Archaeologia Cantiana*, XII (1878), 113–166.

White, H. T. 'The Beacon System in Kent', *Archaeologia Cantiana*, XLVI (1934), 77–96.

# Index